DATE C

In the style of his earlier bo.... **Para Retornar** *men*,
Swartley charts a path through competing voices and inter-preta-
tions in a debate that too often polarizes into two camps.
> —*Lois Barrett, Director, Associated Mennonite*
> *Biblical Seminary–Great Plains Extension*

Swartley addresses Christians with family members or friends with
homosexual issues or who are themselves wrestling with their orientation. Thank you for a serious effort to work with such a divisive
issue.
> —*Henry Kliewer, Conference Minister,*
> *Mennonite Church British Columbia*

The book gives a readable, biblically based explanation in support
of our church's position on homosexuality. I found it easy to understand, scholarly, and credible in its impact.
> —*Miriam Martin, Administrator,*
> *Atlantic Coast Mennonite Conference*

Through his book, *Slavery, Sabbath, War, and Women*, Swartley
has become known as a careful, fair and discerning interpreter of
Scripture—on difficult issues. Once again, in his book, we witness
the same commitments and skills at work. Once again Swartley is
unflinching in his willingness to tackle a difficult subject. And once
again he has offered his considerable gifts to the life of the Church,
helping us to move forward on this contentious issue.
> —*Mark Thiessen Nation, Professor,*
> *Eastern Mennonite Seminary*

Our conference could profit greatly by a study of this book, by those
who want to bring a biblical view from a Mennonite perspective to
this issue.
> —*Ken Nauman, Conference Minister,*
> *Southeast Mennonite Conference*

Because of both the content and how it's presented, I believe this
book can facilitate informed discussion and debate.
> —*Henry Paetkau, President,*
> *Conrad Grebel University College*

Willard Swartley has written a courageous piece of work. I found this to be a most helpful and encouraging book.
—*Keith Weaver, Moderator,*
Lancaster Mennonite Conference

Willard Swartley, well-known biblical scholar, takes up the ever-difficult topic of homosexuality in a book that is both scholarly and pastoral, culturally sensitive and biblically learned, but above all honest and irenic. His analyses both of cultural factors and biblical materials are informed, incisive, and instructive. His solutions avoid quick fixes and invite those who are interested in the important discussion concerning homosexuality, Scripture, culture, and church to think in an open and sophisticated way that will promote better understanding and perhaps even new and better solutions than those previously achieved in less informed conversations.
—*Marion L. Soards, Professor of New Testament Studies,*
Louisville Presbyterian Theological Seminary

Willard Swartley's thoughtful book is a significant contribution to the church's larger debate about same-sex relationships. He summarizes much of the recent literature, providing a distinctively Mennonite perspective even as he engages other Christian traditions. The book is enriched by the prayerful humility, candor, and generosity of spirit for which he is well known.
—*A. Katherine Grieb, Virginia Theological Seminary*

Willard Swartley's essays offer a clear rationale for the church's teaching position on homosexuality. Their high view of Scripture, helpful review of recent scholarship and penetrating analysis of contemporary culture will make an important contribution to the conversations surrounding this combustible topic.
—*John D. Roth, Professor, Goshen College*

Willard Swartley's book is not for the faint of heart. He draws the reader into the biblical text, and with a technician's skill and a pastor's heart holds our faith and life accountable to the Scriptures.
—*Jeff Wright, Executive Director,*
Center for Anabaptist Leadership, Los Angeles

Homosexuality

Biblical Interpretation and Moral Discernment

WILLARD M. SWARTLEY

Herald
Press

Scottdale, Pennsylvania
Waterloo, Ontario

Library of Congress Cataloging-in-Publication Data
Swartley, Willard M., 1936-
  Homosexuality: biblical interpretation and moral discernment /
Willard M. Swartley. —1st ed.
    p. cm.
Includes bibliographical references and index.
ISBN 0-8361-9245-1 (pbk. : alk. paper)
  1. Homosexuality—Religious aspects—Mennonites. 2. Homosexuality—
Biblical teaching.   I. Title.
    BX8128.H67S93 2003
    241'.66—dc21   2003003795

HOMOSEXUALITY
Copyright © 2003 by Herald Press, Scottdale, Pa. 15683
  Published simultaneously in Canada by Herald Press,
  Waterloo, Ont. N2L 6H7. All rights reserved
Library of Congress Catalog Card Number: 2003003795
International Standard Book Number: 0-8361-9245-1
Printed in the United States of America
Book design by Merrill R. Miller / Mary Meyer
Cover design by Sans Serif Inc.

10 09 08 07 06 05 04 03 10 9 8 7 6 5 4 3 2 1

To order or request information, please call
1-800-759-4447 (individuals); 1-800-245-7894 (trade).
Website: www.heraldpress.com

DEDICATED TO

My father, Wm. Henry †1967
My mother, Ida †1976
a humble farmer couple
who nurtured me in the faith

My four closest male friends:

My brother, Henry †1988
who during my teens
instilled in me a passion for mission
with stories of transformed lives
spiced by games and fun

My EMC office mate 1966-67
Jacob P. Jacobszoon †1983
a dear Dutch friend
spiritual father, theological mentor
gifting me with his ten-day visits

My AMBS colleague
Marlin E. Miller †1994
whose wisdom and servant-leadership
I deeply cherish

Willard E. Roth
spiritual friend
for twenty-five years
enriching my life and well-being

Mary
for whose love and loyalty
throughout forty-five years
I am deeply grateful

CONTENTS

But the wisdom from above is first pure,
then peaceable, gentle,
willing to yield, full of mercy and good fruits,
without a trace of partiality or hypocrisy.
—James 3:17

Oh, how we as churches across the denominational spectrum long for this wisdom from above for moral discernment on homosexuality. If these wonderful character traits and behavioral expressions were present in our reflections on and decisions about homosexuality issues, we would be a long way toward resolution. Perhaps the biggest challenge before us is to keep checking ourselves against these criteria, to see whether we desire and manifest this wisdom from above.

Some brothers and sisters took seriously this heavenly wisdom when they came to strongly support their denomination's church membership guidelines in July 2001. My wife, Mary, reports how two men in her round-table discussion group on opposite ends of this issue both came to support a membership guidelines document. One wanted to drop the homosexuality section completely, and the other found it not strong enough along disciplinary lines. In the course of discernment and the table discussion, both adjusted their views so that each submitted positive votes. Even more important, both affirmed and expressed trust in each other as brothers, acknowledging the need for what each brings to the church. Such stories generate hope for the church in the days ahead.

I suggest that this verse from James—in my daily schedule of readings on the day I intended to write this preface—become a theme text for our discussions on this thorny, and often divisive, topic. Practicing this divine wisdom will block the tactics of the evil one to use this issue to divide and conquer God's people. It is an excellent portrait of God's simple folk seeking to know the ways of God for our moral life.

A word about the development of this book is fitting here. Over the years I have written several papers on the topic. The major paper, titled "Homosexuality: Biblical, Theological, Cultural Perspectives and the Church's Response," was used by numerous conference study groups. In light of the wide interest in this paper, Herald Press requested a manuscript from me on this subject. Taking counsel from numerous people, I agreed to develop a manuscript to provide a resource for ongoing discernment.

But beyond this request, what other motivations led me to undertake such writing on such a difficult topic, even in the midst of other larger and smaller projects? The driving forces, both from head and heart, came primarily from two related types of experience. First, over the last thirty years I became acquainted with people, bright, fine people, who struggled with sexual identity, came to me for counsel, and wanted to know how to live with themselves, Scripture, and the church. I did not have easy answers, but I attempted to maintain friendship and counsel, as much as possible.

Second, I was often disappointed with explanations of relevant Scripture texts that, to me, too easily muted those texts in relation to today's needed discernment on homosexual issues. Reading the variety of explanations over time led me to feel the need to speak to the exegetical and hermeneutical dimensions. However, it has become clear in the last several years that my uneasiness has been experienced by numerous others as well. Hence, by now there is a wealth of exegetical literature on the topic from various perspectives, more than I can treat in this modest endeavor. In light of these two factors, my hope is that my contribution will lead to richer understanding of and humble commitment to both Scripture and those with homosexual struggle and/or identity who come to us in the church for counsel and support.

From the start, a key factor in my understanding of the task was the need to distinguish between exegetical work and the hermeneutical task. Moreover, I saw the need for an analysis, largely neglected in these discussions, of western culture and its legacy to adequately understand the role of sexuality in the modern world. The enormous impact of the 1960s "sexual revolution" needs careful reflection and evaluation. The vehemence of Islamic fundamentalists against western culture cannot be fully appreciated until we assess the negative impact of western culture's sexualized media intrusion into cultures worldwide. Hence my call for assessing the formative factors of present-day western culture in relation to sexual freedom has both biblical-theological and political-economic import. In this task we are dealing with the current crisis of cultures in conflict.

I hope also that my work in this book will lead us toward shalom. I have tried to speak in love what I understand to be the truth on this difficult topic. My prayer is that it will enable peace-seeking responses within the church when points of view clash. Though my stance on homosexual practice is expressed in the book, I call for discernment as a continuing task. The word "dialogue" does not adequately describe what needs to be done, for it seems only to have hardened positions already held. Something more fundamental is needed: discernment on our understanding of biblical authority, assessment of the exegesis and hermeneutics on this issue, and a moral assessment of our western culture. I too sit at the table of discernment to listen to how others perceive the crucial issues in this debate. On these matters we need to respectfully engage each other in ongoing discussion.

I wish to acknowledge the assistance of many people who have helped me clarify my thinking and improve my work at various stages. This process began already in the 1980s and the early 1990s when I taught Biblical Hermeneutics at Associated Mennonite Biblical Seminary. Class discussions were insightful and helpful to me as the teacher. When the request from Herald Press came for me to put my papers into print, an early draft was sent at my request to Conference leaders for discernment and critical response. I wanted to know whether this contribution would contribute positively to discussions in conferences and churches. I am grateful to Levi Miller who selected these half-dozen leaders and to these people in both Canada and USA who took time and gave me very helpful critique as well as affirmation. At later stages in my writing, a dozen other readers (family members, friends near and far, pastors, and colleagues) gave constructive counsel. As always, one learns most from those who see things differently from one's own perspective. I extend thanks also to those that have given time to the manuscript and wrote commendations for the book. I am deeply grateful to each one for the time and thought you have given. I express also my appreciation for Herald Press Editor Sarah Kehrberg's care in editing this manuscript, and for the continuing assistance and encouragement of Levi Miller to undertake and complete the project.

Finally, I thank Mary, my wife, for her helpful counsel at numerous points along the way. As a professional business teacher who taught typing to thousands of high school students, she spots typos instantly. I am especially grateful for her intensive work to prepare the indices in a relatively short amount of time. Further, her vision, hope, persistence, and patience to assist the church mediate conflict arising from the issue of homosexuality inspired me in my work and certainly influenced the accent of this book. Her wisdom has made this book better than it would be otherwise.

A fitting reflection as we move into this difficult topic comes from the noted Croatian theologian, Miroslav Volf:

We enlarge our thinking by letting the voices and perspectives of others, especially those with whom we may be in conflict, resonate within ourselves, by allowing them to help us see them, as well as ourselves, from *their* perspective and if needed, readjust our perspectives as we take into account their perspectives.[1]

And a blessing from the New Testament epistles:

May the Lord of peace himself give you peace
at all times in all ways.
—*2 Thessalonians 3:16*

CHAPTER ONE

MY JOURNEY ON HOMOSEXUALITY

In the late seventies I was asked to write an article on homosexuality for *Christian Living*.[1] This was shortly before my book *Slavery, Sabbath, War, and Women* was published (1983), but it was concurrent with my preparation of the Conrad Grebel Lectures that formed the basis of the book. Already then, one of the consultants for the Lectureship recommended that I write on a fifth topic, homosexuality, to show that the church does not always support every new wave that comes along. In accord with the church's developing position, the consultant believed that one must distinguish between orientation and practice, since the Bible speaks against the latter but not the former.[2]

I chose not to include another chapter because the book was already too long. Nor did I write the article for *Christian Living*. I was trying to make sense of the church's thinking in the early discussions, which distinguished between *orientation* and *practice*. From earlier exegetical work (in 1961) on Romans 1:18-32, in a course taken on Romans at Associated Mennonite Biblical Seminary under Howard Charles, I came to understand the text to say that homosexual desires expressed in "unnatural" sexual acts are the consequence of idolatry. That is, people (here Paul is thinking groups, not individuals per se) who substitute the creation for the Creator as the object of worship are "given over" to "unnatural" sexual passions. Hence I struggled with the orientation/practice distinction in light of my understanding of this text.

During the intervening years I have come to see a functional value in the orientation/practice distinction in regard to homosexuality, believing it has a place in the discussion. But I note that the concept of orientation plays into the notion of a fixed and unchangeable identity, which I both then and now question. Further, advocates for the church's acceptance of gays and lesbians rarely make the orientation/practice distinction. Nor do the more liberal, *avant garde* university writers. My own response has been to look more closely at modern culture to discern how it has shaped the thinking and cultural climate of the last forty years, thus producing the present situation (see chapter 5).

In addition, the criteria that applied to the four selected issues in *Slavery, Sabbath, War, and Women* did not apply to homosexuality, namely, that there are Scripture texts that support either side of the argument. I saw clearly that for homosexuality one encounters at the level of the "plain sense" of the text (the meaning that the texts have had for Judaism and Christianity for centuries[3]) only prohibitions, and strong ones at that. Thus, hermeneutical work, assessing the relation between the text in that culture and its meaning for our culture, needed to be done. Such investigation would try to understand the scriptural teaching and try to determine whether the homosexuality we are talking about today is essentially different from what Scripture speaks about.

Seeing Similarity and Difference

Both advocates of abolition of slavery and those affirming gay and lesbian sexual practices appeal to "rights," citing injustice and oppression as wrongs to be denounced.[4] In slavery, rights were denied wholesale to slaves, by virtue of definition. Arguments for women's liberation appealed in part to rights and justice issues, but also to biblical texts that authorized women's participation in leadership ministries in various roles. A similarity between the issue of homosexuality and that of women's liberation is that both same-sex practice and being female may become liabilities in certain employment situations.[5]

Second, both the feminist and gay/lesbian movements are similar in that they are part of the twentieth century great sexual revolution, the roots of which will be described in subsequent chapters. A mighty movement of unharnessed force has been let loose in western culture—so much so that reading texts from other cultures, including the Bible, seems quaint and entertaining to those acculturated to contemporary sexual freedoms.

But while these abolitionist, women's, and gay/lesbian movements are similar in their cultural liberationist impulses, from a Christian and biblical perspective there are also differences. Two fundamental differences between the first two issues and the questions of homosexuality are:

1. From a *surface* analysis one observes mixed signals in the biblical texts on slavery and the role of women (this is also true for discussions of the Sabbath/Lord's day and Christian participation in war). Some texts appear to support one position while others appear to support the opposite position—*apparent* contradiction within the Bible. Conversely, all the texts that speak of same sex practice are of the same mind. In explicit Scripture statements, homosexual practice, i.e. same-sex genital intercourse, is always wrong.

2. On three issues—slavery, war, and role of women—the accusation of the status quo proponents is that those who deem themselves progressive want to "set for [themselves] a *higher* law than the Bible." The new way, argued by abolitionists, pacifists, and feminists, emerges from God's redemptive action, grace, and kingdom justice. It contrasts to practices in that culture in which slavery, war, and hierarchical

gender structures prevailed. God's way is different, liberating and loving, replacing dominion and self-defensiveness with mutuality and trust. In contrast, homosexual practice is not related to grace-energized behavior in even a single text. Nor is the practice *regulated* by permeation of or juxtaposition with a qualifying gospel ethic. For example, the husband-wife hierarchy is virtually transformed by the Christian ethic of *mutual* submission and the christologically rooted husband's self-giving love in Ephesians 5:21-33.[6]

To explicate the point further, homosexual practice on the surface of the biblical texts—aside from the issue of what it meant then and what people today might mean by the term—*always* appears in prohibitive language. It is a deviation from the model of life fitting to God's community. Freeing slaves, refusing war, and celebrating male-female unity and interdependence are possibilities of grace, through nonconforming values to the world's cultural practices of that time. Scripture thus moves in a redemptive trajectory on these issues when compared to the cultures of the Hebrew and early Christian environment. But, on homosexuality, Scripture takes as strong or even stronger a negative view, and consistently so, than does the culture of its environment.[7]

These two differences were and are substantial. However, some of the principles of biblical interpretation used by abolitionists, pacifists, and liberationists[8] are similar to those employed by writers arguing that the Bible does not condemn homosexuality as Christian gays and lesbians experience it today. By giving priority to Jesus and the Gospels over the Old Testament and Paul, many gay proponents note that Jesus and the Gospels never speak about homosexuality, and thus it is not an important issue (see chapter 3, however). Jesus rather shows mercy and acceptance to those ostracized by social conventions and prejudices. By granting more weight to moral principles than to specific instruction given in specific texts, gay and lesbian proponents argue that the biblical bias toward justice for oppressed minorities outweighs the seven scattered biblical texts against homosexuality. Further, employing another key principle of biblical interpretation, that is, understanding the historical and cultural contexts of Scripture, gay proponents argue that the Old Testament proscriptions cannot be made normative any more than the death penalty for a rebellious son. Likewise, the New Testament mention of homosexuality refers either to promiscuous or cultic practices, neither of which fit the genre of gay freedom today.

In a 1984 address at Goshen College's Convocation, I identified basic biblical principles or emphases that have been adduced to argue for the church's acceptance of both homosexual orientation and practice, under certain conditions. I presented also the principles that argue for the church's objection to homosexual practice. See chapter 6 for this hermeneutical analysis.

In 1988-89, while on a sabbatical at Yale Divinity School, where gay and lesbian advocacy was strong, I was much interested in the extensive space and commentary in the *New Haven Register* given to reporting on the First International AIDS Conference, held in Toronto in June 1989. Projected growth of AIDS infection over the next ten years was shocking. It stirred me deeply and I wrote an article for our Mennonite Church weekly publication, which, however, was not accepted. It appears in print only now in this book, in updated form.[9] See appendix 3.

In 1993 and 1995 I was asked to present biblical teaching and my own theological understanding on homosexuality to two churches in Elkhart and Goshen, Indiana. Both were studying the issue and contemplating how, if at all, gays and lesbians might be included in membership. Those engagements led to a paper written first in 1995 and revised annually over the next five years. This paper, entitled "Homosexuality: Biblical, Theological, Cultural Perspectives, and the Church's Response," was distributed by several Mennonite area conferences for study among the ministers. The components of that paper are presented in this volume in chapters 2 and 4-6, in revised, updated form.

In 2000 I was asked to address a conference at Clinton Frame Mennonite Church sponsored by several regional Mennonite organizations. I prepared a new paper, "Jesus and Paul on Homosexuality: Do They Contradict Each Other?" Half of that paper appears here as chapter 3, with updating and additions. The Pauline portion of that paper is incorporated into chapter 4. Drawing on this previous work done, updated, and revised, I now make available my insight for larger dissemination and discernment. My hope is that this contribution will be accessible to pastors and lay leaders who seek study resources on the topic.

I register two concerns as people read this book, one as a "preface" and the other as a concern of an undesired side effect. Addressing the former, I realize that most of the book focuses on biblical interpretation and related hermeneutical concerns, including analysis of western culture. For many, a prior issue is even more important, namely, biblical authority. I make a modest contribution here to that topic, and point to a few resources that one might pursue further.

Marion Soards takes up this issue in his helpful short book, *Scripture and Homosexuality: Biblical Authority and the Church Today.* Writing from the Reformed and Presbyterian context, he cites from several *Confessions* that provided the historic grounding of the church on this matter. He then sums up in four points why Scripture is authoritative, with power to form and transform human lives. It is so because of four characteristics:

> *Vital.* The Scriptures stand in proximity to the original events that formed the church. They testify to God's work among Israel, and especially to the life, death, resurrection, and exaltation of Jesus Christ. The Bible bears witness to God's formative activity among the people of Israel and the earliest Christians.

Discerning. In its articulation of Israel's and early Christianity's beliefs and practices, the Bible testifies to the profundity of Jewish and Christian perception of and reflection on God's revelation.

Trustworthy. The Scriptures were written as information about experiences, beliefs, and practices in order to provide guidance; subsequent generations of believers have proved the Bible's usefulness over and over.

Normative. Above all, the Scriptures provide us with a norm or a means to judge between the spirits. The Bible guides us as we seek faithfully to decide among the competitive claims that arise in the life of the church. It is "the witness without parallel" (The [Presbyterian] Confession of 1967, 9.27).[10]

Walter Moberly, an Old Testament professor, addresses the same issue in his short, superb article that fair-mindedly presents most all the key issues that both sides must consider in dealing with the topic. Given the difficulty of this issue, he poses the question that the more secular minded raise:

Why bother with the Bible at all? In a culture impatient of traditional authorities, why should Christians go through the complicated rigmarole of biblical interpretation? Is it not a prime case of "If you will believe outdated nonsense, then you must expect the consequences"? Why not abandon the Bible and be free? To such siren voices the Christian response is, in essence, simple. When you have found the pearl of great price, the one thing needful, then you are foolish to let it go. There is—in the God revealed in Jesus Christ, to whom Scripture bears witness—a reality, a love, a truth which is worth holding on to, come what may. What is at stake is not petty rules, and restrictions or puzzles about contemporary sexuality, but one's whole understanding of life and death.[11]

Moberly goes on to note that when one ceases to believe in God as depicted in Scripture, eventually one also ceases to believe that humans are made in God's image. Then the understanding of what it means to be human also changes, as has already happened in western culture.

My own work on biblical authority is accessible in my earlier book[12] and is well expressed in *Confession of Faith in a Mennonite Perspective*, Article 4, on Scripture:[13]

> We believe that all Scripture is inspired by God through the Holy Spirit for instruction in salvation and training in righteousness. We accept the Scriptures as the Word of God and as the fully reliable and trustworthy standard for Christian faith and life. We seek to understand and interpret Scripture in harmony with Jesus Christ as we are led by the Holy Spirit in the church.
>
> We believe that God was at work through the centuries in the process by which the books of the Old and New Testaments were inspired and written.[14] Through the Holy Spirit, God moved human witnesses to write what is needed for salvation, for guidance in faith and life, and for devotion to God.[15]
>
> We accept the Bible as the Word of God written. God has spoken in many and various ways through the prophets and apostles.[16] God has spoken above all in the living Word who became flesh and revealed the truth of God faithfully and without deception.[17] We also acknowledge the Scripture as the fully reliable and trustworthy Word of God written in human language.[18] We believe that God continues to speak through the living and written Word.[19] Because Jesus Christ is the Word become flesh, Scripture as a whole has its center and fulfillment in him.[20]
>
> We acknowledge the Scripture as the authoritative source and standard for preaching and teaching about faith and life, for distinguishing truth from error, for discerning between good and evil, and for guiding prayer and worship. Other claims on our understanding of Christian faith and life, such as tradition, culture, experience, reason, and political powers, need to be tested and corrected by the light of Holy Scripture.[21]

The Bible is the essential book of the church. Through the Bible, the Holy Spirit nurtures the obedience of faith to Jesus Christ and guides the church in shaping its teaching, witnessing, and worship. We commit ourselves to persist and delight in reading, studying, and meditating on the Scriptures.[22] We participate in the church's task of interpreting the Bible and of discerning what God is saying in our time by examining all things in the light of Scripture.[23] Insights and understandings that we bring to the interpretation of the Scripture are to be tested in the faith community.

My second concern relates to the undesirable side effect. After one delves into a study of this type or of any such contemporary issue, one may be left with a distorted view of Bible study. However, this use of the Bible is not the primary or even normal use of Scripture. In order to represent the wider use of the Bible, as it functions in the life of Christian formation, I included an appendix in my *Slavery, Sabbath, War, and Women* book that demonstrates from the text of Ephesians how Scripture sustains our thought and life in many dimensions. Yes, the Bible surely contributes to moral formation, but that is to be conceived much more broadly than dealing with specific social issues.[24] It speaks to all of life as the Word and counsel of God. I include this study of Ephesians as Appendix 7. I recommend that several times during your reading of the book you take a pause and turn to this appendix and remind yourself anew of the larger purposes of Scripture.

From the start of my ruminations on this topic, I have felt that analysis of twentieth-century western cultural forces is needed to help us understand our current moral predicament. Many cultural factors are causative of the current pressure toward homosexual practice (perhaps desire as well), in ways not dissimilar to the forces resulting in high rates of divorce and remarriage.[25] Many theories have been advanced to explain the origin of same-sex sexual attraction (see chapter 5), with Freud's high on the list until recent decades. The sexual revolution of the 1960s is most significant because it redefined sexual mores for the society. As a result, the west has developed a sexualized culture, which despite the glamorous face the culture attaches to sex is often productive of sexual abuse in the home or school. Such abuse is a key factor in influencing later sexual development and capacity for expression. If it is true that our societal culture is a determinative factor, we must then, perhaps, regard homosexual persons (gays and lesbians) as, in part at least, products of social cultural forces they did not choose. This does not mean resignation to these forces, but an acknowledgment that we are dealing not only with individual persons, but also with cultural systems that work against God's pattern for human life. And we must recognize that our sons, our daughters, our best friends, and we ourselves have been affected to greater or lesser degrees by these forces.

Then we will be ready to discuss the problem more constructively, relate to homosexual people more compassionately, and strive for true liberation with hope.

Prayer

Lord God, we recognize that we face in our lives today questions that our fore-parents did not face, at least not in public debatable and discerning ways. We pray that you give us wisdom to seek patterns of love in human sexuality that enable us to reflect your divine image. Forgive us for being too judgmental, and forgive us for being too ready to go along with cultural pressures, from one side or the other. Enable us to find your way to be loving and discerning, hopeful that we can be your faithful people in today's world. In the name of Jesus Christ our Savior and Lord. Amen.

CHAPTER TWO

OLD TESTAMENT
AND EARLY JUDAISM

In this chapter and the two following, I focus on biblical interpretation. I begin by looking at the theology of sexuality embedded in the creation narratives, for only in light of this context does the rationale for the Old Testament proscriptions against homosexual practices gain clarity. Indeed, as Mauser puts it, "it is a fundamental mistake to discuss biblical statements on homosexuality in isolation from the positive ethos of human sexuality in scripture."[1]

In the second part of the chapter I situate the homosexuality debate on Old Testament texts among its foremost representatives. I include both those who understand the biblical texts that speak of same-sex relations as relevant to our present cultural realities, and those who regard these texts as best left in first-century realities, for varied reasons.

Theology of Sexuality in the Old Testament and Judaism

In both Jewish and Christian tradition Genesis 1-2 has played a foundational role in shaping moral reflection on sexuality. It is thus essential to understand these formative texts, for they influence not only the Old Testament and Judaism at the time of Jesus, but also the New Testament and the history of Christian thought on sexuality as well. "Human sexuality is seen, in these texts, as a fundamental continuance of God's good creation."[2]

According to God's design, as disclosed in Genesis 1:26-27, humans were created male and female. The text also says humans were created in God's image. What does this mean? Theologians have debated this over the centuries. Some argued that rationality itself is what distinguishes humans from animals and makes us like God. Others have proposed that the human emotional capacities make us unique from all other animals, especially our capacity to love and care for one another. Still others have held that predication, the ability to communicate through speech, is what sets us off from the animal world and makes us like God. God is portrayed as speaking, even in creating the world.

There are elements of truth in all of these, but the biblical text discloses two points that underlie all these proposals. They are: the capacity for relationship and community and the capacity to exert dominion over the created order as portrayed below.

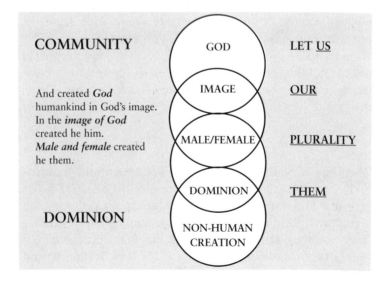

COMMUNITY	GOD	LET US
And created *God* humankind in God's image. In the *image of God* created he him. *Male and female* created he them.	IMAGE	OUR
	MALE/FEMALE	PLURALITY
DOMINION	DOMINION	THEM
	NON-HUMAN CREATION	

In verse 27 we find a poetic parallel in which "male and female" stands in parallel to "God's image." Further, the text begins with a plural subject and singular verb, "Let us (pl.) create (sing.) humans in our image." This is the plurality of the Godhead,[3] which from the later New Testament perspective and early Christian theology we understand as the Trinity. God Almighty is not singular; God is one, a community of being. Just as relationship characterizes God's self, so, we humans are made relational beings, in God's image. Genesis 1 and 2 affirm that we humans exist as male and female, the basic form of community. From infancy until the day we die we exist as either male or female, and we relate to others as persons who are either female or male.[4] As Karl Barth puts it, "[Humankind] never exists as such, but always as the human male or the human female. Hence in humanity, and therefore in fellow-humanity, the decisive, fundamental and typical question, normative for all other relationships, is that of the relationship in this differentiation."[5]

The capacity to relate in this way is one major dimension in which we are God's image in this world, especially so when we relate in caring, helping, respectful, trusting ways. But even this is not the gospel edge of what needs to be said. If indeed in being male and female we connect to God's own being, then we touch the sacred in these relationships, and we respect that sacred dimension in each other, in our maleness and femaleness.

From a biblical perspective sexuality is a good gift of God, bestowed graciously as part of God's good creation. The gift, like the sun and rain, is bestowed upon all people. For those called of God into covenant relationship, sexuality becomes a sacred stewardship. In our knowledge of God's design for our lives, we learn that God intends for sexuality to express the deepest meanings of human life and enhance relationships among God's human creation. Sexuality encompasses all of life, for we exist as either male or female, man or woman. Indeed, "sexuality is far more than anatomy, physiology, and the sexual response system. It is most of all a matter of communication, relationship, and commitment."[6] As one denomination's study document on human sexuality puts it, "Sexuality is a basic dimension of personhood, of maleness and femaleness. It seasons our personality, influences our thoughts and our actions. It helps determine our choice of work, style of life, and way of raising children."[7] Yes, our sexuality is more than the sum of sexual anatomical parts. Sexuality defines the way we live as persons and how we relate to others. Sexuality becomes a part of our way of living, including our relationship to God. It bestows special dignity and purpose. But when sexuality is misused it brings sadness and pain, and in some circumstances guilt and shame, even much anger to those abused.

According to Genesis 1:26-28, humans are "image of God" in this world. Verses 28 and following emphasize the human mandate to exercise dominion over all creation. This may be viewed as analogical to the role of the king in the Old Testament; he was to exercise rule in justice and care for the poor and the oppressed (Ps. 72; 82). Humans, all of us in relation to the created order—the earth, animals, and vegetation—are to be stewards of nurturing care and justice in our dominion over creation.

Note that here man is not told to exercise dominion over woman. To both together is given the cultural mandate, namely, to exercise responsible stewardship in dominion over the created order. The great challenge of our stewardship is to own these capacities, both community and dominion. When men exercise dominion over women, or vice versa, they transgress against community and corrupt God's design. Humans are then oppressed by offenses in our world about which we know well: sexual harassment, sexual exploitation and perversion, rape, and violence. God's design is mocked; sexuality is profaned, and appreciating human sexuality as sacred is forfeited. Humans spiral downward. Horrid newspaper accounts of sexual violations, often involving murder, depict just how degenerate humans become when the sense of the sacred is lost. If we suppress the innate capacity for dominion by stressing only community, we violate from the opposite side. Creativity is stifled, productivity of all sorts lags, and the community turns in on itself, creating serious tensions in relationships. What we can learn from the Genesis creation emphasis is that both dimensions of our human being need to be affirmed, respected, and nurtured. Each should enhance the other.

In Genesis 2 the creation narrative culminates with marriage, a parallel to the first creation narrative that climaxes with the Sabbath. In Jewish communal life, Sabbath and marriage constitute the twin pillars of society. Here, however, is where Christianity differs, I believe, from Judaism. Not only is Sabbath redefined, but singleness is introduced as an option, as good or even better, when life is fully committed to God's kingdom work. See appendix 4.

Proscriptions Regarding Homosexuality

Numerous contributions have attempted to show the several streams of opposing interpretation on this issue. Several scholars (including at least two of my colleagues) have contributed summaries of these contrasting interpretations; such summaries also appear in the spate of edited books that contribute to the debate (I cite ten such edited volumes in the bibliography. They are designated with an asterisk.) People on both sides of this issue appeal to Scripture, stating they seek to be faithful to Jesus Christ.[8]

First, I identify the influential sources that gave rise to the newer interpretations, which have been identified as "revisionist"[9] since they propose new ways of reading the texts with meanings different from those traditionally held by the Christian church over the centuries.[10] I will also identify the writers who over these last fifteen years have pointed out the weaknesses and problems of such interpretations. I am well aware of the church's past abuses in using Scripture to defend views that now seem clearly wrong (most notably, support of slavery). I believe, however, that the traditional reading of Scripture on this issue is more truthful, since the biblical texts are quite consistent and this position fits the overall scriptural view of sexuality as well. In terms of effect upon human and societal health, I believe it is also more compassionate, provided the position is held with love for even those who hold opposing views and engage in sexual practices thereby deemed sinful.

Three influential books have pioneered the exposition of the new interpretations of Scripture and have shaped numerous church people's thinking on homosexuality.[11] These studies explain the biblical texts that forbid or condemn same-sex genital unions in such a way as to put distance between what the biblical texts are speaking about (i.e., in New Testament pederasty or cultic prostitution) and what the church is dealing with today (i.e., loving, caring homosexual relationships). Their interpretations argue that some of the biblical texts are ambiguous in meaning at points (we don't really know what the Greek words mean and the stories in Genesis 19 and Judges 19 that were long thought to condemn same-sex intercourse really condemn inhospitality). Thus some people, generally reflecting the Boswell and/or Scroggs arguments, conclude that the seven biblical texts that explicitly speak of same-sex practices (Gen. 19; Judg. 19; Lev. 18:22; 20:13; Rom. 1:24-27; 1 Cor. 6:9; 1 Tim. 1:10) do not address the issue of loving homosexual relations. Other considerations, therefore, such as justice and compassion for the marginalized, are more important factors in shaping the church's response.

But is this really true? Numerous scholarly essays have considered the exegetical work of these contributions and have found them both flawed and unconvincing.[12]

These dozen authors span the Christian communion and cannot be dismissed as grinding a conservative ax. Rather, the fact is that careful scholarly work on these texts does not support dismissing them as irrelevant to today's issue of same-sex relationships. A very good accessible brief discussion of these texts is by Richard B. Hays in *Sojourners* (July 1991).[13] See also Hays's helpful treatment of the topic in his excellent monograph *The Moral Vision of the New Testament.*[14]

Three points sum up the exegetical data, in my analysis. First, no one word appears in these texts that translates conclusively as *homosexuality.* The King James Version (KJV) and earlier translations prior to the Revised Standard Version (RSV) didn't use the term, simply because it was not in the vocabulary at that time (the first known use of the term is in German, *homosexualität,* in a pamphlet published in Leipzig in 1869).[15] The RSV (first edition in 1946, 1952) uses the term *homosexuality* in 1 Corinthians 6:9, but the second edition in 1972 drops it, apparently because of the changing climate in North America toward homosexuality. The seven biblical texts clearly speak of same-sex genital relations. Since only in modern times has the concept of "sexual orientation/identity" arisen,[16] we must remember that the biblical teaching speaks to behavior—same-sex genital acts. The concept of orientation to denote same-sex preference or attraction is not on Scripture's radar screen. The term *desire (epithymia)* is used in Romans 1 to denote that which leads to same-sex relations. The same term is used more widely to denote also heterosexual behavior that falls outside morally approved conduct. Many of the Pauline uses refer to the desires of the old life, frequently translated *passions* (Rom. 6:12; Eph. 2:3; Col. 3:5). On occasion the term can also be used in a positive sense (1 Thess. 2:17). In biblical thought, sexual desires (passions) for genital relations outside the heterosexual marriage relationship when acted upon fall into the negative connotation of *porneia,* a term used widely in the New Testament.

Second, the stories in Genesis 19 and Judges 19 are rightly said to narrate God's judgment upon homosexual rape and

inhospitality and therefore hardly address—nor condemn—
loving homosexual relations. But this doesn't mean these
texts do not speak to the issue of homosexual practices. In
Genesis 19 it is precisely (homo)sexual lust that precludes
hospitality. Hence, the story judges against not only Sodom's
inhospitality, but also against homosexual lust, since it fore-
closed the possibility of the townsmen welcoming the male
strangers in a truly hospitable manner.[17]

Some of these sources assert that "to know" in Genesis
19:5 refers not to sexual intercourse but to the *general* relational meaning of know, since the majority of uses elsewhere
in the Old Testament carry this broader meaning. Several
scholars, however, have argued persuasively that the Hebrew
word *yadha* (*to know*) in 19:5 certainly intends carnal (sexual)
knowledge (compare Gen. 4:25), as the use of the same verb
in Genesis 19:8 makes clear, "I have two daughters who have
not known *(yadha)* a man."[18] The view of John Boswell that
Genesis 19 shows no sexual interest is, as Gerald D.
Coleman puts it, "an interpretation [that] is erroneous and
should sustain no credibility."[19]

Further, in about a dozen instances in later writings, especially during the intertestamental period, there are references
to the sin of Sodom as sexual. Another equal number refer to
Sodom's sin without specifying the sexual aspect; some specify wealth or rebellion (see appendix 1). Within the Old
Testament itself, Isaiah 1:10 and 3:9 do not specify Sodom's
sin but utilize Sodom as symbolic of people departing from
the ways and deeds of God. Jeremiah accuses the prophets of
Jerusalem of committing adultery and walking in lies, thus
becoming like Sodom to God (23:14). Ezekiel names the sins
as pride, excessive food and prosperity, and failure to aid the
needy (16:49). Jude 7, however, specifies Sodom's sin as sexual immorality and unnatural lust.[20]

Third, several Old Testament and several New Testament
texts do speak about and against the practice of same-sex
intercourse. Leviticus 18:22 and 20:13, in the Holiness

Code, and 1 Corinthians 6:9 and 1 Timothy 1:10, in Pauline literature, condemn the action of *a male lying with a male* (i.e., sexual intercourse). The New Testament texts will be treated in chapter 4.

The Old Testament Leviticus texts regard same-sex relations as an abomination (Hebrew *toevah*—compare with transvestism in Deut. 22:5 and cult prostitution in Deut. 23:18). Other *toevah* type abominations are idolatry and child sacrifice (Deut. 12:31; 20:18). Lesser violations of food laws are said in English also to be an abomination, but the Hebrew word (*sheqets/shaqats/shiqquts*) is different, meaning filthy or unclean (Lev. 11:11ff.). Boughton regards *toevah* as linked to those violations that are contrary to a person's true identity, thus far more serious than violation of food laws.[21]

Seow, however, lists more texts from the Pentateuch where *toevah* is used: for unclean food (Deut. 14:3); idolatrous practices and child sacrifice (Deut. 12:31; 13:15); magic (Deut. 18:12); remarriage of divorced wife (Deut. 24:4); idols (2 Kings 23:13; Isa. 44:19), to argue that these sanctions are not obligatory beyond that historical context.[22] However, the sins in these texts involving idolatrous practices, magic, and child sacrifice are indeed grave offenses.

A recent contribution on clean/unclean foods may provide a new window of understanding. Basing his article on his doctoral dissertation, Jirí Moskala reviews fourteen theories to explain why certain animals are clean and others unclean. Among these are the theories that (1) unclean animals were those offered by pagans in sacrifice; (2) only those animals acceptable to God for sacrifice were suitable for humans to eat; or (3) the clean/unclean distinction is rooted in moral/ethical purposes, specifically to teach reverence for life.[23] A newer anthropological theory, based on Mary Douglas's work, has dominated recent literature on the topic. It holds that clean animals are "a perfect specimen to the category of being to which one belongs" and unclean animals are not a *pure* type of the category.[24]

Moskala, a professor of Old Testament exegesis and theology, presents the strengths and weaknesses of all the theories. According to his conclusion, the best explanation is that the proscriptions represent accordance with creation theology. This view draws together elements from several theories considered, which, however, in themselves are inadequate. These elements are: "holiness, natural repulsiveness, respect for life, health, a wall against paganism, etc." Moskala sums up: "there is enough biblical material to demonstrate a close relationship between Leviticus 11 and Creation from the exegetical point of view and to present a *theological interpretation* with the Creation-Fall-New Creation pattern and stress on the life-death principle behind the dietary law in the Pentateuch."[25]

In light of this thesis, still to be tested in scholarship, it is possible to see a common denominator to all the *toevah* prohibitions in the Levitical code.[26] All cases cited above relate to creation theology (not the same as natural law or natural theology), in that these offenses violate what, on the basis of revelation, God intends in creation order. Idolatry is refusal to own and worship the Creator; magic is its expression. The remarriage prohibition (Deut. 24:4), in which the first husband takes back the wife he divorced after she was defiled by a second husband, is likewise *toevah* because it threatens the one flesh union of Genesis 2:24. A second union has defiled the first. Incest, sex between humans and animals, and same-sex relations undermine the male-female union enunciated in creation theology.

William J. Webb, in his literary analysis of Leviticus 18, observes that verse 21, in its condemnation of the worship of Molech (cf. 2 Kings 16:3; 23:10), introduces what appears to be an extraneous topic in a sequence of sexual violations:

—Incest (vv. 6-18)
—Menstruation (v. 19)
—Adultery (v. 20)

—Sacrificing children to Molech (v. 21)
—Homosexual relations (v. 22)
—Bestiality (v. 23)

Webb notes that some interpreters regard verse 21 as indicating the context in which homosexuality was practiced, namely, pagan male cult worship (cf. Deut. 23:17-18; 1 Kings 14:24; 15:12; 22:46; 2 Kings 23:7). These interpreters then contend that the homosexual prohibition is culturally particular, and has no sting against same-sex relations in committed relationships. Webb refuses this explanation and argues that the Molech prohibition represents a literary marker, a shift from sexual offenses that involve offspring to those that preclude offspring. The latter are more serious, and each stands as an offense in its own right. Verse 22 is categorical, prohibitive of all male-to-male sex relations, not only those in cultic prostitution. Thus "the lack of covenant relationship and the lack of equal-partner status are simply not substantive issues" in this proscription.[27]

While Webb makes an important point in his analysis, the admission of Molech worship as a cultural context for the prohibition does not disqualify the text from broader application to homosexuality. A particular context does not disallow universal moral sanction in its application (of greatest import here is Jesus' crucifixion!).[28] The fact that same-sex male relations and Molech worship, which involved sacrificing offspring, are linked may be "telling" of the seriousness of the same-sex offense. This link also parallels the thought of Romans 1:18ff. that connects same-sex practices with idolatry.

In his recent extensive, critical study of homosexuality, Robert A. Gagnon exhaustively investigates Genesis 19, Judges 19, and the two Levitical prohibitions (18:22; 20:13). After examining parallel Near Eastern background texts on homosexuality, he thoroughly examines the practices of homosexual cult prostitution in Israel. He goes on to say that the prohibitions in Leviticus derive basically from violating God's design in the creation of distinct sexes for heterosexual pairing. In his study of Genesis 1-2 Gagnon sees God's design for sexuality, manifest in the male-female anatomical, sexual, and procreative complementarity. Gagnon argues against the scholars who discount the normative value of the prohibitions against homosexuality, whether because it is associated with idolatry, constitutes a procreative dead end, involves contact of semen with excrement, or represents status inversion in gender dis-complementarity (see the work of Nissinen and Brooten). While these factors may have more or less significance in the prohibitions, Gagnon shows that if these alone were the sole reasons, then other prohibitions logically should have been included.[29] That Paul in Romans and 1 Corinthians depends upon the Levitical prohibitions is therefore not to be discounted. It is a theological grounding of sexual ethics in Israel's Holiness Code and is congruous with the normative understanding of first-century Judaism, especially Philo and Josephus.

Philo (ca. 10 B.C.–A.D. 45) and Josephus (ca. A.D. 37-100) represent Judaism's view on sexuality in the first century A.D., and thus provide the context for the world of sexual mores that influenced Jesus (more on this in chapter 3). Philo links the destruction of Sodom with God's hatred of homosexual intercourse. He speaks of such unions as "strange and unlawful"; therefore God "extinguished them."[30] When commenting on Leviticus 20:13, Philo connects the proscription to the pederasty practiced in the Roman world of his day. These unions stand condemned because the lover "pursues a pleasure that is contrary to nature (*para physin*)." He links this to the failure of the union to procreate and populate the earth, echoing Genesis 1:27-28.[31]

Josephus writes similarly, saying that our (Jewish) marriage "law recognizes only sexual intercourse that is in accordance with nature (*kata physin*)," intercourse of a man and woman that leads to procreation of children.[32] Later, Josephus notes that the Greeks attributed same-sex desires to their gods (who presumably also had intercourse between males) and accuses them of "inventing an excuse for their pleasures, which were disgusting and contrary to nature (*kata physin*)."[33]

Other writings from roughly this era present similar perspectives (see the citations in appendix 1; cf. *Sibylline Oracles* 5.430; *Testament of Levi* 17:11 where pederasty is listed among sins that characterize debased Gentile practices). Gagnon, whose contribution on this historical period is quite extensive, sums up the reasons for such negative views in intertestamental Judaism toward homosexuality. The predominant "against nature" contention functions as the underlying rationale. This rationale consists of: (1) such "intercourse cannot lead to procreation;" (2) it "represents an affront to God's sexual stamp on males and females by uniting two non-complementary sexual beings (with emphasis on the inherent degradation of males penetrated as if females); (3) homoerotic desire constitutes an excess of passion; and (4) homosexual intercourse is not practiced even by animals."[34]

That same-sex relations were negatively regarded in the Old Testament and Judaism can hardly be doubted. The evidence points all in the same direction. One can, of course, debate whether the strong emphasis put upon procreation or the strictness of purity laws can be used to mitigate the force of this proscription. But as we shall see, the New Testament corroborates this moral view of proscribing same-sex relations, even though it valorizes celibacy, which also does not mesh with the priority of procreation. The New Testament certainly does relax some of the purity laws, but proscription of same-sex relations does not appear to be one of these.[35]

To conclude this chapter focusing on the understanding of the human within God's whole creation, I cite Psalm 8, a paean of praise to a majestic God for the wonder of the human creation:

Prayer (Psalm 8)

O LORD, our Sovereign,
   how majestic is your name in all the earth!
You have set your glory above the heavens.
Out of the mouths of babes and infants
   you have founded a bulwark because of your foes,
   to silence the enemy and the avenger.

When I look at your heavens, the work of your fingers,
   the moon and the stars that you have established;
what are human beings that you are mindful of them,
   mortals that you care for them?

Yet you have made them a little lower than God,
   and crowned them with glory and honor.
You have given them dominion over the works of your
   hands;
you have put all things under their feet,
all sheep and oxen,
   and also the beasts of the field,
the birds of the air, and the fish of the sea,
   whatever passes along the paths of the seas.

O LORD, our Sovereign,
   how majestic is your name in all the earth!

CHAPTER THREE

JESUS AND
THE GOSPELS

Does Jesus speak to the issue of homosexuality? One anecdotal quip is:

"Did you see the book *Jesus and Homosexuality?*"
"No, what does it say?"
"Well, when you open it you find only blank pages!"

But is this really true? If Jesus said nothing directly on homosexuality, does it mean that he gives no moral guidance on the issue? In my judgment, Jesus never said anything directly against his followers participating in war (he commended the faith of the centurion in Matt. 8:5-12; see also Mark 15:39). Nor did he ever speak directly against the institution of slavery, so widespread in the Roman world of his time. But does this mean that Jesus taught nothing pertinent to the issues of war and slavery? My 1983 study, *Slavery, Sabbath, War, and Women*, saves me from this hermeneutical folly. Jesus did teach on sexuality, which by logical consequence speaks to homosexuality in ways parallel to how his teachings on justice-liberation and "love of enemies" speak to slavery and war respectively.

I see eight teachings of Jesus in the Gospels that have import for ethical discernment on homosexuality. I believe that all eight of these teachings reinforce the commands of love for God and love for neighbor.

1. Jesus' strong and unequivocal teaching against lust (Matt. 5:26-28). To be sure, the moral pitfall applies to both heterosexual and homosexual desires and relationships. This teaching signals a prime danger in sexual relationships, since today sexual intercourse is often how a relationship begins (a September 2000 National Public Radio newscast reported that over fifty percent of American youth are sexually active before age 15). Our culture is sex and lust oriented. But, thankfully, new winds are blowing. *Newsweek* reported in its December 9, 2002, issue that virginity among high school students has increased ten percent in the last decade.[1]

Similarly, Jesus' judgment against *porneia* (often translated fornication) counts also (see Matt. 5:32, 19:9; and especially Mark 7:21, Matt. 15:19), since it denotes all sexual genital relations outside heterosexual marriage. In *porneia*, sexual desire runs ahead of whole person relationship. In my view, it is not possible to address adequately the homosexual issue without also addressing this larger cultural phenomenon of extra- and pre-marital sex. But certainly, in first century Judaism homosexual intercourse would have been considered one of the worst of *porneia* offenses.

2. Jesus and the divorce trap-question. In Mark 10 (see also Matt. 19) Jesus is asked to declare himself between the liberal and conservative camps of interpretation regarding circumstances that legitimate divorce. Jesus identifies with neither, but appeals to the original will of God for marriage. He says that Moses granted divorce, with conditions, *because of* the people's hardness of heart, whereas God declared his will in original creation. Jesus quotes lines from Genesis 1:27 and 2:24: "from the beginning of creation, 'God made them male and female. For this reason a man shall leave his father and mother and be joined to his wife, and the two shall become one.'" It seems to me that this answer, so typical of Jesus who does not engage in casuistry, would also have been his answer had the question of same-sex covenant unions (unthinkable in Jewish culture) been posed to Jesus.

Most scholars believe that the "exception clause" ("except for unchastity") in Matthew 19 represents the later church's concession to Jesus' unconditioned declaration of God's will. But numerous interpreters have explained this as Jesus' own word as an exception to guilt, that is: since only the man could initiate a divorce in Jewish culture, he makes his wife to become an adulteress, unless (*except* if) she has already committed adultery. In any case, this 'exception' represents a decree of casuistry, though the two interpretations differ in that one assigns the exception to Jesus and the other to the later church's accommodation to cultural needs. For fuller treatment of these teachings of Jesus and their applicability to today's sexual crisis, see Robert Gagnon's seminal study, *The Bible and Homosexual Practice*.[2]

When this text is put into the light of an analysis of current culture, in which 200 years of western thought and culture have twisted understandings of sex in the corporate essence of society (see chapter 5), one might raise the question: does the church have the authority to accommodate to personal cases of homosexuality, either because in this text Jesus himself did so for divorce, or because the later church did? For example, if an adult homosexual was, as a child, molested for a protracted period of time by the same-sex parent, does this provide a basis for concession to the divine norm? In this case, might one make allowance within the theological rubric of God's permissive will, due to the hardness of the heart of the people that created a society in which such transgression occurs? Note that in this case the hardness of heart is not assigned to the child now become adult (rather, every ounce of mercy and support is merited on behalf of this person). Extended therapy may change this person's desire.

3. Jesus and the "eunuchs who have made themselves eunuchs for the sake of the kingdom of heaven" (Matt. 19:10-12). It is clear that Matthew attends to the consequences of Jesus' teaching, in that the declaration of the divine will is now followed by the disciples' conclusion that such a hard position on divorce makes it "better not to marry." Jesus acknowledges that not all will be able to accept the moral rigor of his teaching, so he then gives an alternative, which by today's cultural standards, at least, is no less rigorous and austere. Jesus speaks of three types of eunuchs: those so from birth, those made eunuchs by humans, and those who freely choose such sexually ascetic behavior "for the sake of the kingdom of heaven." It is striking that in our culture the possibility of freely choosing to be a eunuch in order to avoid violation of the divine will in sexual relationships is rarely considered or mentioned. But it is a text of the Jesus tradition. Further, celibacy has been honored by Jesus and Paul, by the Roman Catholic Church for centuries, and by some Protestants as well.[3] When taken seriously in its pertinence to the current debates on homosexuality, it is indeed difficult to say that Jesus never spoke to the homosexual issue (if any hermeneutical parallel is to be drawn between homosexuality and slavery or Christian participation in war).

4. Jesus on adultery (Matt. 5:31-32; Luke 7; John 4; 8:1-12). In both Mark 10 and Matthew 5:32, Jesus clearly indicates that adultery violates God's will. But in both Luke 7:36-50 and John 4, Jesus does not shun the adulteress (possibly the woman in Luke 7:36-50 was not married but a town prostitute). Rather, Jesus clearly breaks Pharisaic norms in socializing with and speaking to the adulteress and prostitute, in Luke 7 even receiving her affection, which in context is contrition for sin. When applying this teaching to the homosexuality issue, we should be quick to say that the Christian way is not to shun or ostracize those who are homosexual, but to provide a 'third way' (neither accepting their sin nor condemning

them) that frees them from their social marginalization, offering transformed self-understanding through forgiveness of sins, as Jesus clearly did on both occasions. We should also note that in John 8 there is a double judgment: against the male accusers and in the word to the woman, "Go, and sin no more." Consistently in the Gospels, Jesus does not flinch from mercy toward those regarded as sinners.

5. **Association with outcasts (sinners and tax collectors, a leper, the poor).** Almost all readers of Scripture observe that Jesus associated with the outcasts of his society, much to the dismay and chagrin of the Pharisees. Scholars do not agree as to how the word "sinner" is to be defined—whether it includes the poor who could not buy the proper sacrifices, the unclean,[4] or the Gentiles per se. But there is general agreement that the tax collectors were those who compromised Jewish loyalty through collusion with Roman rule. Lepers were most ostracized and put outside the community, for fear of contamination with the same disease. The poor were many and were judged negatively by observant Jews because their professions either forced purity contamination or precluded purchase of prescribed animals for sacrifice.

Clearly, Jesus turned the tables on all these cultural marks of status and rank. His first Beatitude promises blessing for those who are poor (Matt. 5:3 says "poor in spirit," which means the "brokenhearted"—broken because of their status in society). It seems to me that this clear and strong emphasis in the Gospel portrait of Jesus means that true followers of Jesus, regardless what position they take on homosexuality, must be welcoming and extending of hospitality to people of homosexual orientation and practice. But that commitment in and of itself does not resolve the issue, for two reasons:

a. The homosexuality debate hinges on whether or not to regard homosexual practice, not orientation, as sinful. Some people in the church, sometimes in leadership positions, say it should not be regarded as sinful, but normal, with no stigma attached to it. But if that is/were the case, then this strong strand of Jesus' teaching does not fit the situation under discussion, since gays and lesbians do not regard themselves as sinners and don't want society to regard them as such. Such a non-prejudicial society is then the transformed society that Jesus came to establish. But this scenario obtains only if homosexual practice, though regarded as sin by Scripture and the church through the ages, is not really sinful.

b. It is striking, in my opinion, that Jesus nowhere condoned the sin of the sinners to whom he graciously related. Rather, he empowered them into a transformed status in society, be it Levi the tax collector, the sinful woman, or the prodigal son (a story that epitomizes the stance of Jesus and the Father toward the outcast sinner).

6. **Jesus' ethics of compassion and holiness.** A companion emphasis to Jesus' association with the outcasts is what has been called in recent Jesus literature an "ethic" or "politics of compassion," which competes against the Pharisaic ethic of holiness. Marcus Borg has argued this point in his book, *Jesus: A New Vision.* And he is right, so long as 'Pharisaic' is kept in the claim. But to hold that Jesus disregards the fundamental call of his Scripture (Old Testament) to holiness is a false claim. The entire gospel testimony, including association with tax collectors and sinners, is the embodiment of God's holiness. In my judgment, it is a cheap deal to sacrifice holiness for compassion. Jesus' uniqueness lay precisely in his embodiment of both simultaneously. This lies at the heart of the incarnation. Were Borg's axiom accepted, it would make the Gospels contradict Paul and Peter, since in both sets of writings the call to holiness of life is unambiguous.

7. **Justice, judgment, and mercy.** In the New Testament, righteousness and justice translate the same Greek words (noun or verb forms). Luke's special emphasis is to show that Jesus, in contrast to the Pharisees, is the truly "righteous/just" person (23:47).[5] In Luke's narrative this contrasts to the pretended righteousness of the Pharisees. The "righteousness" of Jesus is linked, to be sure, to Jesus' inauguration of

a new society, which neither courts nor condemns Rome, nor sanctions Pharisaic piety. The charge the Jews put on Jesus, in turning him over to the Romans, is that he was a disturber of society, even of national security (23:2).

We must acknowledge that the modern notions of justice (so often used in homosexuality debates) are not present in the Gospels. Rather, the Old Testament notion of justice combined with mercy is more prominent.[6] In Paul, justice is part and parcel of justification, in which God justifies those who believe, even while they are weak (helpless), sinners, and enemies in relation to God (Rom. 5:6-11).[7] Romans 1-2 prepares for this declaration, setting the stage to make all people culpable and potentially redeemed through the work of Jesus Christ, for his shed blood covers all our sins.

The Gospels, as well as the whole New Testament, contain consistent emphases on judgment, especially upon those who fail to heed the word of Jesus, by not responding in repentance and seeking forgiveness of sin. Even Sodom (notoriously perverse) and Tyre and Sidon (Gentiles who know not the God of Israel—except for some) will fare better in the judgment than will Chorazin, Bethsaida, and Capernaum, who heard the word and witnessed Jesus' mighty deeds, but spurned the opportunity to believe and enter the kingdom of God. Contrary to popular emphasis, Jesus is not soft on judgment, even in Matthew and Luke where the wisdom (*sophia*) traditions appear.

8. Jesus' call for both discipline and mercy. Matthew 18:15ff. is a key passage, in story sequence, that combines the church's call to exercise discipline with the admonition to practice unlimited mercy. Verses 15-18 describe the process of addressing offense or sin within the congregation. The three stages (personal address, seeking another brother/sister in the discernment, and the congregation acting to regard the offender as a Gentile and tax collector) are motivated by the strong desire to keep the congregation faithful and by concern for repentance when needed, to be followed by forgiveness and reconciliation.[8] That is why the text focuses on forgiveness immediately after this. Peter queries, with anxiety, about how often one is to forgive another. Jesus' shock-answer, seventy times seven, is followed then with the parable of the unmerciful servant. Even though the lord of the servant released him from his debt, the same servant went out and tried to wring from those who owed him everything to the last penny, even throwing in prison those unable to pay. Then the lord summoned that unmerciful servant, scolded him for his actions, and threw him into jail until he could pay his debt to him. Jesus then says, "So my heavenly Father will do to every one of you, if you do not forgive your brother or sister from your heart" (Matt. 18:35).

Using this text and others in Matthew, Richard Hays characterizes Matthew's ethic as one of both rigor and mercy.[9] On the one hand, Jesus' followers are called to the ethic of perfection (or completeness in love), and on the other, to an unlimited bestowal of mercy and forgiveness toward those who sin against us (Matt. 18:21-22). These are important words for us as we seek to find our way on the issue of homosexuality. It seems to me that we as church have failed in carrying out direct address to those who offend, with the purpose of seeking restoration through love. How to do this in our present situation is not easy, since the debate often turns on whether any offense exists. But the motivation of mercy that forgives is the attitude that we should all have as we seek to find the way and live out our views on this subject.

Where do these eight forays into the hermeneutical significance of Jesus' teaching leave us with regard to the issue of homosexuality?[10] I suggest three points of summary.

1. From a hermeneutical standpoint, it cannot be held that Jesus said nothing to guide us in the homosexuality debate. His citation of Genesis 1:27 and 2:24 to answer the trap-question of divorce is as pertinent to homosexuality as is the command to love the enemy for the issue of war, or the text in Mark 10:35-45 for slavery.[11]

2. Jesus' teaching and example calls us to be welcoming and accepting of all people, including those of homosexual orientation, and even those practicing, whether in covenant unions, or more promiscuously. It was precisely a promiscuous sinner in Luke 7 whom Jesus received and declared forgiven before God.

3. Our response in daily life is to accept all people, but not to approve of conduct that violates God's will as declared in Jesus and Scripture more broadly. We need not trade holiness for compassion, nor compassion for holiness. It would be wrong to pit the first four emphases from Jesus against the last four. All eight are essential if we strive to be Jesus-type people. Only in the power of Jesus and God's Spirit, which anointed Jesus for ministry, will we be able to bring to bear upon the present situation the transforming power of the Gospel, to be an ecclesial witness to all eight dimensions of Jesus' being and teaching.

Given the exception clause in Matthew (5:32), we may need to recognize that the church lives with a certain degree of accommodation to culture. But this should not mean that we lose the vision of what God wills for human life (as also on divorce and remarriage). Just as God used people and institutions (kingship and war) in the Old Testament within a context of permissive will,[12] so God can use the church today in the midst of the homosexual reality and struggle, to work out the divine purpose to bring salvation to all people. Above all, let us not neglect the church's call to mission by haggling endlessly over this intractable issue of homosexuality.

Amid our efforts to understand and hear each other, those with whom we disagree, we should remember two essential points:

1. On many aspects of this issue there is general agreement:[13]

- condemnation of abusive and promiscuous
  heterosexuality and homosexuality

- recognition of the reality of homosexual orientation (though differences lie in understanding causation and feasibility of change)[14]
- commitment to love and respect all people, including homosexual people
- Christian ethics are for Christians
- ethical discernment on this matter is a communal issue, not a private affair.

2. This issue is essentially a pastoral issue, in the pastor's care for members, not a political issue, as it has become in our society and even in the church. Unfortunately, this issue has become so politicized that moral discernment is often marginalized in attempted conversations.[15] My concern is expressed well by Kathryn Greene-McCreight in her helpful article, "The Logic of the Interpretation of Scripture and the Church's Debate over Sexual Ethics":

> I fear that this debate may ultimately be "resolved" as it was in the APA, that is, with political lobbying and jockeying for power. If this is the case, whichever side "wins," the church will have lost an opportunity to witness to the love of Christ, that perfect love casts out all fear and which demands our obedience and deepest gratitude.[16]

It is my hope and prayer that as the church continues to deal with homosexuality, we might be able to de-politicize the issue in the church context and seek the wisdom from above.

Prayer

May God help us to heal the hurts of homosexual persons and their families, and not to use this issue to divide the church. Help us to acknowledge elements of the unknown in this issue, and to seek the Holy Spirit to guide us into all truth, as Jesus promised. May your wisdom, mercy, and grace, together with your transforming love, abound!

Jesus' prayer

"Our Father in heaven, hallowed be your name.
Your kingdom come.
Your will be done, on earth as it is in heaven.
Give us this day our daily bread.
And forgive us our debts,
*   as we also have forgiven our debtors.*
And do not bring us to the time of trial,
*   but rescue us from the evil one.*
[For yours is the kingdom, and power, and glory.
Forever and ever. Amen.]

—*Matthew 6:9-13*

CHAPTER 4

UNDERSTANDING PAUL ON HOMOSEXUAL PRACTICE

The storm center in understanding biblical teaching on homosexual practice focuses on certain Pauline texts, particularly Romans 1:24-27 and 1 Corinthians 6:9-11. The moral admonition of the later text recurs in the later pastoral epistle, 1 Timothy 1:10, at least in part. Some commentators also regard 1 Thessalonians 4:1-8 as directly related, since they regard an ambiguous Greek term to mean homosexual abuse of brothers in the community. Others translate the text more generically in regard to moral practice. This chapter examines these texts in sequence.

Romans 1:24-27

This is certainly the most pertinent and important text on the issue, since its function is to describe theologically the nature of humanity's condition outside salvation in Jesus Christ. The text contains a triple recurring motif: God gave them (humans) up (vv. 24, 26, 28). In verse 24 it is to their desires *(epithymiais)*: impure lusts and the degrading of their bodies. Why did God give them over to this? Because they exchanged the truth of God for a lie and worshiped and served the creature rather than the Creator. In verse 26 humanity is given over to degrading passion *(pathē)*, in which the natural sexual use *(chrēsin)* is replaced by the unnatural (or, literally, beyond nature—*para physin)*: females with females and males with males. The triple repetition of "God gave them over" is matched by a triple repeating of humans "exchanging" a God-intended practice for another:

> "and they exchanged the glory of the immortal God for images resembling a mortal human being or birds or four-footed animals or reptiles" (v. 23)
> "they exchanged the truth about God for a lie and worshiped and served the creature rather than the Creator, who is blessed forever! Amen" (v. 24)
>   "Their women exchanged natural intercourse for unnatural, and in the same way also the men, giving up natural intercourse with women, were consumed with passion for one another" (vv. 26-27)

In sum, the word *exchange (metellaxan)* is used thrice: exchanging the glory of God for images (v. 23), exchanging the truth of God for a lie (v. 25), and exchanging the natural use for the unnatural (vv. 26-27). Since "being given over" corporately is the result of these exchanges, any given person's desire is hardly freely chosen. Paul is not discussing the status of individuals.[1] But same-sex *desire* and *practice* are regarded as the result of a God-disowning culture, one that substitutes worship of the Creator with worship of creation (v. 25). This plight of the human condition arises from suppressing, through wickedness, elemental truth about God knowable through creation. Humans are without excuse because the "exchange actions" are ours, and the divine actions of "giving up" are the consequence. Now all of this, together with God's condemnation of people judging one another and boasting in the law but continuing to sin, leads to the eventual conclusion: "all have sinned and fall short of the glory of God" (Rom. 3:23). Thus, the gospel-gift is to all people: the righteousness of Christ is for us. We are to die to the old and resurrect to the new in baptism, and become sanctified by walking according to the Spirit that gives life and peace.

The context of Romans 1:24-27 is Paul's appeal to idolatry to make his larger case that both Gentiles *and Jews* stand condemned in the face of God's righteousness. The core of the argument is that those who suppress the truth by their wickedness do not know what they could know about God based on what is visible in creation.[2] Why? Evil deeds prevent them from seeing what could otherwise be seen in nature—that it is a manifestation of the sovereign Creator. They then worship creation, making idols to represent the God they do not know and cannot know unless the gospel of Jesus Christ is proclaimed to them, which they may then hear, understand, and receive (Rom. 10:14-17).

Paul uses same-sex desire and behavior as his most persuasive case, which, among other sins also (Rom. 1:29-31), illustrates the extent of blindness and self-justification of their deeds as "approved," not only for themselves but for others too (1:32). This text is usually understood as Paul's description of the pagan Gentile world, but nowhere does this text specify Gentiles as the object of description.[3] After Paul declares God's condemnation on those who judge others (2:1-8), he summarizes as follows in 2:9-11, "There will be anguish and distress for everyone who does evil, the Jew first and also the Greek, but glory and honor and peace for everyone who does good, the Jew first and also the Greek. For God shows no partiality." This is the first occurrence since 1:18 of Jew and Gentile, in the same order as in 1:17.

John E. Toews, in his commentary on Romans (which delimits as one section Rom. 1:18–2:3), perceives the structure of the text differently than most and calls this point of assumed Gentile reference into question:

> This section has a distinctive structure that uses the logic of the Jewish scheme of just judgment (*ius talionis*): crime,

judgment, punishment. The scheme is repeated four times, 1:22-24, 1:25-27, 1:28-31, 1:32-2:3.

Crime	God's Reaction	Moral Consequences
v. 22: claiming to be wise, they exchanged (*allassō*) the glory	God gave them up	v. 24: therefore (*dio*), impurity, dishonoring of the body
v. 25: who (*hoitenes*) exchanged (*metallassō*) the truth	God gave them up	v. 24: therefore (*dio*), vv. 26-7: sexual perversion
v. 28: they not thinking fit to know God	God gave them up	v. 28: just as (*kathōs*) vv. 28-31: unthinking mind, social vice
v. 32: who (*hoitenes*) know the just judgment of God	no excuse	v. 2:1: therefore (*dio*), judge yourself, judgment of God

The issue in verses 22-24 is idolatry; humanity exchanges the glory of God for a form of humanity and animals. Verse 23 refers to Israel's worship of the golden calf at Sinai by citing Psalms 106:20 and Jeremiah 2:11. "God gave them up"— the language involves an act of divine judgment—to impurity and the dishonoring of the human body. The most patent manifestation of both is sexual perversion. The linkage of idolatry and perversion is a common one in the Old Testament and Judaism. Idolatry is the root human sin in Jewish thinking and in Paul. It leads to all other sins. But the logic of "idolatry leads to perversion" is usually applied to the Gentiles. The surprise here is that the illustration Paul uses to document idolatry is the unfaithfulness of Israel itself, not the Gentiles.[4]

True indeed, the argument of Romans 1:18ff. leads to the conclusion of 3:9, "we have already charged that both Jews and Greeks are under the power of sin." Also, in 3:23, "all have sinned and fall short of the glory of God." Thus, the gospel-gift is to all people: the righteousness of Jesus Christ is for us.

This text in Romans is quite clear, but to what extent is it stereotypical of the Gentiles—even though Gentiles are not specifically mentioned? Likewise, to what extent is the description in chapter 2 stereotypical of Jews—even though Jews are not specifically mentioned in 2:1-2? But the fact that 1:18–2:8 does not designate Gentiles or Jews and that 2:9 includes them in parallel offenses or good deeds mutes the point of stereotypical description.[5] Clearly, Paul's theological purpose is to lead up to his basic point in chapter 3 (cited above), and again in chapter 5—that God justifies us while we are yet weak, sinners, and enemies. In this respect no distinction between Jew and Gentile may be made, nor indeed *shall* be made.

As we would expect, the text does not distinguish between homosexual orientation and behavior. On the contrary, they seem to be blended in the text with no consideration of their difference as we have come to perceive and speak of it today. How then does the text speak to the phenomenon of same-sex practice prevalent in western urban cultures in these recent decades? Scholars have "explained" the text in various ways, in order to remove it from the canon of ethical obligation for the life of the contemporary culture and church. I identify seven of these interpretations and the rationales they give, and then test the adequacy of each interpretation. The seven can be subdivided. Two come to new understandings by proposing new meanings within the language of the text (though both perceive this from background studies). Five gain new insight by focusing more on the historical and/or cultural backgrounds of the text, i.e. the world in which the text was constructed.

Textual Proposals

1. Key issue: "against nature." John Boswell's interpretation holds that Romans 1:24-27 speaks only about homosexual acts that are alien to one's nature (i.e. in conflict with one's desire). These acts only are condemned.[6] Thus it is wrong for a heterosexual person to engage in a homosexual act. But for homosexuals, who act in accord with their nature (not against or beyond [*para*] their nature), same-sex practice is not sin.

This interpretation is not persuasive in regard to what Paul and Scripture intended. It can only be a read-back into the text from the assumed superior knowledge of our contemporary culture. In the larger context of Romans, such a maneuver discounts the main point, that all are caught in the web of sin. Thus such a reading not only undermines the intent of the text, as Richard Hays points out, but it is anachronistic.[7] The point of the text is to say precisely that natural desire has gone awry.[8] Or, as Christopher Seitz, Old Testament professor formerly at Yale Divinity School and now at St. Andrews University, Scotland, says, it contradicts the "plain sense" of Scripture.[9]

Paul's appeal to "nature" here, as in 1 Corinthians 11, renders his argument less than perspicuous, however, and especially so in light of similar appeal by Philo and Greek writers from Plato to the Stoics. Numerous writers (Grieb, Schoedel, Fredrickson, et al.;[10] but see Countryman's explanation below) note this problematic aspect of the text. Even apart from this text and the particular issue of homosexuality, Paul's referral to 'nature' for warrant in moral imperative has been discussed widely in commentaries and articles over the last century. Is Paul appealing here to conventional cultural views of what is natural and unnatural or to a theological doctrine of natural law? "Natural theology" as such contradicts the very argument Paul is making, since humans cannot know apart from divine revelation what is evident in natural revelation, due to being blinded-sided by sin. One might even argue further, as Jeffrey Satinover does, that Paul's primary reference to nature makes the point that by nature all are sinners, in collusion with Adam and Eve.[11] Only through regeneration by God's grace and the power of Christ and the Spirit are we able to live the new nature (see Rom. 6; Eph. 4:17–5:13).

Gagnon's extensive study of the varied proposals to understand Paul's use of natural/unnatural concludes,

> That Paul was thinking of "nature" not as "the way things are usually done" (i.e. cultural convention) but rather as "the material shape of the created order" is also apparent from his previous illustration that idolatry entails the suppression of truth.... In other words, *visual* perception of the *material* creation that God has made . . . should lead to a mental perception about the nature of God and God's will....
>
> Similarly, the reader should expect that the appeal to nature in 1:26-27 had to do, at least primarily, with the visual perception of male-female body complementarity (the fitness of the sex organs).[12]

The persuasiveness of Gagnon's view for me is that it does not contradict the widespread notions in Paul's cultural environment that "natural" equals heterosexual sexual acts and "unnatural" equals homosexual sexual acts, nor the specific view of "nature" set forth by William Countryman (in accord with an organism's past and usual functioning), nor the view that what is "natural" or "unnatural" is based simply upon what one perceives via visual senses. But beyond all this it recognizes Paul's theological heritage, that his belief in the Genesis 1-2 teaching that male and female were created for union with each other foundationally determined his negative view of same-sex relations.

2. Erotic passion, not homosexuality per se. David E. Fredrickson examines the Romans text from the context of both Jewish and Gentile cultures to observe just what precisely it is that is condemned in sexual relationships, homosexual and/or heterosexual. He proposes that the deviance and sin that stirs God's wrath, or, to use modern language, is inappropriate, is failure to control sexual passion. Thus in Romans 1 he zeroes in on such terms as *epithymia* (v. 24), *pathos* (v. 26), *ekkaio* (v. 27), *orexis* (v. 27) and *planē* (v. 27). He contends that all these focus on unrestrained lusts of various sexual desires, of whatever kind, that have mastered a person. Thus the text should be viewed as condemning not really homosexuality per se, but unrestrained sexual desire in both homosexual and heterosexual relations.[13]

Without doubt, Fredrickson has identified a key emphasis of the text, and it is true that many Greek writers, and even the Old Testament, would agree that burning passion is the cause of moral downfall. But, as with Boswell, this interpretation dodges the clear appropriation of this passion to the homoerotic expression. Nothing in this text is said of unrestrained passions in heterosexual relations, even though the general New Testament word *porneia* would include it. If we are fully to understand this text, we are not helped much by this nuance. It prevents perceiving just how this particular text connects unrestrained passion and lust with same-sex erotic desire.

Background Understandings

3. Cultural context issue: pederasty. Robin Scroggs' interpretation contends that Romans 1:24-27 refers to pederasty, a practice quite common in educated Greek culture. Pederasty was when an older man assumes a type of foster parent relation with a young boy, taking responsibility for his development holistically but also receiving sexual favors from him.[14] Since this is so different from the type of loving mutual same-sex relations we speak of today, Scroggs reasons, this text doesn't speak to our contemporary situation. Thus this text does not address the issue of loving, covenant same-sex relationships that we currently consider.[15]

But is this really true?[16] Since Paul didn't use the Roman cultural and Greek terms for pederasty, we need to question Scroggs' interpretation. If Paul had pederasty in mind, he could and likely would have used the rather common Greek word, *paiderastēs*.[17] Hence Scrogg's view is inadequate. Paul had in mind not only pederasty, but the wider range of same-sex relations in the Gentile world, though this likely did not include the notion of "homosexual *orientation*" (but see Brooten below).

Significantly, Romans 1:24-27 not only speaks about and against male same-sex desires and practices, but also includes female same-sex desire and practices. This fact in itself discounts the pederasty explanation, since pederasty in Greco-Roman practice applied to men and boys.

4. Dirt (and Greed), not Sin. William Countryman has approached the study of this topic by examining how the worldview of that time influenced biblical writers on topics of sexuality. He says every culture has its own way of defining what is dirty. In our western culture we teach children not to put certain things, like coins, in their mouths, because they are dirty. From this perspective we can understand that practices such as cross-dressing and same-sex sexual acts were considered unacceptable, because they violated purity laws and were regarded as dirty. The same logic is used to explain why sex during menstruation was forbidden.[18] Sexual practices among the Gentiles were also somewhat stereotypically regarded as dirty.

Using this grid, combined with his extensive study of the relation between property and greed as also bearing upon sexual proscriptions, and with reference to the contemporary honor/shame culture, Countryman analyzes Romans 1:24-32 in the context of these emphases. Contrary to the common notion that Paul regards homosexual acts as sins, Countryman rightly points out that such acts are not designated as sins in the text (none of Paul's usual words for sin, such as *hamartia, asebia,* and *adikia* occur here). Language of sin is used in relation to idolatry in 1:18-23 and in vv. 29-31, mentioning first *wickedness (adikia)* and then immediately greed *(pleonexia).* But in verses 24-27 a reading of the texts that takes in a neutral sense the key words (such as *epithymias,* which could mean anything from lust to eagerness) discloses that the text regards these as *purity* offenses (i.e. uncleanness) together with *shame* in the dishonoring of the body. While this is true, it could be argued that v. 18, which contains two *sin* words *(asebia* and *adikia)* functions as an introduction for the entire section, not just the verses speaking of idolatry.

This treatment of Paul's use of natural/unnatural is instructive, for Countryman regards it as more in keeping with the notion of that which is in continuity with its past; that is, the grafting in of the Gentiles in Romans 11:24 is over against nature *(para physin),* whereas Israel was according to nature *(kata physin).* Countryman considers Paul's use of nature in 1 Corinthians to be in a different sense, that of "widespread social usage." If that were the meaning in Romans 1:24-27 this argument would fall flat, since the Greek world accepted homosexual intercourse (at least some earlier Greek writers considered pederasty the highest form of love). Rather, what Paul is saying in 1:26-27 is that this "over against nature" (as in 11:24) meant "that Gentiles experienced only heterosexual desire before God visited uncleanness on them and have therefore changed their 'nature,' that is, lost a certain continuity with their past."[19]

Summing up his view, Countryman says, "While Paul wrote of such acts as being unclean, dishonorable, improper, and 'over against nature,' he did not apply the language of sin to them at all. Instead, he treated homosexual behavior as an integral if unpleasingly dirty aspect of Gentile culture."[20] Countryman thus contends that homosexuality is viewed not as sin, but was in that culture a part of "dirty" Gentile culture. Thus Paul regards it a "purity" issue, not a moral issue.[21]

Countryman's other main contribution examines the role of "property" concepts in relation to sexual ethics, in both Testaments but in detail in the Old. He holds that both Jesus and Paul punctured and transformed the property notion of sexual relations to a major degree, by prioritizing the reign of God over sexual relations and family. But Old Testament views continued in the culture, and thus sexual offenses were regarded in part at least as violation of patriarchal authority and hierarchical order, and were thus also motivated by greed, coveting that which belongs to another. Adultery, for example, was wrong because it violated another man's property rights.

By explicating the meaning of biblical sexual teaching within these two worldviews, purity and property combined with greed, Countryman argues that we cannot move from the specifics of the text to contemporary life on sexual ethics. Based on his study he proposes six principles that arise from the text and that call "for an exercise of judgment in relating them to the facts of our sexual life" today.[22]

Countryman's extensive study is helpful, but somewhat global in his portrayal of how pervasive male property notions were in determining sexual codes of conduct, especially for the Old Testament. For if one looks closely, for example, at the rationale for not "uncovering nakedness" in the commands of Leviticus 18, it is said that while the mother's nakedness is the father's, it also says the father's nakedness is the mother's (Lev. 18:7). In several verses following, the concept of "one's own" occurs, which seems to defy the "property" conception. The point becomes even clearer in the New Testament, in both Paul and Jesus, as Countryman observes. But Countryman does not stress adequately the radical nature, given the cultural property conceptions, of

1 Corinthians 7, for example, which portrays man and woman in marriage and celibacy as fundamentally equal in initiative, rights, and forgoing of rights. Likewise, Ephesians 5:18-33 shows that the gospel has broken the "property" view of husband-wife relations. The gospel, initially in Old Testament and more fully in the New, has broken the cultural hegemony of male domination.[23]

I agree with Countryman that a distinction must be made between impurity and sin (see my citation of Paula Fredriksen, chapter 3, note 4). As numerous scholars point out, being impure or unclean is rectified not by confession of sin, but by observing purification laws.

Another weakness in Countryman's effort to claim impurity (dirt), not sin, as the problem with "unnatural" sexual relations is the lack of considering how the Scripture throughout the Old Testament considered idolatry. Countryman does identify idolatry as the cause for God's "giving over" the Gentiles to unnatural desires and the sins of verses 28-32. But how can one hear the fierce castigation of the Old Testament prophets against idolatry and think that Paul, steeped in Judaism, would regard its consequences as impurity? I suppose exile can be viewed as a drastic punishment consigning Israel to impurity (but that would require evidence and extended argumentation), but to regard idolatry's consequence as merely impurity does not do theological justice to the scriptural tradition found in the Old Testament. It seems to belittle the seriousness of religious heritage out of which Paul wrote.

To illustrate the point, I quote two portions of Psalm 106, from *The Jerusalem Bible*, vv. 36-37 and 47:

Serving the pagan's idols,
they found themselves trapped
into sacrificing their own sons
and daughters to demons.

Yahweh our God and Savior,
Gather us from among the pagans,
To give thanks to your holy name
and to find our happiness in praising you.

To note that no word for sin occurs in v. 37 of this Psalm counts little. Consequences of idolatry for Israel were of ultimate seriousness. In fact, the concept of sin as "falling short" of God's will would be too weak in describing the consequence of idolatry from a Hebraic point of view. Nor does Levitical-type "impurity" fit, except perhaps in the sense that God in the exile *gave them over* to the impure pagan Gentile world. But there are no simple cleansing rules for the consequences of idolatry, such as bathing, waiting until the next morning, etc. Even so, Yahweh God in his steadfast love rescued Israel time after time (v. 42), even bringing them back from exile. Further, Countryman assumes that Gentiles are the subject of Romans 1:18-32. As noted above, there is reason to question this.

In addition, the Leviticus proscription against same-sex relations makes no provision for cleansing from impurity. Rather, the penalty is most severe—death. This, along with other major violations of sexual boundaries that entail death as well, are grave moral offenses, not just simply trespassing purity laws.[24] The grace of God in Jesus Christ overcomes the severe penalty for such offenses; likewise, the many other sins humans commit are forgivable (those in verses 30-32 and more besides).

5. **Paul, a child of his time.** Another take on reducing the force of this text for the contemporary issue is represented well by William R. Schoedel.[25] Schoedel explicates in some detail the homophobic disgust and repugnance toward same-sex eros and genital relations found in several leading Greek writers, in which same-sex desire is often connected to unrestrained passion. Since negative assessment of same-sex practice is found in Plato, Philo, and also from a medical standpoint

in Soranus—as well as in the Old Testament—it is to be expected that Paul as a child of his time would look at same-sex eros in similar fashion.[26]

However, Schoedel contends that, in addition to purity concerns, the underlying factor in this negative assessment of same-sex practice was the view held of the degradation, through casting in the female role, of the feminized boy or young man in the relationship.[27] First Corinthians 11, in its expectation of long hair for women and short hair for men, is adduced as a corollary, rooted in views of nature expressed by Philo, Epictetus, and other Greek writers. But because of the contextual character of these views, the same judgment need not apply to same-sex relations today. Schoedel also recognizes that in both Judaism and Christianity new conceptions of the family were emerging that forbade the male the prerogative to sexually penetrate "at will not only a wife but also his male and female slaves or a young male favorite. Sexual politics were undergoing a sea change. And a good deal can still be said in favor of the new model of the family that was emerging."[28] But since this new model "tended to ignore aspects of the physiological and psychological realities of sexuality," Schoedel concludes by saying we should be willing to accommodate, for it "is surely not unimaginable that a God who seeks the outcast would call those to him whose sexual orientation sets them apart from the majority."[29]

What is striking about this analysis is its articulation of two factors of our contemporary reality: a revolution in attitude during the last decades to value equally the female and male, and the need to accommodate to cultural realities. Both are key factors in the gradual normalization of acceptance of same-sex practice. Note, however, that Schoedel's theological grounding spoke of God as accepting those with same-sex orientation. Many draw the line between orientation and practice.

Depending on one's church tradition, the call to accommodate is compelling, if generally there is accommodation of

Scripture to contemporary culture, often with social pressure to do so. But some Christian groups, particularly those in the Anabaptist tradition, have resisted this line of reasoning. For similar arguments are used to justify the church's participation in war. Cultural accommodation, even though often done, is not inherently a theological value in Anabaptist history and theology.

   6. **Patriarchy and gender asymmetry.** Writers in the feminist stream, represented well by Bernadette Brooten, argue that New Testament views on same-sex relations were a by-product of a patriarchal culture that enforced gender asymmetry, which Jesus came to critique and replace with egalitarian relationships. The New Testament condemnation of same-sex relationships, which threatened patriarchal control, represents the residual influence of the patriarchal culture.[30] Brooten, summarizing her argument, says,

> I have argued that Paul's condemnation of homoeroticism, particularly female homoeroticism, reflects and helps maintain a gender asymmetry based on female subordination. I hope that churches today, being apprised of the history that I have presented, will no longer teach Rom. 1:26f. as authoritative.[31]

   John Nolland, however, critiques Brooten's emphasis on the "gender asymmetry by female subordination,"[32] Brooten may be misrepresenting Paul, whom many have argued was a strong feminist liberationist. Brooten does not take into account, Nolland rightly says, Paul's teaching on sexual equality so evident, *against prevailing culture*, in Galatians 3:28 and 1 Corinthians 7:3-4. Precisely because of this revolutionary theological insight, in Romans 1:26-27 Paul puts in close parallel male and female homosexuality, most likely reflecting Genesis 1:26. If Brooten were correct, how could the *parallel* logic hold, since the woman is not put into either gender asymmetry or female subordination in a lesbian relationship? The *parallelism* between male and female same-sex practices refutes Brooten's explanation. Nolland rightly observes, "Whatever is wrong with these practices [in 1:26-27], it is evidently the same thing that is wrong with both" gay and lesbian relationships.[33] Thus it cannot be claimed that Paul judged female homoeroticism to be wrong *because* it involved female trespassing into the male role domain. Other reasons for this moral judgment are determinative.

Thus while Brooten has persuasively critiqued the many explanations previously set forth, which attended more to male homosexuality than to female, her own argument, rooted in the immorality of the view in ancient culture that females were inferior, is also not convincing, given the larger Pauline literary context. For in that context God's act of gospel-grace levels the field between male and female (see Paul's daunting freedom to make God's *royal* promise to David effectual for both "sons and daughters" in 2 Cor. 6:18, an inclusiveness with no textual precedent). Romans 1:26-27, with its rare parallel of males and females in Paul's treatment of same-sex practice, is further evidence of the same. Moreover, Paul ends this same epistle with a great tribute to the significant role of women in the missionary and leadership roles of early Christianity (see Rom. 16).

7. **Total cultural disconnect.** Walter Wink argues for a total cultural disconnect in ethics on sexuality. As a whole, the Bible, says Wink, contains such a wide and inappropriate set of sexual practices and thought that to make it a guide for sexual ethics today is highly questionable. We would not want to include in our sexual practices polygamy, concubines, or levirate marriage. And we also don't practice the death penalty for the transgression of the list of sexual offenses in Leviticus 20:10-16, including those who engage in same-sex genital relations. Of twenty rules on sexuality, Wink says we today generally disagree with sixteen and agree only with four: prohibition of incest, rape, adultery, and intercourse with animals.[34]

Clearly, Wink's argument cannot be dismissed lightly, for there is much truth in it. Its chief weakness, however, is that it does not take intracanonical dialogue seriously (almost all his twenty cases are from the Old Testament), as is necessary also in speaking about how Scripture speaks to slavery, war, and the role of women.[35] It does not develop the positive contribution that Scripture in both Testaments provides for sexual ethics. Wink holds that "[t]here is no Biblical sex ethic," but that our sex ethic must simply express Jesus' love command. This is too easy a dismissal of biblical authority for sexual ethics (see e.g., 1 Thess. 4:1-8), regardless of ones personal views on same-sex covenant relationships.

Despite the many efforts (and there are more strategies than reported here) to explain the biblical text to gain space for freedom to affirm same-sex relationships, the variety is itself telling. So many attempts, of different and sometimes contradictory nature, have been used to reinterpret the text that the effort appears exegetically suspicious. Any one explanation, when viewed in comparison to others, remains unconvincing. I prefer—and it seems to me to be more honest—to not attempt to rework what the texts say and mean with or by tenuous interpretations. In principle, however, I am certainly not opposed to new interpretations of Scripture. But in the cases I've examined above, they simply are not persuasive.

Rather, it seems to me conclusive that:

1. Same-sex genital practices were considered morally wrong by Scripture, and Romans 1:26-27 is a clear case on this matter (on this Wink agrees).

2. There is likely a gap between the consistent biblical repudiation of same-sex genital *practices* and contemporary understandings of sexual *orientation*, even though some writers are now arguing the Greco-Roman world also recognized aspects of orientation.[36]

The issue of current debate is whether, in light of this gap between Scripture and current understandings of homosexuality (and there is wide variety here also), we hold that Scripture condemns contemporary homosexual practice in any and every form. Is current homosexual practice—especially of a covenant union quality—now to be regarded differently than homosexual practices were regarded in Scripture? Before we can adequately answer that question, we need to ask why there is such distance between contemporary sexual views and the sexual ethical ideals of the New Testament and early church. The next chapter on western culture proposes that numerous contemporary factors have created this dilemma.

1 Corinthians 6:9 and 1 Timothy 1:10

In discussing 1 Corinthians 6:9 and 1 Timothy 1:10, Robin Scroggs recognizes that the term *arsenokoites* is likely derived from the Septuagint (LXX) version of the two Leviticus texts discussed above. It is a compound word, derived from *arsenos* (male) and *koiten* (compare English work *coitus)*, both of which occur in the Greek translation of Leviticus 18:22 and 20:13.[37] Scroggs is likely correct on this matter, and this is an important factor in assessing the situation. This word may have been coined by Paul, since it occurs only here in the New Testament and not in earlier Greek textual sources where homoerotic acts are discussed.[38] As David Wright asserts in his careful study, the two texts in Leviticus had influence also upon early Christian thought, beyond what John Boswell acknowledges. For the term *arsenokoites* appears both in these two New Testament Pauline texts and in the early church fathers.[39]

My colleague, Jacob Elias, presents the issues surrounding the debate:

> In 1 Corinthians 5:9-11 and 6:9-11, Paul includes several lists of condemned kinds of behavior. The longest of these lists includes the two terms frequently linked to homosexuality:

1 Cor. 5:9	1 Cor. 5:10	1 Cor. 5:11	1 Cor. 6:9-11
I wrote to you not to associate with *pornois,*	not at all meaning *tois pornois* of this world, or the greedy and robbers, or idolators, since you would then need to go out of the world.	But now I am writing to you not to associate with anyone who bears the name of brother or sister who is *pornos* or greedy, or is an idolator, reviler, drunkard, or robber.	Do you not know that wrongdoers will not inherit the kingdom of God? Do not be deceived! *Pornoi,* idolators, adulterers, *malakoi, arsenokoitai,* thieves, the greedy, drunkards, revilers, robbers—none of these will inherit the kingdom of God.

The word which occurs in all four contexts is *pornoi,* meaning "one who practices sexual immorality" or more specifically "fornicator." The meaning of the other two underlined terms is much debated (as is evident when comparing Bible translations, see below):

1. The adjective *malakoi,* meaning "soft," occurs in the New Testament only two times. In 1 Corinthians 6 and in Jesus' query whether the crowds had expected John the Baptist to wear soft robes (Matt. 11:8; Luke 7:25). Who then are (literally) "the soft ones" in 1 Corinthians 6:9? Attempted explanations have included:

  a. effeminate, or the submissive partner in a homosexual relationship, whose lifestyle is thought to resemble that of a woman (Phillips)
  b. catamite, or the passive and normally younger partner in a pederastic relationship (Jerusalem Bible)
  c. male prostitute, or an effeminate call-boy (NIV, NRSV, Scroggs)

2. The term *arsenokoitai*, etymologically "a man who has intercourse with another man" (reminiscent of words used in Lev. 18:22; 20:13), appears in the New Testament only here and in 1 Timothy 1:10. This may be an original word coming from Paul himself or another Hellenistic Jew, and derived from the Greek Septuagint translation of Leviticus 18:22 and 20:13. Proposed meanings:

   a. pederast, or the older man who takes the dominant active role in a pederastic relationship (Scroggs)
   b. sodomite, or a male person who engages in sexual relations (often abusive) with another man (KJV: abusers of themselves with mankind; NIV: homosexual offenders; NRSV: sodomites)
   c. male prostitute, or a man available for contracted sexual services for women and/or men (Boswell)
   d. some translations propose one generic expression to convey the combined meaning (TEV, NEB: homosexual perverts; RSV: sexual perverts)

All this begs some reflection on the relevance of these texts for Christian understanding. In addressing the problem of sexual immorality in Corinth (including an instance of incest, 1 Cor. 5:1-5), Paul warns the believers in Corinth not even to associate with those within the church who persist in such behavior (5:9-13). Such wrongdoers will not inherit the kingdom of God, Paul warns (6:9-10). Addressing the Corinthian believers, however, Paul reminds them that "such were some of you" and then reassures them "but you were washed, you were sanctified, you were justified in the name of the Lord Jesus and in the Spirit of our God" (6:11). A key question: In Christ are homosexual person (also drunkards, robbers, the greedy, and the others) saved from their nature and/or behavior?

The most fiercely debated question, however, is whether the terms *malakoi* and *arsenokoitai* refer generally to all persons engaging in homosexual activity or more specifically to persons involved in abusive homosexual activity.[40]

Indeed, the issue as to whether the meaning of these terms denotes same-sex relations generally or some particular type has been hotly debated. Given Corinth's reputation of sexual libertinism, it is most likely Paul and his readers knew of same-sex relations of different types, from more stable long-term partnerships to more abusive ones, though neither temple prostitution nor pederasty would necessarily have been considered abusive in that culture. That Paul does not make such distinctions is important to observe. Rather, the reasons for his judgment must lie elsewhere.

After thorough consideration of the scholarly debate on these texts, Robert Gagnon holds that *arsenokoitai* (and *malakoi*) in 1 Corinthians 6:9 are to be understood in relationship to what Paul has already said on why same-sex relationships are wrong in Romans 1:24-27. Gagnon sums up Paul's view, which concurs with that of first-century Judaism in Philo and Josephus:

> What was wrong, first and foremost, for Paul in the case of same-sex intercourse was the fact that the participants were members of the same sex rather than the opposite sex. It was not a question of whether the sexual relationship was characterized by mutual affirmation or exploitation, parity in age or age disparity, procreative capacity or procreative incapacity, innate sexual urges or contrived sexual urges, or any other extrinsic set of antinomies. In order to determine the semantic spread of the term *arsenokoitai*, it is a mistake to focus exclusively on the one or two most common forms of same-sex intercourse in Paul's day at the expense of ignoring Paul's reason for opposing same-sex intercourse, which has little or nothing to do with factors that could distinguish unacceptable forms of same-sex intercourse from acceptable forms. [41]

I believe Gagnon is correct on this matter. In Romans 1:18-32, 1 Corinthians 6:9, and 1 Timothy 1:10, Paul was thinking in accord with the Jewish tradition of his moral upbringing, and secondarily, from the popular view of Gentile vices. He was speaking of homosexual practices. He was not making fine distinctions, since all homosexual practices were off limits for Jews (cf. Jesus' silence).

Interacting with numerous contributions to this debate, Anthony Thiselton comes to a similar conclusion in discussing this text in his recent commentary on 1 Corinthians. He regards C. Wolff's study convincing, arguing that Paul would have witnessed both abusive relationships and "genuine love" between males in his travels. The distance between then and now is not so great on this subject: "The more closely writers examine Graeco-Roman society and the pluralism of its ethical traditions, the more the Corinthian situation appears to resonate with our own."[42]

In assessing the arguments that these texts in 1 Corinthians and 1 Timothy refer to pederasty, he says, "many [scholars] tend to regard the evidence of restricting the term to contexts of *pederasty* linked with male prostitution as at best indecisive and at worst unconvincing."[43] Observing that the first five vices in the list are sexual in nature and the last five are "grasping, greed sins," he rightly says that the two that "concern same-sex relations receive no greater emphasis than the other eight."[44]

1 Thessalonians 4:1-8

1 Thessalonians 4:3-6 merits consideration especially because it addresses a key moral principle as well as possibly the specific topic under discussion. Here Paul calls the believers to holiness, to abstain from sexual immorality, to learn to control your own body, and not to "exploit or transgress" your brother in this matter. While the interpretive decisions are difficult in the Greek text, as Jacob Elias notes in his commentary on 1 and 2 Thessalonians, the text clearly calls for holiness in regard to sexual matters.[45] Larry Yarbrough, in his extensive study of this text, believes that verse 6 refers to homosexual relations when it prohibits

"exploiting a brother in this matter" (i.e., the area of sexuality).[46] While some interpreters and translators think the phrase "in this matter" *(en tō pragmati)* means *business* (KJV says "defraud his brother in any matter"), most think it refers in context to *sexuality*. Holiness in sexual relationships is prescribed by this apostolic admonition. Whether homosexual relations are specifically intended by the generic wording is doubtful, but not impossible, given the notion of "exploiting a brother" in this same admonition. Even in the broader sense of sexual relations, the call to holiness in all relationships certainly assumes ethical boundaries in sexual practices and poses for reflection the question whether homosexual practice would not thereby be proscribed.

Acts 15

Acts 15 has come into the current discussion in order to remind us that sometimes God's people have to make a 180-degree turnabout in their thinking. By appealing to Acts 15, Jeffrey Siker, in his *Theology Today* article, which is reprinted in his edited volume on homosexuality, has made a strong case for the church to undergo a heart-shift on this issue.[47] He says that like the Gentiles, gays and lesbians have received God's welcome into the faith community by his bestowing the Holy Spirit upon them, and who are we to contradict the work of God? Almost I am persuaded, until I read Acts 15:20, and realize that the included Gentiles are now expected to conform to the Jewish sexual codes that forbid *unchastity* (*porneia*), a generic term matching our popular word (sexual) *immorality*.

The New Testament texts cited above leave no doubt whether same-sex intercourse is included as one expression of immorality. Further, inclusion of Gentiles was an anticipated sign of eschatological fulfillment, the time and work of the Messiah. But I find no analogy in prophetic Scripture regarding inclusion of practicing gays and lesbians into Christ's body (Isa. 56:3-8, in its inclusion of foreigners and eunuchs, hardly applies. Jesus does privilege eunuchs who become so for kingdom challenges—and this serves as a clear biblical basis for celibacy, not only for the homosexual person).[48]

The mission of the church is to all people, and this is indeed the strongest argument for the church to reconsider its stand on this issue. Certainly this means acceptance of all people regardless of their sexual identity. But here, as I note below, sexual identity gets in the way of the fundamental issue of sinners becoming saints. And, in that process, Scripture and the church have always assumed that thinking and action changes in many ways, including sexual commitments and freedoms.

In concluding such analysis of Paul on this difficult topic, it is important to hear also the depth of spiritual intimacy Paul knows with God, and his prayer for believers. Indeed, this prayer is one we can use in praying for our brothers and sisters in the church, whether they think as we do on this topic or whether they think differently:

Prayer

For this reason I bow my knees before the Father, from whom every family in heaven and on earth takes its name. I pray that, according to the riches of his glory, he may grant that you may be strengthened in your inner being with power through his Spirit, and that Christ may dwell in your hearts through faith, as you are being rooted and grounded in love. I pray that you may have the power to comprehend, with all the saints, what is the breadth and length and height and depth, and to know the love of Christ that surpasses knowledge, so that you may be filled with all the fullness of God.

Now to him who by the power at work within us is able to accomplish abundantly far more than all we can ask or imagine, to him be glory in the church and in Christ Jesus to all generations, forever and ever. Amen.

—*Ephesians 3:14-21*

CHAPTER FIVE

ANALYSIS OF CONTEMPORARY WESTERN CULTURE

The biblical interpretive task includes not only understanding the texts in their cultural contexts, but also seeking to understand ourselves as interpreters in our cultural context. What are the forces bearing upon us today that are facing the church and its position on this issue, even though the Christian church has had for nearly two millennia a consistent tradition?

I propose that the current issue of homosexuality as it has emerged in western culture in the recent decades, especially the politics surrounding it, is the fruit of the larger western cultural legacy of the last two hundred years, together with certain specific cultural influences of the last three decades.

Even the exegetical work in chapters 2-4 reflects post-Enlightenment influences. The historical-critical method, rooted in the rational quest for truth, has been employed and deployed to explain texts or perhaps even to explain them away, as some would say. In recent decades the historical-critical method has been much critiqued,[1] but nonetheless it remains a basic mode for scriptural study in the western world.

This chapter seeks to understand western culture to help explain why homosexuality (whatever one's views) has become a cultural *cause*. To the extent that culture itself is a generative force of homosexuality, the chapter may also contribute to our understanding of *causation*. On this there are widely divergent theories, from behavioral-genetic to prenatal and/or childhood developmental to parent-child relationships to macro-cultural and/or environmental factors to spirit-world to simply no *cause* at all.[2]

General agreement exists that homoerotic attraction to some degree occurs in some males and females in all cultures. But while in the cultures of the majority (two-thirds) world it does not exist as a cultural cause, it has become a dominant issue in western culture. To put it more starkly: it has become part of the dominant cultural agenda of the west, especially in United States, while less so in Canada.

The following features of western culture contribute to this in different ways, with some not directly related to the homosexual agenda, but strategically providing underlying conditions that enable others to have become potent factors. These are thus more directly related to why the homosexual agenda has become a cause. In my judgment, factors 4-7 below are more directly explanatory of the origins of this dominant cultural cause.

The status of religion in the west no longer gives cohesion to culture, instead representing conflictive forces in society, especially on moral issues. Pluralism in beliefs necessarily characterizes western culture, given its wide ethnic and religious diversity. The liberal/conservative rainbow, crosscutting religions and politics, is crucially potent in aiding and abetting this issue as a *cause*. One of the best acknowledgments and delightfully charitable treatments of this matter is Barbara G. Wheeler's article in which she reflects upon what she as a liberal has learned from living on the campus of several conservative Christian seminaries.[3] Agonistic exchanges between Walter Wink and Robert Gagnon illustrate the same point.[4]

At stake here is the issue of both biblical authority and strategies of interpretation, which chapters 1-4 above have sought to exemplify in specific textual investigations. But there is also another important factor, that of accommodation to the dominant sexual culture since the 1960s sexual revolution. This is often authorized from the liberal side by a popular appropriation of Augustine's version of Jesus' love command, "Love, and then what you will, do," popularly translated as "love, and do whatever you please." This mode of moral reasoning harks back to the provocative books of Joseph Fletcher and Bishop John A. T. Robinson in the 1960s and underscores the point that the sexual revolution of the 60s is a paramount factor in understanding why the homosexual issue has become a cause in western society. Those arguments are most clearly represented today by John Shelby Spong.

Since I am not a scholar with specialty in analysis of western culture, I hope that this fledgling endeavor will stimulate further work, perhaps a full-length monograph, which it deserves, by others who have made cultural analysis their vocation or avocational interest. The following appear to me to be prominent factors:

1. **The value placed upon human autonomy with its fruit of individualism.** The greatest influence of the Enlightenment upon modern western civilization has been the conception and valorization of the "individual self." As Middleton and Walsh put it, "Autonomous human beings are the self-normed masters not only of their own destiny but of the destiny of the world. . . . Western culture is founded on human *autonomy*. This tower is built on a foundation of radical, self-determining freedom. But far from being a valid, life-enhancing freedom, this very closely resembles what is described in Genesis 3 as the primal human sin, which results in death. . . . It means that we seek to transcend the norms offered by God and to define for ourselves, instead, the parameters or limits of right and wrong. We become quite autonomous: a law (*nomos*) unto ourself (*autos*)."[5]

This view, coupled with scientific, technological capability and belief in the "ineluctable and inevitable march of progress," enables humans in the modern world to live "unimpeded by threats such as tradition, ignorance, and superstition," so that we can devise our own remedies for whatever problems arise. This modern worldview now blends with a post-modern one regarding all knowledge as perspectival, with no way of checking whether any particular belief or value corresponds to some larger reality.[6]

In contrast to this worldview, in the world of the Bible and in many societies worldwide still today, the individual's self-concept, identity, and role are formed as a matter of course within communal solidarity and prescribed roles. Not individual autonomy, freedom, and rights, but rather community solidarity, purposes, and communal identity are foremost values. In such cultures one does not consider individual differences as determinative of identity. In Scripture, one's identity emerges from one's group, and specifically from belonging to the people of God and, in the New Testament, the body of Christ. One's role in the faith community provides the context for self-reflection and thinking about personal identity.

In contrast to biblical assumptions about personal identity, our modern culture has made sexual identity a foremost value. In public schools, sex education is considered most important; religious education counts little. Granted, secularization and pluralism demand it be that way. But the point that should not escape us is: basic assumptions about what counts as important to personal identity are vastly different in our modern society than in the time and culture of the Bible.

2. Materialistic values. Underlying the above is the western ideal of material success and prosperity. Indeed, consumerism is one of America's distinctive cultural maladies. As biblical scholar Walter Brueggemann put it in a recent lecture, ours is "a technological, therapeutic, military culture of consumerism." Robert Bellah's seminal work, *Habits of the Heart*, describes the individualistic, therapeutic, and managerial consumerist character of American culture. He notes that even with a tightly integrated culture along these lines, "the individual can only rarely and with difficulty understand himself and his activites as interrelated in morally meaningful ways with those of other, different Americans."[7]

Because this is so basic and pervasive, it is hard to speak credibly in our society of self-denial, the servant ethic, and the pursuit of a vision for life that forgoes personal freedom for a corporate good other than material success. It is striking that from Ezekiel 16:49 through the church fathers, wealth, and especially greed and injustice, are linked to homosexuality.[8] They were seen as a cultural whole. This, perhaps, is revelatory of our contemporary cultural reality. Notable also is the reality that homosexuality flourishes in societies of luxury, and thus appears to have a strong link to economics (connected to points 6 and 7 below).

3. The industrial revolution and its impact upon family life. While in traditional societies the family was always the primary social unit and focus of one's energies, the forces impinging on western social structure due to the industrial revolution have crippled family structure and cohesion. In more recent years, this dissolution of family solidarity has been fueled by direct ideological attack on the family, not because of radical commitment to the vision of the kingdom of God of which the Gospels speak, but because the family has been deemed an impediment to realization of one's self-fulfillment. Critiques of the family, some from more radical feminists, are a prominent force in this larger negative valuation of the family. The disintegration of the family is a primary factor behind the sexual revolution that directly bears on the homosexuality crisis of our time. See appendix 4, especially note 7, for more on this topic.

4. The sexual revolution of the mid-1960s is perhaps the strongest influence on our present sexual crisis, although this is in reality only a focalization of a force at work much longer in western society: the sexualization of culture generally. The justification of this trend, and perhaps its empowerment, is

its negative assessment of the older puritan ethic and the horror of the witch hunts in which sexuality-in-the-closet had horrible negative impact upon people's lives.

Be that as it may, in the 1960s a sexual revolution engulfed American culture, epitomized by the great concert in Woodstock, New York, where sex and marijuana freely flowed. This too was the period of "situation ethics," which legitimized liberation from earlier sexual mores, and whose only moral criterion was love, defined as what pleased self and didn't violate another. The stage was set for a series of mutations in sexual ethics. Sexual experimentation became a cherished American freedom, which, tragically enough, has now led to a very high out-of-wedlock pregnancy rate for teenagers.[9] The only climate in which homosexuality could become a key cultural factor in personal identity is one in which being "sexually active" precedes a committed relationship that entails marriage and potential family responsibilities.

5. **Secular (I say secular, not Christian) feminist ideology** that sought liberation and identity of the feminine on the trajectory of values in points 1-3 above. In its most extreme forms this has been empowered by new religious ideologies such as goddess worship, Wicca, and/or (neo)paganism.[10] With this turn to new forms of nature worship, the freedom of sexual expression, especially lesbianism, becomes a matter of religious liberty in a pluralistic society. In these "new religions" the turn to worship of the creation, rather than the Creator (Rom. 1:18ff.), is evident. That same-sex practices follow is predictable, according to the Romans 1 analysis.

Jeffrey Satinover links this development to what he considers a revival of gnosticism, which could take an ascetic view toward the body and sexual expression or a thoroughly libertine view. He regards the emergence of paganism as a "religion" of significance in our time as a replay of the gnostic libertine dimension. While this may be linked to new age spirituality, it has little or nothing to do with the Christian church and its most fundamental beliefs regarding Jesus as Savior and Lord.[11]

6. **Urban dynamics.** David Greenberg's massive sociological study, *The Construction of Homosexuality,* argues persuasively that homosexuality is a societal force with certain cultural characteristics, chief of which are its development as a social force in western *urban* society and its transport from there to other urban locations worldwide.[12]

At the time of his publication (1988) Greenberg was professor of sociology at New York University with specialty in criminology, law, and theory of deviance. His research is expansive, extending to ancient societies as well as contemporary western society. In primitive societies *transgenerational* homosexuality is pres-ent, where an older male or tribal leader initiates a young male into sexual relations, but which ends at the time of marriage. *Egalitarian* homosexuality also occurs in some societies, often among children. But this is not lifelong, nor an exclusive mode of sexual behavior. *Transclass* homosexuality occurred in more hierarchical societies where older, wealthy males related sexually to the young, weak, poor, or slave. The western conceptions of homosexuality have developed in relation to the social conditions and constraints of a culture in which market economy, bureaucracy, and medicalization of homosexuality have played dominant roles (compare Michael Foucault's view later in this chapter). The modern view of a homosexual identity is just that—the product of modern culture. This development and view of homosexuality are interconnected with the forces of modern urbanization, which he documents with sociological data.

The factors in points 1-5 above all bear more intensely on urban culture. Thus the urban environment, with its lack of primary relationships of accountability, becomes the seedbed for actualizing homosexual impulses. The urban setting provides for freedom and self-realization on individualistic terms, without communal accountability, exactly what is culturally needed for homosexual experimentation in relationships of numerous types.

7. **The sexualizing of culture through the influence of entertainment, leisure, sports, and the media-oriented**

culture—where roles on stage distort identity. In explaining the prominence of homoerotic relations in the Greco-Roman world, Smith cites the gymnasium and theater as two contextual influences.[13] The novel, film, and art in the last thirty years have exerted powerful influence on activating thought and practice in the direction of homosexuality. This reality is often intensified in university settings, where exposure to the arts has raised issues of what may be taught and viewed in film. Cases of alleged pornography have come into the state courts. This of course pertains to both hetero- and homosexuality.

8. Loss of the New Testament teaching on the "higher good" of celibacy as an alternative to the option of marriage, or celibacy within marriage for extended periods of time. Recall that both Jesus and Paul were unmarried and that 1 Corinthians 7 regards the unmarried state better than the married. The loss of celibacy as an honored preference is much related to the development of the romantic view of marriage in western culture and the sexual revolution of the twentieth century, with a major shift in understanding regarding the primary purpose for sexual intercourse. These shifts in values have made it popular to value "God and family" above "God and kingdom service."

Consider this factor in the context of the current marital status of the U.S. population: 40 million single men and women, 15 million divorced, and 14 million widows or widowers. Post-marital sex is as big an issue as premarital, and post-marital celibacy is actually more difficult, since the person has already known an active sexual life in marriage.[14] Certainly, in terms of population, even within the church, celibacy looms as an issue as important to address as homosexuality. Indeed, the church's call to celibacy for homosexually oriented persons, with which I fully agree, lacks the ring of integrity if we address homosexuality without addressing heterosexual premarital sex and post-marital celibacy (also celibacy within marriage for the sake of kingdom purposes).[15]

9. **The belief that sexual preference/orientation is impossible to change.** This notion has developed over the last three decades, but lacks grounding in empirical data, despite the many claims otherwise (see further discussion below). Because advocacy for gays and lesbians has become so strong, and often politicized—unlike the divorce-remarriage issue the church faced some decades back—it is difficult to know how pastoral care should be undertaken for those who struggle with homosexual desire (see further in chapter 7).[16]

10. **A culture of equal rights and fairness.** As Wheeler notes, these values are powerful American civic values, strongly espoused in advocacy for gays and lesbians.[17] While these may lack biblical theological strength as values in and of themselves, they are readily harnessed in the service of justice, since the Greek legacy regarding justice is often commonly associated with the biblical call for justice (*mishpat*; see e.g. Deut. 16:20, Amos 5:24, Micah 6:8, Isa. 42:1-4). We have already noted in chapter 4 that what drives the biblical view of justice is not so much equality but mercy, kindness, and compassion. In the New Testament God's justification (effecting justice) of sinners arises from divine grace and love.

In various forms these virtues, Greek and Christian, are blended to make strong appeals for "inclusion" of all, so that any hesitation to advocate for gay and lesbian causes can appear to be unchristian and an expression of homophobia. The opposing conservative stance is to appeal to other biblical values, holiness and disciplinary love, and thus dig in against advocacy voices.

Salvation by God's grace through Jesus Christ is not rooted in arguments that all should be saved because they have equal merit or rights, though that is a primary value for treatment of all citizens in America public life, and certainly should be. Rather, salvation and entrance into the body of Christ is always by God's grace, extended to all who acknowledge and repent of their sin(s). The biblical doctrine of election, beginning with Abraham and culminating in

Christ for Christians, testifies against the notion that God accepts us because of any personal merit, identity, status, or even piety. No one may claim standing before God or the *right* to be included in the Christian body *because* they are Anglo or Hispanic, male or female, hetero- or homosexual. On the other hand, the New Testament is crystal clear that no one is to be excluded from the invitation to respond to God's salvation because of any of these distinctions (Acts 10:34). But to say that no one is to be excluded from salvation and being part of the church does not yield the conclusion of "inclusiveness" on the basis of some "human right" based in some form of justice, as is often assumed. Rather, the route to be included in God's salvation and the body of Christ is through repentance and confession of sins, baptism, God's free justification, and the gift of the Spirit.

These *cultural factors* are determinative of where we are today. A responsible cultural analysis must also include the cost in health, including mental and physical disorders, especially the HIV-AIDS cultural tragedy. See appendix 3 for data on HIV and AIDS.

As part of this culture, we need to ask what it means to be a faithful church in mission in and to this western culture. The church in most all its branches has been shaped by this culture. The nature of our culture poses three agonizing questions.

First, might western culture have become a God-disowning culture similar to that spoken of in Romans 1:18-32, where basic norms of morality have been subverted by what now seems to be culturally appropriate? Might our cultural deeds of wickedness have suppressed the truth and blinded our ability to see what is evident if we were not deceived? But if this is the case, what can we do about deception that is culturally empowered? One is not free to choose readily against the dominant culture (see appendix 2). In this sense we are all victims, and survival apart from that victimization is hardly imaginable. (The very concept of victimization is also an effect of our culture upon our self-concept.)

Second, do we make specific persons (or congregations) pay in an unfair way for the church's assimilation into these western cultural forces, when we know that all of us have assimilated at crucial points? Many aspects of western culture are good and need to be affirmed. But many dimensions of it are also evil. The impact of our culture upon the church's moral code is greater than we generally consciously acknowledge. North American Christianity is not only in the world, but also *of* the world. Many Christians are wealthy, and greed is ever lurking at our door (in Eph. 5:5 and the early church fathers, greed is connected to idolatry, which in Rom. 1:18-27 is linked directly to "unnatural" sexual desire).

Third, is all homosexuality cut from the same cloth? Amid this struggle to know and do the truth, I am convinced it is not. Causation is not easily explained.[18] Some is more freely chosen, and some appears more innately—genetically and biologically—shaped. A dominant explanation is that it arises in early development without the child's will or knowledge.[19] Other factors, many rooted in western culture may also contribute. These are:

—use of mind-altering drugs.

—influence of theater, film, and pornography.

—homosexual practice arising from enforced situations, such as life in prison (but which may not arise from homosexual identity as such).

—psychological developmental issues between parent and child.[20]

—disappointment over a failed heterosexual relationship.

—result of sexual abuse during childhood or early teen years.

—compensation for loneliness and need for intimacy.

—lesbian desire empowered by the fight against straight culture and patriarchy, coupled with neo-pagan religion and ritual.

This listing is not *causal* in the sense of explaining ultimate origins (a debate that may never be settled) but rather identifies those factors of western culture that have immediate explanatory significance. Like all sexual practice, once activity begins, though it is possible to stop, it is not easy, since it readily becomes habitual.[21]

One of the fallouts of this culture is the assumption that freedom for sexual activity is an inalienable right, especially in advocacy for gays and lesbians, and perhaps also for all singles. But this directly counters the teaching of the church over the centuries. We must, therefore, remember what we expect of heterosexual singles in our congregations. Given our cultural reality, we may need to interpret celibacy as part of the suffering that unmarried Christians are called to bear (Matt. 19:11-13, though Paul in 1 Cor. 7 regards it a freedom enabling response to kingdom opportunities). We need celebrations for singles that compensate for the lack of "passage" that marriage marks for couples in the congregation. Further, our social groupings need to incorporate singles. Christian faith challenges the assumption that self-fulfillment or achieving happiness accords with the gospel. In other words, resistance to western culture, including its preoccupation with sexuality (especially homosexuality and homophobia), needs greater theological critique than we have given it. In this light we will better understand our calling to be alternative cultural communities of love for everyone. We will seek to be inclusive in our brotherly-sisterly affection for each other, including those with stronger same-sex attractions. At the same time we will refuse to reduce personhood to the concept of sexual orientation. We need also to resist the cultural pressure to funnel friendship into fondling.

Should the church say the same thing to all? Certainly not, not from a perspective of pastoral care. The church faces the challenge of becoming more proactive in compassionate and redemptive ministry to these varied realities, honoring the distinctiveness of each person and situation, with conviction that God can change through Jesus Christ's transforming power those aspects of behavior that reside in the *human will*. We need to be modest in claiming or expecting change as possible for everyone, since for some, same-sex desire may arise from genetic and biological traits.[22] We need to pay more attention to both the findings of scientific literature and the church's healing ministries that indicate that change from homosexuality to heterosexuality is possible, especially when the person desires the change.[23]

Psychiatric experiment in Britain in the 1970s with two separate groups of homosexual men showed a 71 percent change rate to stable heterosexual marriages (100 percent to heterosexual relationships) for those who were clear at the outset of therapy that they desired to change. In the second similar-size group of fifteen, where the participants were ambiguous in their desire to change, only 7 percent made a solid shift to heterosexuality.[24] Satinover cites—mostly from the 50s and 60s—seven psychotherapeutic and two psychoanalytic practitioners who report in scientific journals percentages of persons who experienced change. The composite is 50 percent of a total of 341 persons undergoing treatment. He reports also that in "1984 the Masters and Johnson program . . . reported a five-year follow-up success rate of sixty-five percent."[25]

More recently, Dr. Robert Spitzer, who led the movement in the early seventies for the American Psychiatric Association to stop defining homosexuality as a "psychiatric disorder," has challenged the "new orthodoxy" that sexual orientation is fixed, and thus it is unacceptable for clinicians to assist a client to change. Based upon a sample of 200 in-depth interviews, Spitzer found that many have "made substantial changes in sexual arousal and fantasy—not merely behavior."[26]

The NARTH Association (National Association for Research and Therapy of Homosexuality) of over one thousand members bears witness to a major movement in psychoanalytic practice that change is possible for many who desire it. This change-reality is affirmed by Joseph Nicolosi and other studies as well.[27] Gagnon holds that the evidence for the possibility of change in behavior, even desire, is overwhelming to those open to considering it, and he cites numerous professional studies and asks that we consider the testimonies of ex-homosexuals as well. In light of well-documented change in practices and even desire (including those in mid-life who shifted from heterosexual to homosexual practice), it needs to be acknowledged that sexual desire is fluid over the course of one's life.[28] We need to learn also from those within our own church organizations who report that change is possible by combined prayer and treatment efforts.[29]

Satinover, in his important book, *Homosexuality and the Politics of Truth,* laments the "silencing" of the professional learning during the last decades regarding the psychoanalytic and psychological research and knowledge relative to treatment that leads to potential change of sexual orientation for those who desire it. He documents the dwindling of research and published articles in the medical literature (MEDLINE) due to the strong pressures to normalize homosexuality, especially in the two decades of the mid-70s to the mid-90s.[30] He claims that the research data shows a 61 percent successful change rate for those who desire to change and, with psychiatrist Spitzer, claims it is unethical to deny this treatment to those who desire it.

Past president of the American Mental Health Counselors Association Warren Throckmorton says:

> If there is no research, how can professional associations be certain that sexual orientation cannot change? . . . Even if one accepts the presumption that sexual orientation cannot be changed, how does one know when a client's sexual orientation is settled? . . . Clients who want to change cannot reliably be told that they cannot change, since we cannot say with certainty that they have settled on a fixed trait.[31]

My own perusal of the professional journal *Psychological Reports* over the last five years verifies the conspicuous lack of literature on such research.

To hold that all homosexual people can change goes beyond the evidence, though some people, like Leanne Payne, make such a claim through "healing of memories."[32] For some people for whom the desire is more innate, the change in "orientation" may need to await the time when both homo- and hetero- are eclipsed by the heavenly body. This eschatological element too must be kept in view, and it helps us keep in perspective just how important this issue is. Richard Hays' article is aptly titled, "Awaiting the Redemption of the Body."[33]

Certainly the church should not exclude anyone because of "orientation." At times I have doubted that this notion is helpful, since it tends to make sexuality the primary mark of one's identity, reduces personhood to sexuality, and thus accepts the western cultural legacy too uncritically. Why would one want to construct such an identity concept except to stigmatize people as homosexuals, which seems to have been the case in the early history of the use of the term in late 1900s and first half of the last century? More recently it has served the causes of building sub-group identity, gaining of "rights" and recognition, and to some extent authorizing homosexual practice. Mary Stewart van Leeuwen, in her excellent article, has critiqued this conception as well.[34]

The concept of a "sexual orientation" has figured much into the church's deliberation on the matter. But some gays and lesbians outside the church claim same-sex practice as their choice.[35] In church discussions and official documents we have accepted the concept of "orientation." But we have not dealt with bisexual preference and practice,[36] much less multiple partners, both homo- and heterosexual, and the moral issues this presents.

In our present dilemma we are culturally under the impact of the natural wisdom of Aristotle: one's happiness *(eudaimonia)* lies in the fulfillment of one's nature. Aristotle was not focusing on sexuality in his discussion, but more on vocational aptitude. But our culture in its preoccupation with sexuality has virtually identified human nature and sexuality. Achieving happiness is also a given in western culture. In light of the forces of our culture, here is the dilemma: given the currently strong cultural ethos to normalize gay and lesbian sexual experience, how can the church ask a homosexually oriented person, so self-identified, to forgo sexual pleasure—when happiness is the fulfillment of one's nature? Is it fair to ask homosexually oriented persons to remain celibate? Marva Dawn is most helpful on this, speaking as one with physical disabilities and also as a single person for many years.[37] As she notes, many situations in life are not fair, and she recounts her impaired walking and seeing. Her sufferings from these limitations were greater than those of being a celibate single.

Few writers on homosexuality have addressed the issue of cultural analysis,[38] and the part that such analysis should play in our discernment of the homosexuality issue. The work of David Greenberg and Martti Nissinen, who both affirm acceptance of homosexual practice and lifestyle, shows through depth of research that the current phenomenon and modern way of viewing homosexuality has been constructed by our western culture.[39] Jeffrey Satinover's book is also pertinent to the discussion, as it documents cultural forces at work during the last four decades. Michael Williams, while excepting homosexual covenant union relationships, regards the lust that dominates gay and lesbian practices, and other sexual sins such as rape and pornography, to be "an idolization of a desire that turns it into an evil."[40] This is the sexual and political entropy of destructive forces in the cultural system.

In considering postmodern trends it appears that modern western culture continues to write its own moral script. An influential postmodern French thinker, Michel Foucault, regards discourse itself as creating reality, especially in the history of sexual understandings. Foucault contends that power issues lie at the heart of the discourse. Further, the western media culture has created a discourse that has, to a great extent, brought about a matching reality.

While we in our church discussions have talked about homosexuality as an orientation, the more radical trend in university thought these days resists that idea, as Ron Fogleman's review of Robert Goss's book, *Jesus Acted Up: A Gay and Lesbian Manifesto*,[41] points out. Fogleman objects to Goss's emphasis on homosexuality as an identity, quoting Foucault to substantiate his point (Goss too appealed to Foucault):

> We must be aware of the tendency to reduce being gay to the question: "Who am I?" and "What is the secret of my desire?" . . . The problem is not trying to find out the truth of one's sexuality, but rather, nowadays, trying to use our sexuality to achieve a variety of different types of relationships. And this is why homosexuality is probably not a form of desire but something to be desired. We must therefore insist on becoming gay, rather than persisting in defining ourselves as such. [42]

Fogleman's critique is made within his commitment to deconstruction, which allows nothing to stand by virtue of essence. Rather, he pleads for a liberating deconstruction of homosexuality that will not enclose it in "identity" terms, thus selling out to the "dangerous illusion of moral authority bestowed upon those who claim to speak in the 'name' of 'truth.' "[43]

Here then is a current example of not only how our culture might write its own moral script, but also a plea for it to do so. Nothing is to be assumed as given, or "normal," or "truth." Rather, humans construct as they live, for whatever purposes they wish to achieve.

Apparently spurred by Fogleman's critique, Goss has since published *Queering Christ: Beyond "Jesus Acted Up,"* in which he contends that to speak of a person as being gay or lesbian or straight is too "identity" oriented and "essentialist." Rather, we should seek to break "identity" barriers, recognizing that one can be gay *and* bisexual or even heterosexual and bisexual. Sexual practices should be free to be constructed, to realize one's full potential through multiple forms of expression.[44]

This faces us with a great challenge: what role does Scripture and faith have in a postmodern world? And what role, if any, do Christians have in constructing the world of the future, in the context of such trends?

Indeed, culture, arising after the first fraternal murder, has potential for both good and evil. Jacques Ellul's book *The Meaning of the City* discerns both dimensions of the city and culture in the dialectic between Genesis 4:17, 20-22 and Revelation 21:1-3.

Scripture takes us on a journey from one city to another, from one founded on fraternal murder (René Girard's emphasis) to another founded on the lamb slain by human violence for the atonement of all our sins, because of God's unending love for us:

> Cain knew his wife, and she conceived and bore Enoch; and he built a city. Adah bore Jabal; he was the ancestor of those who live in tents and have livestock. His brother's name was Jubal; he was the ancestor of all those who play the lyre and pipe. Zillah bore Tubal-cain, who made all kinds of bronze and iron tools. (Genesis 4:17, 20-22)

> Then I saw a new heaven and a new earth; for the first heaven and the first earth had passed away, and the sea was no more. And I saw the holy city, the new Jerusalem, coming down out of heaven from God, prepared as a bride adorned for her husband. And I heard a loud voice from the throne saying, "See, the home of God is among mortals. He will dwell with them as their God; they will be his peoples, and God himself will be with them. (Revelation 21:1-3)

Prayer

"Teach me your way, O LORD, that I may walk in your truth; give me an undivided heart to revere your name" (Psalm 86:11). "Make me to know your ways, O LORD; teach me your paths. Lead me in your truth, and teach me, for you are the God of my salvation; for you I wait all day long" (Psalm 25:4-5).

For I know that you promise: *"I will instruct you and teach you the way you should go; I will counsel you with my eye upon you" (Psalm 32:8).*

Amid the culture wars of our present era, help us to pray with St. Francis:

Lord, make me an instrument of thy peace;
where there is hatred, let me sow love;
where there is injury, pardon;
where there is doubt, faith;
where there is despair, hope;
where there is darkness, light;
and where there is sadness, joy.
O Divine Master,
grant that I may not so much seek
to be consoled, as to console;
to be understood, as to understand;
to be beloved as to love;
for it is in giving that we receive,
it is in pardoning that we are pardoned,
and it is in dying that we are born to eternal life.

CHAPTER 6

HERMENEUTICAL ANALYSIS AND REFLECTION

In this chapter we engage in hermeneutical analysis, focused on whether and how basic emphases in the larger canonical witness affect our understanding of the specific injunctions regarding same-sex genital relations. The pro and con aspects of this debate beg for theological reflection. What are the primary theological values of Scripture that bear on understanding sexuality and the purposes of sexual, genital relationships? Do the sexual ethics of Scripture, influenced by the times in which the texts were written, apply authoritatively to our contemporary western cultural situation? To answer such questions I point to some basic considerations arising from the emphasis of the biblical text.

The first consideration is recognition that Judaism placed high value upon procreation as the visible fulfillment of the sexual relationship (Gen. 1:27-28; Ps. 127:3-5; Ps. 113:9; Prov. 17:6). To be without children and descendants was to experience leanness in God's favor, even disfavor (Gen. 16; 30:1-8). Corollary to this understanding of sex, Israel regarded man *and* woman as the highest gift of God's creation (Gen. 1:26-27; 2:18-24). Thus for a man to spurn sexual relationship with a woman for homosexual relations was viewed as refusing God's treasured gift of creation and the blessing of offspring (cf. Rom. 1:18-29).

A second consideration is that Israel (and the church) developed its morality in the context of its relationship with pagan nations. In Leviticus 18:22, 24-30, for example, Israel's sexual ethics are reinforced by appeal to Israel's difference from the pagan nations. However, the list of sins in 1 Corinthians 6:9 is regarded by many biblical scholars as a catalogue of Gentile vices found also in Greek philosophical writings. Be this as it may, in both the Old and New Testaments homosexual practice is condemned as morality unacceptable within God's redeemed community.

A third and most important consideration is that the genius of the biblical message is not upon "classifying the vices" of humans, but in beckoning men and women into God's community of love, healing, and forgiveness. Here is where the church must do its homework in dealing with homosexuality today. We must ask, at fundamental and theological levels, what is the relationship between these foundational biblical emphases on love, forgiveness, healing, and homosexuality? Different answers arise from both sides of the debate. Perhaps it is most helpful not to seek specific answers, but to explore at length what these emphases mean both for the issue of homosexuality and for the health of the church and individual families. Too little love and forgiveness, as well as illness, personally and corporately as a church, has surrounded the debate. The determination to convince others of the rightness of one's own or the church's position has stifled the health and well-being, indeed shalom, of the family and church. It has also taken its toll on the mission and witness of the church.

Rather than seek quick and specific answers, I suggest we reflect over time on the interconnectedness between these realities. Then we might better understand what God's healing for us as a church and as individuals means on this thorny, most divisive issue.

Broader Hermeneutical Considerations

Granted that Scripture is uniform and consistent in its witness against same-sex genital practices (unlike its voice on slavery, Sabbath, war, and role of women), how does this connect with our situation today? A crucial learning in my earlier study of *Slavery, Sabbath, War, and Women* was that one must consider not only what isolated texts say, but how such statements are to be assessed in light of the overall biblical theological moral principles that emerge in the biblical revelation. Thus the exegetical task must be followed by hermeneutical work in which the dominant moral and theological emphases of Scripture are assessed in relation to the weight of specific texts. Tension can exist between specific moral injunctions and the overall moral-theological direction of the canon. So it is important to assess overall biblical teaching to see if broader principles confirm or question conclusions derived from exegesis of specific texts. Further, the factor of cultural distance between the biblical text and our life today must be assessed.[1]

On this matter of pervasive biblical, theological, and moral teaching, the Scriptural teachings on creation and marriage, on the one hand, seem to exclude the homosexual option, since humanity is defined in its basic communal nature as male and female. On the other hand, both Jesus and Paul seem to relegate marriage and family to secondary importance in relation to the call of discipleship in God's kingdom (though Jesus explicitly upholds the sanctity and permanence of marriage and condemns lust).

Again, on the one hand, the biblical call to holiness and nonconformity to the world's way, especially its sexual sins, is strong and clear. On the other hand, Scripture as a whole (not only Jesus as seen in chapter 3) is equally strong in its call for justice-mercy and acceptance of the marginalized, which might thus lead us to accept gays and lesbians together with homosexual practice in light of their being stigmatized by religion and society. Resolving these tensions is the hermeneutical-interpretive task, as we live with Scripture in our world today.

How do we manage these mixed ethical signals in the biblical text? How do we balance biblical justice with its concern also for boundaries and discipline? How does biblical holiness fit with compassion and inclusion? Does the strong gospel principle of inclusion override the texts that call for boundaries and discipline (Matt. 18:15-18; 1 Cor. 5)? Are inclusiveness and discipline incompatible? As James Lapp rhetorically asked in his sermon at the 1995 Mennonite assembly: Do we need to choose between inclusiveness and discipline? Further, as Ron Sider suggested, we seem to have "confused compassion with relativism," and the "tragic result is that our sexual practices, divorce rates, and economic lifestyles look more and more like those of the rest of North American society."[2] Does Jesus' acceptance of sinners mean he is soft on sin? Matthew 5:28 and Mark 10:1-12 do not support such a conclusion, and these texts speak to sexuality issues. Further, when Jesus relates to and accepts the marginalized he offers transformation and healing, so that the person is not only accepted but changed (though some texts, like John 4, are silent in portraying the moral result of the encounter—but as noted before, silence is not evidence).

Numerous basic biblical moral teachings are pertinent to the church's discernment of the moral nature of homosexual practice and the consequent response of the church to people in such practice. I list eight moral principles, three in Set A and five in Set B. Set A principles are often used to argue for a change in the traditional position of the Christian church, while Set B principles are often used to reinforce the traditional position. Set B voices also value Set A principles, but apply them so Set B is not muted.

Set A Principles

1. The Bible as a whole, and Jesus in particular, calls God's people to take the side of the oppressed and to stand

for justice, the equitable treatment of all people. Those who are homosexual, who have not chosen their orientation and have experienced oppression and injustice, must become the object not of condemnation but of special grace. The church must stand for their cause. Just as Jesus fellowshipped with and accepted those ostracized by his society, so must we.

2. Love, mutuality, and covenant relationships are basic biblical values. When homosexual relationships, especially covenant unions, conform to these moral qualities of love, mutuality, and covenant faith, the church must accept and affirm such people and such relationships.

3. The kingdom of God introduces a new order for society. Traditional family ties, sexuality practices, and vocation must all take secondary status to allow for freedom and new practices, whatever best enhances kingdom vision. In Christ there is neither male nor female. Marriage and reproduction are no longer primary values. In light of these priorities, homosexual lifestyle can take its place alongside heterosexual lifestyle.

Set B Principles

1. Genesis 1:26-27 teaches God's basic sexuality-design for humanity: male and female together reflect the divine image. Homosexual practice flies in the face of this creation design. It is against the nature of creation. Further, it lacks the potential of God's mandate for procreation, a not insignificant point in the moral theology of the church over the centuries.

2. Genesis 2 teaches that marriage is for the union of male and female, man and woman. In both the Hebrew and Christian Scriptures, genital sex outside the marriage covenant is sin, designated *porneia* in the New Testament. Further, promiscuity is forbidden, as well as lust that leads to sin.

3. Biblical covenant is linked to law that provides the theological basis for regarding marriage not as a private event, but a public affair. Covenants manifest themselves in social

public structures, through laws and community sanctions. Life in God's community means becoming part of a corporate society that sanctions and blesses marriage covenants. Through centuries of literature and communal practice, the Hebrew and Christian communities have not sanctioned homosexual covenant relationships (cf. John D. Roth on this point and his caution against accepting too easily what has developed only in recent church history at the expense of the longer church tradition[3]).

4. Jesus' teachings on justice and kingdom priority are directed specifically and clearly against the breakup of male-female marriage unions (Mark 10:1-10). When this word on the permanence of the male-female marriage union is too hard to heed, then Jesus dares to advise celibacy, as modeled by both Jesus and Paul. Paul's manifesto, "In Christ there is neither male nor female" (Gal. 3:28), does not suggest the legitimacy of alternative sexual lifestyles, but the unity of women and men in the kingdom community.

5. God's people are expected, from Genesis to Revelation, to be nonconformed to the practices of this world and to exercise discipline among its members. Moral discernment is a basic necessity for those who seek to be faithful and liberated from the seducements of the world in which God's people live. Because some types of homosexual practices were cited by Paul as illustrative of the pagan Roman world ignorant of God's revelation, the church today must discern what is sin and what proves the acceptable and perfect will of God. A foundational teaching that permeates Scripture is that both moral discernment and discipline are essential.

But Is Our Situation Different?

Numerous considerations have developed in the course of the homosexuality debate over the last several decades. Some address the appropriateness of applying Old Testament and New Testament texts to the contemporary gay/lesbian situation. Today's culture is quite different from that when those texts were written; so perhaps the rules and tenets are not applicable anymore.

In this regard, Robert Gagnon has taken up the hermeneutical challenge from the standpoint of examining carefully the arguments made that put distance between biblical moral proscriptions against homosexual practice and our contemporary situation. He treats at length seven such hermeneutical escapes.[4] Gagnon borrows and modifies Richard Hays's method in *The Moral Vision of the New Testament*, combining the descriptive and the synthetic, and the hermeneutical and the pragmatic. He considers carefully the leading reasons that have been put forth to discount or mute the relevance of the scriptural homosexuality texts for today:

> The Bible condemns only exploitative, pederastic forms of homosexuality.
> The Bible primarily condemns homosexuality because of its threat to male dominance.
> The Bible has no category for "homosexuals" with an exclusively same-sex orientation; same-sex passion was thought to originate in over-sexed individuals.
> Homosexuality has a genetic component that the writers of the Bible did not realize.
> There are only a few biblical texts that speak directly to homosexuality.
> We do not follow many of the other specifically sexual injunctions of the Bible, so why should those against homosexual practice be binding?
> Since we are all sinners anyway, why single out the sin of same-sex intercourse?

In his response to these points, Gagnon gives reasons why they cannot be maintained under careful scrutiny. In some cases the exegesis that supports the point is flawed and not convincing. In other cases he points to faulty logic or to evidence that is not conclusive. One important point he makes is that the idea that the ancient world had no notion of sexual orientation can no longer be held in an unqualified manner. Concurring with Bernadette Brooten, and drawing on his earlier quoted Greco-Roman texts, Gagnon documents levels of recognition that some people were inclined toward same-sex relation—to the extent that some Greek writers (e.g., Aeschines, Protogenes in Plutarch, Pausanias) extolled homosexual love as the highest form (extending reflections on love in Plato and Socrates).[5] The evidence reminds us that in Greek homosexual practices, as well as in citations by first century Jewish writers, some persons and certain types of relationships were considered expressive of natural sexual tendencies. Certain conventions of who might join with whom also prevailed, involving status and social relationships. Some homosexual relationships were lifelong. These facts render no longer tenable the claim that the contemporary understanding of homosexuality is historically novel.

While Gagnon makes a welcomed contribution here, it must also be said that the concepts that might be classified as "orientation" in Greek literature, cited by Brooten and Schoedel[6] as well, are not identical to what orientation has come to mean in current understanding. Nevertheless, I have argued that the notion of set orientation does not square with the plasticity of sexual desire evident over a life span for given persons (for example, once homosexual, then later bisexual, and even in *some* cases, heterosexual). Also, voices from the secular avant-garde on this issue downplay the notion of a set orientation and stress rather that we humans construct what we desire to be sexually attractive (see last part of chapter 5).

In considering the claims for a genetic component (brain size, genes, etc.), Gagnon, while not eliminating genetic dispositional factors as in other phenomena such as violence or alcoholism, holds that environmental influences are by far the more determinative and cites numerous scientific studies with statistical data—and critique of them—to support his discussion. Similarly, the evidence for the possibility of change in behavior, and even in desire, for those who expressly want change is overwhelming. Gagnon cites numerous professional studies (see chapter 5). In light of this documented potential for change, he claims that it needs to be acknowledged that sexual desire is not determined from birth on. His section on health risks and harmful effects on church and society is also relevant hermeneutically, for it counts against the easy dismissal of clear biblical teaching. His conclusion calls for the overflow of love, joy, and peace in Christian bodies that will enable us to figure out those things that will make a difference in being pure and blameless in the day of Christ.

In my assessment of Gagnon's tour de force on the subject, I deem it difficult to show contrary exegetical or hermeneutic rationale on most all the issues. Anthony Thiselton, in his extensive hermeneutical study of the issue, says that the various newly proposed explanations of the texts prohibiting same-sex relations "raise only illusory problems."[7] I too have questioned the varied, too easy explanations of the texts that seek to mute their ethical import for our contemporary situation. At the same time, I have developed a related conviction that the hermeneutical task cannot be completed without careful and critical analysis of western culture, which provides both the impulse for and a legitimating acceptance of same-sex relationships (therefore the writing of chapter 5). We face the challenge of critically engaging the culture in which we live, specifically the politics that govern discussions of this issue. Are the driving forces in our culture those we desire to underwrite? My own sense is that just as we contest the "myth of redemptive violence" that is so much a part of our western culture (see Walter Wink's good work here[8]), we also need to challenge the "rights" and individualistic ethos of our culture, especially when it devalues one's identity in community. For Christians, "in-Christ" identity should transcend sexual identity.

Consideration of Hermeneutical Analogies

I have already addressed the analogies of slavery and the role of women in their hermeneutical status. On divorce and remarriage, Jesus clearly teaches against them, but the Old Testament, Matthew perhaps, and Paul make concessions to allow for divorce, at least, in certain situations. The Old Testament (Deut. 24) and Matthew (5:32) allow for remarriage in certain cases, but Deuteronomy prohibits the first husband from remarrying the wife after she was another man's wife. For Matthew, the exception clause may be grounded in the same rationale, since the majority of commentators take it to mean: "if the wife already has had sexual relations with another man, thus defiling the marriage relationship," divorce may be permitted.[9] Paul's counsel is not to remarry if it is deemed necessary to separate or divorce, but to remain single and celibate. But his logic at the beginning of 1 Corinthians 7 might also allow for remarriage if passion is strong. The variations of biblical teaching in this matter disqualify it from being a sound analogy to the uniform proscriptions against homosexual practice.

In chapter 3 I also considered warfare and kingship. On warfare I noted that the moral basis for the pacifist view that Christians are not to participate in war appeals to moral commands of Jesus, specifically love of enemy, which by inference means one cannot participate in war since it requires willingness to kill the enemy. In the same way, Jesus' teachings on the union of male and female as one flesh would disallow homosexual practice. The appeal to kingship signaled another analogical dimension. Though kingship was not willed by God, God continued to work with his people, instructing kings toward moral ideals (Ps. 72; 82), and birthing messianic hope on the kingship metaphor.

Gagnon has examined oft-used analogies to the homosexuality issue (circumcision in Acts 15 with the Gentile inclusion, slavery, divorce/remarriage, and women-in-ministry). He shows that these examples are not analogous. Rather, he points to other sexually related sins that have the same characteristics as homosexual practice: incest, bestiality, adultery, prostitution, and soliciting prostitutes.[10]

In addition to the sexually based analogies that Gagnon mentions, with which I agree, two others might be considered: singleness and money, for different reasons and in different ways. If one allows for the legitimacy of homoerotic desire but proscribes homosexual practice, the situation is quite analogous to the situation of the heterosexual single. Certainly most have sexual desire, but are expected not to develop sexual practice. This analogy may be the most significant of all, since it requires us to be consistent in applying the Christian moral expectation that sexual union is restricted to heterosexual marriage. The fact that our culture shows considerable deviation on this matter points again to the importance of analyzing and critiquing our western culture.

The option of singleness with celibacy prompts deeper insight into sexual desire. I quote Walter Moberly in the context of noting how sex and sexuality fit into the larger goal of human life: to be transformed into God's image revealed in Christ (Luke 9:23; 2 Cor. 5:17):

> First, "sex" is not a necessity, nor even a priority. What matters most in human life can be achieved without it, and missed with it (consider 1 Cor. 13, Gal. 5:22, and famous Old Testament summary statements such as Deut. 10:12-22; Mic. 6:8). A distinctive and recurrent form of Christian witness to this has been the monastic life—the vows of poverty, chastity, and obedience embody the claim that neither money, nor sex, nor power is indispensable to the living of life to the full; for Jesus lived life fully without them. It is a hard witness, to which in its full form only some Christians are called, but one which captures something central to Scripture.[11]

Moberly then speaks further of Jesus as "the model of the fulfilled human being" and presents his life as attractive and fulfilled, socially and spiritually (Paul's life also testifies to this). Clearly, this is one feature of our contemporary culture that seems to have gone awry. As I point out in appendix 4, we have fallen short in expressing this dimension of the gospel. Some have compared homoerotic desire to alcoholism. Perhaps this is valid in some respects. In both cases a person lives with a condition that he or she did not freely choose, and causation explanation is complex. Further, once one begins to practice either, it is most difficult to stop, true also for heterosexual practice as well. However, hermeneutically, there is limited correlation in this analogy, for Scripture, while speaking against drinking in excess, does not proscribe categorically against it, but regards it as folly and downfall of the person. The similarity between the two may be to say that Scripture did not understand alcoholism or homosexuality in the manner which we do today. Another similarity, according to some, is that both are social maladies. Current gay and lesbian proponents would object to this, however. Though they may regard drinking for an alcoholic to be a social malady, their sexual preference, they would argue, is not a danger to society.

Moberly has insightfully suggested the analogy of money to illustrate the distance between biblical teaching and contemporary practices. Scripture and the early church fathers taught strictly against charging usury, and warned incessantly against the perils of wealth. In modern culture this has changed, but not because debt, greed, and extortion have disappeared. A new economic system has changed the nature of money—our way of viewing it. Thus the older proscriptions no longer apply. He puts it pointedly: "If money can retain the same name, yet become a different reality, may not similar considerations apply to same-sex attraction also?"[12] As I noted earlier, proscriptions against sexual sins and greed are often coupled in biblical and early church vice lists. This analogy is arresting and may be significant in the moral debate. Would our new scientific understandings of sexual desire be parallel to the development of the capitalistic economy in which money is viewed differently from earlier times? If one holds that the homosexual phenomenon, as we now experience it, is largely a cultural construction, then this analogy is quite apt, since capitalism is also a social construction. And, strikingly, there is little freedom to escape from it.

From Text to Present: How?

How does one assess whether teachings in Scripture are to have binding authority on Jesus' followers centuries later, when culture and worldview perceptions differ? Gagnon answers by showing the inadequacy of reasons put forward to argue that we in our setting today must go beyond the biblical proscriptions against homosexuality. I call attention to other helpful models in making this assessment, the contributions of Richard Hays and William Webb.

Richard Hays, in *The Moral Vision of the New Testament*, develops a methodology to assess how Scripture functions for the church. This consists of a fourfold task. First we undertake a descriptive task, in which one seeks to read the text carefully. Second, we seek a synthetic analysis for which the focal images of community, cross, and new creation function for theological-ethical assessment. Hays argues that these three images permeate New Testament literature and are therefore essential "benchmarks" for determining authority of any specific teaching for the ongoing life of the Christian community. Third, Hays then employs hermeneutical considerations in which he considers the modes of Scripture's address of the issue. These modes are rules, principles, paradigms, and symbolic world. For the issues Hays considers, he examines the modes by which Scripture addresses that specific issue. In this step he also considers other authorities, specifically tradition, reason and science, and experience. Fourth and finally, he takes up the pragmatic task, seeking to discern how the teaching is to be applied to the present-day community of faith, both in ethical sanction and in communal life.[13]

In chapters 2-4 of this book I focused on the task of textual reading, seeking to understand each text in its specific setting as well as in its relation to and coherence with the entire canonical witness. Here I consider more directly Hays's focal images for assessing the continuing moral mandate of Scripture on this issue. How is the biblical teaching against same-sex activity to be assessed in relation to community, cross, and new creation? Hays prefaces his discussion by briefly pointing to larger theological beliefs: God's creative intention for sexuality (see my chapter 2 above on this); the fallen human condition; and the Bible's demythologizing view of sex. These points are helpful, especially in reminding us that this issue should be approached within the context of fallen creation. This, of course, is Paul's argument in Romans 1:18–3:20, to make way for the wonderful good news of God's salvation.[14] In assessing the biblical teaching in relation to the focal image of the cross, Hays rightly says, "The biblical strictures against homosexual behavior are concerned not just for the private morality of individuals but for the health, wholeness, and purity of the elect community."[15] Paul makes clear that point in his admonitions on sexual conduct in 1 Corinthians 5-6, concluding with the rationale: "For you were bought with a price: therefore glorify God in your body" (6:20), expressed well in the worship song,

> "Lord, prepare me to be a sanctuary;
> pure and holy, tried and true,
> with thanksgiving I'll be
> a living sanctuary for you."

Paul's treatment of the church as a body with many members also makes clear that when one hurts or offends or when one is hurt or offended it has impact upon all.

While no New Testament text connects homosexuality directly with the focal image *cross*, as Hays observes, the cross is the power that delivers us "fallen" humans from the powers of evil, and indeed from the wrath of God as expressed in Romans 1:18. Texts such as Romans 6:12-14 and 8:1-17, among many others, speak clearly about the new life that Jesus Christ makes possible.[16] An even more direct connection between the cross and issues entailed in homosexuality is Jesus' teaching on becoming eunuchs for the kingdom's sake (see chapter 3 above). Here it is clear that faithfulness to the way of the cross may require celibacy, both for homosexual and heterosexual people.

The *new creation* criterion is especially important for this issue. In 1 Corinthians 6:11, after listing sins in verses 9-10, including same-sex relations, Paul writes, "And this is what some of you used to be. But you were washed, you were sanctified, you were justified in the name of the Lord Jesus Christ and in the Spirit of our God." This is more than most of us can handle, to think that the new creation in Christ has come so fully into our lives, indeed our corporate life as a church community, that we can claim that all the old sins are gone, once and for all. We know that we live in the tension between the "already" and the "not yet." Not all the "goodies" of God's salvation have been fully given. Paul recognizes this in his famous "groaning of all creation" declaration in Romans 8:18-23. This is an important text for the issue of homosexuality since it so clearly reminds us that "not only the creation, but we ourselves, who have the first fruits of the Spirit, groan inwardly while we wait for adoption, the redemption of our bodies" (v. 23). This is also significant for the discernment process (see chapter 8) as we seek to make decisions in the congregation on how to treat specific cases. The text also calls us to humility on the degree of transformation we might expect in relation to homosexual orientation. We simply must acknowledge that not all the "change" of salvation's gift is realized in this life. Not until we get new bodies can we claim the full restoration of God's original creation shalom.

Regarding the *modes* of Scripture's address on homosexuality, Hays rightly observes that while the "New Testament contains no passages that clearly articulate a rule against homosexual practices," the Leviticus texts do.[17] If, however, 1 Thessalonians 4:1-8 is about same-sex relations, as we considered in chapter 4, then v. 6, "that no one wrong or exploit a brother or sister in this matter," is a rule. Also, as Hays notes, if *porneia* in Acts 15:28-29 includes homosexual acts, then this too is a rule of prohibition.

On *principles*, yes: the teaching in Romans 1:18ff. enunciates a distinction between 'natural' and 'unnatural' (see chapter 4 above), denoting one type of sexual intercourse that is acceptable to God and another that is not. To "glorify God in your body" is also a principle applicable to the issue of homosexuality. While Hays excludes *love* and *liberation* from his focal images, because they are not found in all the major portions of the New Testament literature, it seems to me that "love for the neighbor as for oneself" functions also as a principle, in light of the potential health hazards (see chapter 5 and appendix 3).

The *paradigms* that apply, Hays notes, "are the emphatically negative and stereotypical sketches in the three Pauline texts (Rom. 1:18-32, 1 Cor. 6:9, 1 Tim. 1:10)." Further, seeking for paradigms that might sanction homosexual sexual relations, Hays puts it well: "The New Testament offers no accounts of homosexual Christians, tells no stories of same-sex lovers, ventures no metaphors that place a positive construal on homosexual relations."[18]

The Romans 1 description of a world in rebellion against God's created intention for humans reflects also the *symbolic world* in which Paul understands same-sex relations. It is "an account of how the ordering of human life before God has gone awry."[19]

In considering *other authorities*, a stage in Hays' hermeneutical assessment, he rightly says that *tradition* is clear, and for "*reason* and scientific evidence, the picture is cloudy."

Even if it were clear (e.g., genetic origin), "the etiology of homosexual orientation is not a significant factor for the formation of normative Christians ethics,"[20] as I too have argued elsewhere in this book. His discussion of experience is also helpful, and moves in much the same direction that I have taken. The tricky issue here, as noted in chapter 1, is that experience differs from person to person. How does one assess the experience of Mel White in his book *Stranger at the Gate* and similar stories, alongside those told by Bob Davies and Lori Rentzel in their book *Coming Out of Homosexuality*? Simply put, *experience* turns out to be an unreliable guide on this issue.

The *pragmatic* task, how to discern and live out the ethical vision, I take up in chapter 8 on moral discernment. What Hays offers is a methodology, the best one I know, on how to move from text to moral mandate applicable for followers of Jesus centuries removed in time from sacred story inscripturated.

Underlying the issue of how one discerns normative moral guidance from Scripture texts for contemporary issues are numerous considerations. Charles Cosgrove contributes a careful analysis of the reasoning that functions in the valuing processes in five hermeneutical assumptions.[21] These are applicable to both Hays' work, and to William Webb's contribution that I now describe.

William Webb has also made a significant hermeneutical contribution, by examining in depth widely regarded analogies to homosexuality in Scripture. His study focuses on the issues of slavery, the role of women, and homosexual practice. His endeavor seeks to show similarities among and differences between these issues, by using an analytic grid of eighteen hermeneutical principles. His argument is that it is possible to assess whether moral commands are intended only for a given time and culture, or whether they are to be regarded as transcultural, with universal moral significance. He labels his approach "redemptive movement"; it can be evaluated on a model he calls "the X-Y-Z Principle." Y denotes the words of the text, X denotes the world of the text (the original culture), and Z denotes the final, authoritative, transcultural ethic.[22]

To illustrate his procedure, one of his eighteen criteria is "Break Out." Does a given teaching in a text (be it "go, buy a slave" or "women shall keep silent" or "male shall not lie with a male") concur with the X reality, the culture of the time? *And* does the larger biblical witness (i.e., the whole canon) show any indication of "breaking out" beyond that command? Webb subdivides his eighteen criteria into three levels of witness—or how the biblical evidence stands on each of the issues: persuasive, moderately persuasive, or inconclusive. For the Break Out criterion, Webb sees contrast between the issues of slavery and the role of women, on the one hand, and homosexuality on the other.[23] On the two former issues there is canonical textual breakout; that is, other texts critique slavery and silencing of women. For homosexuality, however, there is no such breakout.

The same obtains for his criterion of "Purpose/Intent Statements"—*why* certain restrictions were given. Do they reflect accommodation to achieving a larger goal? Webb cites numerous texts on the wife's submission to her husband. In each of six cases there is a purpose statement that connects to the mission of the church so that no one will malign the word of God (Tit. 2:4-5) or so that the unbelieving husbands will be won over by the behavior of the wives (1 Pet. 3:1; cf. 2:12). Because there is a specific *purpose* or *intent* statement connected to the admonition, it does not stand as an absolute command for universal application. But there are no *intent* or *purpose* qualifications for homosexuality. Thus Webb reaches the same conclusions on this criterion as he did for Break Out.[24] Holding that there are no limiting factors, nor is there significant dissonance in the biblical data proscribing homosexual practice, when analyzed by these eighteen criteria, the biblical commands for homosexuality apply to all cultures.[25] They are morally transcultural and universal.

Of the eighteen criteria that Webb utilizes to test the Y-Z relationship, whether a text is normative for all cultures, for homosexuality, he regards six as persuasive for clear moral outcomes, six as only moderately persuasive, and six as inconclusive.[26] For those that are inconclusive, several do not apply to this issue: for example, "theological analogy." There are no theological or christological analogies of thought for homosexuality such as obtain for husband-wife relationships (God as husband to Israel, and Christ who loves the church and gives himself for it). Unlike the diverse signals for the role of women that reflect "redemptive movement," there are no textual clues for a "redemptive movement hermeneutic" for homosexuality.

Webb's work concurs with findings I described above.[27] Webb devotes one chapter to "What If I Am Wrong," a good reminder that all our efforts to understand truly, rightly, and fully on such a complex issue are to be put under such a rubric. It reflects a level of humility amid the quest for the truth.

The Route of History

Numerous writers have described the history of the Christian church regarding same-sex practices. John Boswell has argued that certain liturgical texts from the early fourth century through the late medieval period contained a special ritual blessing for same-sex committed relationships.[28] But the evidence he cites does not prove more than a blessing upon two brothers (or sisters) in connection with special kingdom tasks, usually involving church mission.[29] Sexual union is not specified.

Rather, as Stanley Grenz shows in his accessible treatment of the topic, from the early second century through the medieval period and into the post-Reformation period, the church consistently condemned same-sex relations.[30] Many of the prohibitions, beginning with the epistle of Barnabas, commanded against pederasty: "thou shalt not corrupt boys." The *Apostolic Constitutions* (late fourth-century Syrian writing) says, "Thou shalt not corrupt boys; for this wickedness is contrary to nature, and arose from Sodom, which was therefore entirely consumed by fire from God."[31] While it may appear that only pederasty is specified, both Boswell and Grenz believe these statements should not be narrowly applied to boys, but also to same-sex partners of any age. Citations from various church writers appealed to both the prohibitions in Leviticus and Paul's judgments against same-sex relations. They also argue on occasion that the relations are unnatural because they don't result in procreation (Clement of Alexandria) or that such practices violate one's relationship with God (Augustine).[32]

One intriguing aspect of this history of proscription against same-sex practices is that female same-sex relation is rarely mentioned.[33] Grenz is likely correct in explaining this as arising from the fact that the society was strongly patriarchal and women did not have such options. Consequently, it was not a problem to be addressed. The one-sided proscription may also have been related to the contemporary (mis)understanding of how conception occurs, that it arises from the "seed" of the male, planted into the female, like a seed in the field. But this theory, like that which attributes the proscriptions to the shame of a male playing a female role, are flawed and inadequate, in Grenz's judgment.[34]

Much more could be cited from the long history, but nothing really new. The tradition is consistent through the medieval period and through the post-Reformation writers. In some medieval texts, same-sex was also considered illegal, as it was also in Calvin's Geneva and among New England Puritans. In King Henry VIII's reign in Britain, sodomy cases were considered a felony and were transferred from ecclesiastical jurisdiction to the civil courts. At times, but quite rarely, homosexual offenders were publicly executed, as late as 1750 in Paris. It remained a violation of law in England until 1967.[35]

The long and short of this hermeneutical tack, to trace how we move from text through history to the present, provides only corroboration for the hermeneutical conclusions of Hays and Webb. There is no pathway from then to now, except through the "sea changes" that occurred in the last half-century, and especially as a consequence of the sexual revolution in the 1960s. But, as I argued in chapter 5, other earlier changes in western thought and value-priorities fed into the great sexual revolution of the 1960s. We live now in the post-1960s, and are faced with new, unprecedented challenges, when viewed from the long course of history.

I conclude this chapter with a meditation that helps us to ponder God's guidance for us.

Prayer

And the peace of God, which surpasses all understanding, will guard your hearts and your minds in Christ Jesus. Finally, beloved, whatever is true, whatever is honorable, whatever is just, whatever is pure, whatever is pleasing, whatever is commendable, if there is any excellence and if there is anything worthy of praise, think about these things.

—*Philippians 4:7-8*

CHAPTER SEVEN

THE CHURCH'S BELIEF AND RESPONSE

Especially in light of the cultural analysis in chapter 5, response to the gay and lesbian reality needs careful thought. What does the church do in this dilemma? Show compassion? Or speak prophetic judgment (cf. Hosea 4:1-3) toward homosexual practice, as part of our culture's distortion of sexual values? Biblically, there is precedent for both, and thus we are called also to do both. Let us remember that this same sexualized culture has power over us all, urging us to express and fulfill sexual desire. It is so strong that we are all victimized by its allure and seduction. I believe our modern culture is more responsible than genes or brain size, though genetic tendency cannot be excluded in our discernment on the issue.[1]

My own response to this matter has been difficult. On the one hand, I often feel prophetic judgment against homosexual activities—especially when deep pain is caused, marriages are broken, or a young person (in one case I know, a minor) is violated by an older person. On the other hand I feel compassion toward people who have strong homosexual desire, the origin of which they do not understand. Perhaps we should let grace and love cover a multitude of sins, and trust

God for forgiveness. But I know that this is an easy dodge of the dicey task of exercising discipline in love, both a biblical and strong Anabaptist emphasis.[2]

Richard Hays speaks helpfully to this matter. After treating the issue at the levels of textual reading, synthetic analysis, and hermeneutical considerations, he takes it up in his final section: "Living the Text: The Church as Community Suffering with the Creation."[3] He raises the question: "Can homosexual persons be members of the Christian church?" His answer:

> Yes. This is rather like asking, "Can envious persons be members of the church?" (cf. Rom. 1:29) or "Can alcoholics be members of the church?" De facto, of course, they are. Unless we think that the church is a community of sinless perfection, we must acknowledge that persons of homosexual orientation are welcome along with other sinners in the company of those who trust in the God who justifies the ungodly (Rom. 5:4). If they are not welcome, I will have to walk out the door along with them, leaving in the sanctuary only those entitled to cast the first stone.[4]

He then raises a following question: "Is it Christianly appropriate for Christians who experience themselves as having homosexual orientation to continue to participate in same-sex erotic activity?" His answer:

> No. The only one who was entitled to cast a stone instead charged the recipient of his mercy to "go and sin no more." It is no more appropriate for homosexual Christians to persist in homosexual activity than it would be for heterosexual Christians to persist in fornication or adultery. Unless they are able to change their orientation and enter a heterosexual marriage relationship, homosexual Christians should seek to live lives of discipled sexual abstinence.[5]

I believe the church is called to be a discerning and discipling community, and this involves moral formation as central to the nurture of the church. Set within the context of the church's worship, this becomes an empowering resource for moral development and growth. When a church body's standards are violated, the kind of discipline that Hebrews 12:4-11 presents as God's way with loved believers provides a model for us. I earlier referred to key sources on church discipling and discipline (see note 8 in chapter 3). Taking this aspect of the congregational life seriously is an important context for everything else said in this chapter.

How Might the Church Respond?

In this section I speak of (1) the range of the church's response to our present situation, (2) what I think needs doing most, and (3) some ideas as to how church conferences might respond to congregations that have accepted practicing homosexuals, as well as to how congregations might respond to requests for membership by those engaging in same-sex activities.

First, we examine the range of the church's response. James B. Nelson, in his book *Embodiment*, has described at length four responses of the church, which he labels as:[6]

1. A "rejecting-punitive" response. Homosexuality is sin. Persons who practice homosexual acts should not only be rejected by the church, but punished for their acts (historically this has included stoning, burning, sexual mutilation).

2. A "rejecting-nonpunitive" response. Homosexual acts, but not homosexual persons, are condemned. Heterosexual marriage is the biblical norm, and other forms of sexual copulation go against the will of the Creator God. Nelson appeals to Karl Barth as representative of this position.[7] Though this appears to be a harsh position (Barth on occasion uses the term perversion to refer to homosexual acts), it accords with both Scripture and the church's teaching over many centuries. But finally, Barth stresses God's overwhelming grace that is for all people, for all sin, whatever the condition giving rise to that sin.[8]

3. A "qualified acceptance" response. We must come to grips with the reality of sexual orientation, which for many cannot be changed. While Scripture regards homosexual practice as sin and while celibacy is recommended for homosexually oriented persons, yet the church must be open to new understanding of this issue and be welcoming of people with same-sex *desire*. Helmut Thielicke in *The Ethics of Sex*, written in 1964, is representative of this approach.

4. A "full acceptance" response. Same-sex desires are God-given, not contrary to creation intent. Christian love allows no less than full acceptance of the person as he or she is in this regard. Nelson describes his own position as having shifted from number two as a teenager to number three later in life, and upon having several wonderful gay friends, now to number four.

Certainly, one can hold a position that does not fit neatly into these four classifications. I myself value aspects in positions two through four, and accept some inconsistency or tension in that spectrum. That tension arises from seeking to honor the authority of the biblical text and also to be accepting, even affirming of gays and lesbians, without condoning homosexual practice.

Gerald D. Coleman argues that none of these four responses describes accurately the Catholic teaching on this subject. He classifies the Roman Catholic responses into one of three general approaches in evaluating homosexual *activity* morally: (1) homosexual acts are wrong; (2) homosexual acts are neutral; and (3) homosexual acts are wrong—but homosexual behavior for *some people* does not fall under the total condemnation of the first approach. Coleman then identifies the Catholic approach as holding forth chastity as the expected norm for those homosexually inclined.[9]

Second, what most needs to be done? Teaching and pastoral care are on the top of the pressing agenda (and here Coleman's book is most useful). The teaching task is huge, and it should not focus on homosexuality per se. The larger issues of sexual standards, and the cultural consequences of promiscuity, must be addressed. Officially, some denominations have been slow to support some current movements to promote premarital sexual abstinence. Why? Do we fear being labeled old fogeys? Or, maybe as parents we fear that what we come down hard on is surely what our children will do. My sense is that much of our present homosexuality crisis could have been avoided had we been clear in our stand against premarital sexual experimentation, that is, becoming sexually active. In several cases I know, being jilted heterosexually provided the context for same-sex experimentation. Or, simply not making it into heterosexual activity pressures one toward same-sex experimentation. We have a massive teaching task, and we need courage and God's strength to take it on.

On the pastoral care end, we need to minister compassionately to people who are homosexually inclined, for whatever reason. But we cannot treat all the same. The causative dynamics interrelated to sexual attraction to same-sex persons or strong desires for homosexual relations need to be assessed in the context of pastoral care, and this task requires more than most pastors are trained for. When does one advise special therapy? And where does one send an individual looking for therapy—since many counselors today would be unsympathetic to seeking change of desire or practice? Certainly the listening ear that is willing to reflect on family dynamics, personal pilgrimage, past hurts, and failed goals is an important part of the pastoral task. Most important, an effort must be made to understand the person as a person holistically, and not just as a homosexual.[10]

The church should arrange for seminars to assist pastors in this process. Counseling and pastoral care initiative should be done long before church membership questions are considered. Unless this is done, the church membership question seems phony, and it is the issue, not the person, that is being either refused or baptized. We must know people well before we can mediate healing and hope, and pledge brother or sister care. Further, if a homosexual person comes to a congregation from another congregation and requests membership, the person's status in the congregation from which she or he has come needs to be ascertained and carefully assessed. I would think that a congregation would need some extended time to learn to know and care pastorally for the person before membership is considered. If after such care the person is not ready to commit to the standard of the church in this regard, membership may be delayed or associate membership might be given, with a reevaluation date set also. Why such caution? Because the church has not walked this way before. Indeed, pastoral care and spiritual discernment are needed every step of the way.

A related but equally important task is pastoral care of parents whose son is gay or daughter is lesbian. How do we listen to their stories, anguish, and point of view? In the congregational setting, it would be wise to pull together a small group that functions as the care-giving resource, with primary commitment to listen, care, pray, and support in friendship. Not everyone in the group needs to have the same point of view on the matter, but only to be committed to listen, discern, and speak in love what they through prayer come to discern as God's word for the situation. Those best equipped to help will be those who minister out of some sense of their own brokenness, and God's finding them in the midst of their own lament.

Also, on the point of what needs doing most, I think it is important not to let this issue overwhelm the mission and energy of a congregation. Institutional and congregation leaders must be alert to the way homosexuality tends to stop everything else and becomes an all or nothing bargain. This happens both in the discussion and discernment time and even in the position that is taken. In this respect it becomes a very divisive issue, and the life of the church is pressured to a halt. The fact of this phenomenon has often made me wonder where the empowerment for this debate comes from. For this reason, it is most important in all aspects of this process to be spiritually alert. As one enters into discernment and processing of this issue, some signal tests might be adopted for oneself and for the congregation or institution. How is my prayer life? How free is our praise to God and to Jesus Christ as our Savior from sin, death, and evil? How warm is our love to our brothers and sisters, and what are our feelings to those with whom we disagree?

Third, how might conferences or dioceses, or other overseeing bodies, respond to churches/congregations that have covenanted gays and lesbians as members? This question may be framed differently depending on the polity of the church body. A biblical case can be made for excommunication (with the incest case of 1 Cor. 5 as textual support analogically).[11] Or the overseeing body (perhaps the denominational executive body) might censure the church/congregation by calling it to accountability to the church's standards in its adopted statements. This would be a form of church discipline, the exercise of the prophetic word.[12] At its best, church discipline combines judgment and compassion, saying: "Yes, homosexual or bisexual practice is wrong, but the issue is bigger than the situation of certain individuals. It is the reaping of what has been sown by our western culture over the last several centuries," or while we can't comprehend the complexity of the case, our best understanding is that same-sex sexual unions depart from God's intended will for humankind. While we expect accountability to the church's standards, we also extend compassion and desire to work with you toward healing, whatever that may mean in this situation.

Because accepting homosexual practice within the church takes a radical departure from both Scripture and the church's tradition,[13] the governing body might request that the congregation not advocate at delegate sessions for its position. To ask this does not mean silencing discussion of the issue—which may continue in arranged sessions—but that some exercise of discipline is deemed appropriate. Governing bodies might also request that the congregational leaders teach against homosexual practice, just as we continue to teach against divorce (and remarriage) when it exists in the congregation.[14]

Is it possible to do this and maintain loving relationships with those with whom we disagree? Extending Christian charity does not mean approval of conduct.

One of the dominant emphases of Scripture is that God is a God of enduring steadfast love. Also, God's love and mercy outlast God's anger and punishment (Ps. 30:5; Isa. 54:8; Jer. and Hos.). Jesus pointed to both God's mercy and judgment. Matthew 5:44-48 anchors Jesus' most startling teaching, love for enemies, in the merciful nature of God, who sends the rain on both the good and the evil.[15] In other situations, Jesus tells parables that speak of judgment for various responses of disobedience, negative attitude, or loss of opportunity (most notably Luke 19:11-27). It is striking to note that Paul, whose voice is strongest against same-sex practices, is the New Testament witness that most strongly urges mission to all people. Paul lived this mission, as well. At points it seems that he envisions that all will somehow be reconciled to God (Rom. 5:15, 18-19; 11:26-36; Eph. 1:9-10; Col. 1:20). Paul never speaks about condemnation of some to hell, though he does speak about everyone giving an account of deeds done in the body (2 Cor. 5:10). Paul speaks about God's judgment, to be sure (e.g. 1 Cor. 3:12-17), but he declares that nothing in all God's creation can separate us from the love of God that is in Jesus Christ our Lord.

This dominant emphasis of Scripture must temper our judging of sin (which, after all, besets each of us), so that we seek transformation and reconciliation for all people with God and fellow humans. The vision that guides us is a holy vision for the church, the vision of unity and faithfulness to Jesus Christ.

Prayer

Elect from ev'ry nation yet one o'er all the earth,
Her charter of salvation: one Lord, one faith, one birth.
One holy name she blesses, partakes one holy food,
And to one hope she presses, with ev'ry grace endued.

Though with a scornful wonder the world sees her
        oppressed,
by schisms rent asunder, by heresies distressed,
yet saints their watch are keeping, their cry goes up,
        "How long?"
And soon the night of weeping shall be the morn of song.

—*Samuel J. Stone*

CHAPTER EIGHT

A MODEL FOR CONGREGATIONAL DISCERNMENT

As indicated in the preface, it is important to keep basic biblical instruction central as Christians seek guidance on moral issues, whether in the local congregation or as a denomination. Such a biblical text is Colossians 3:12-17:

> As God's chosen ones, holy and beloved, clothe yourselves with compassion, **kindness**, humility, meekness, and patience. Bear with one another and, if anyone has a complaint against another, **forgive** each other; just as the Lord has forgiven you, so you also must forgive. Above all, clothe yourselves with **love**, which binds everything together in perfect harmony. And let the peace of Christ rule in your hearts, to which indeed you were called in the one body. And be **thankful**. Let the word of Christ dwell in you richly; teach and admonish one another in all wisdom; and with **gratitude** in your hearts sing psalms, hymns, and spiritual songs to God. And whatever you do, in word or deed, do everything in the name of the Lord Jesus, **giving thanks** to God the Father through him (bold emphasis mine).

The Jerusalem Conference process found in Acts 15 can provide us with a basic model for how to walk through discernment and decision-making together as a community. Though I differ with Jeffrey Siker's use of the Jerusalem Conference process to accept and bless homosexual relationships of covenant union,[1] I believe that this Scripture offers us fundamental principles for moral discernment on this issue. Ross T. Bender, former dean of the Associated Mennonite Biblical Seminary, outlined these in a study process some years ago:[2]

—All points of view are presented.
—An appeal is made to history (how did we get here?).
—An appeal is made to Scripture (what does it say and mean?).
—An appeal is made to basic theological convictions.
—Testimonies are given about Christian experiences.
—Those present speak *and listen.*
—A respected brother—James—gives his judgment.
—The assembly comes to consensus and reports its common mind.

This sounds simple, but it was not simple for the Acts 15 issue of whether non-Jews need to be circumcised to become part of the messianic body of faith. Nor is it simple for many Christian bodies of faith today to follow those steps and work toward consensual judgment on whether congregations should accept as members those in practicing gay and lesbian relationships. The Jerusalem Council reaffirmed certain tenets of Jewish faith that were not to be compromised in the admission of uncircumcised Gentiles into the community. Since one of these tenets is proscription of sexual immorality, it becomes difficult to "bracket" this conclusion when utilizing the process for discernment on the homosexuality issue.

Another biblical guideline helpful to us in discernment and decision-making is that developed by Paul Minear in his treatment of Romans 14-15, where eating food offered to idols and holy observances threatened to divide the congregation.[3] The text refers to those who think they can eat food offered to idols without defilement as "the strong." Those who believe they will be defiled by eating such food are "the weak" in this and the 1 Corinthians 8-10 texts. As Minear helpfully points out, there were actually five positions or groups in this debate:[4]

—The "fors" who scorn and despise those who are "against"
—The "againsts" who scorn and despise those who are "for"
—The doubters who can be swayed one way or the other
—The "againsts" who do not condemn but accept the "fors"
—The "fors" who do not despise but accept the "againsts"

The first two groups are bound to aggravate and perpetuate any potential cleavage in the group,[5] while the last two bring the groups closer together and leave a way clear for reconciliation. Romans 14 sets forth four points of truth that all are to keep in mind as they seek to "welcome one another in Christ" (14:3; 15:7):

—Each of us will give an account to God.
—If one is persuaded to do what one considers wrong, it causes one to fall.
—If one's action injures a brother or sister, the stance does not proceed from love.
—Whatever does not proceed from faith is sin. [6]

In addition to these guidelines, other strong theological convictions bear on discernment of this issue. I refer to these in my "Response" in the book *To Continue the Dialogue*, edited by C. Norman Kraus. The key task here is to adjudicate properly among the four sources of authority recognized widely by the Christian church. These may be conceived as a quadrangle in relationship to each other, as in this diagram at the top of page 126:

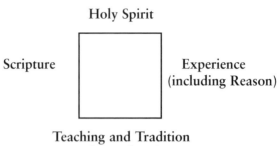

Holy Spirit

Scripture

Experience
(including Reason)

Teaching and Tradition
of the Church

Scripture and church tradition clearly regard same-sex genital relationships to be morally wrong.[7] Even if one accepts interpretations of the seven key Scriptures that neutralize these texts in relation to current same-sex practices,[8] it is not possible to construct a *biblical* case authorizing same-sex genital relations as morally right.[9]

Appealing to the authority of the community in interpreting Scripture gains little in solving the problem.[10] Numerous voices from experience call for rethinking the issue, but as several writers point out, experience dons many faces. Experience is ambiguous as a source for moral authority. Marion Soards makes the point, saying it is ambiguous because "it is simultaneously objective and subjective. To put the question another way, all experiences are not equal. Which experiences count? Why? Why not? Do all persons perceive it the same way? Whose perceptions are most valid?"[11] Richard Hays, in considering the role of experience, makes the point that it must extend beyond individual testimony to the experience of the community to be validated, and to have any normative status in moral discernment.[12] Experience is thus a chameleon as an ethical authority. It counts, and should be heard, but it is not definitive. Marcus Smucker appeals to experience to highlight the need for (pastoral) support of homosexual people and their families.[13] Then too, voices from experience also speak of transformation from same-sex preference and practice to heterosexual preference and practice.

Often it is said that science, in its various branches, biology, pyschology, social science, etc., is another source of authority.[14] On this I demur. It can provide helpful, even crucial, information, but it does not function as a moral authority. The empirical *is*, in contrast to the *is* of God's deeds in salvation history culminating in Christ, does not produce an *ought*. To put this matter simply: the invention of the automobile, or the Internet, has revolutionized our way of living, but it has not altered the moral authority of the Ten Commandments. It is true, however, that science does offer explanations of phenomena that help us understand in new ways. The scientific proposals and efforts to explain homosexuality have not yielded proven results to date.[15]

When we include empirical data from the sciences, the contribution of social science and cultural analysis comes into play as well (the content of chapter 5). If indeed the forces of culture have contributed to the present situation, how shall they be assessed and how does the church respond? What aspects of the culture does the church affirm, and what does it contest, even condemn? Should the church's response be focused on individual gay or lesbian persons (which may involve misplaced anger on the part of the church) or more on these cultural factors, critiquing the sources of the present dilemma? Should individual people be made to pay when they are "victim" of this long-developed cultural legacy? To what extent does the church want to be counter-cultural, given other areas of its accommodation to culture?

We continue to search for the leading of the Spirit on this matter. I propose an experiment to help in this discernment: same-sex partners and their congregation or support group read and prayerfully reflect daily for forty days on Romans 8:1-27—a text that connects us to the Holy Spirit in multiple ways—and 1 John 4:7-21—a text on God's love and love for one another—and seek to discern what happens to thought, attitudes, commitments, and behaviors, as well as sexual desires on the part of the covenant couple. Reporting from a dozen cases, where both partners confess Christian identity, would be helpful. It would be practical field research to illumine further Mark Thiessen Nation's article on discernment of this issue.[16]

Nation proposes eight points that might be affirmed by Christian bodies as they begin the process of discernment:[17]

1. The social and biological sciences have raised complicated questions about how people come to be gay and lesbian, questions that present puzzles we do not pretend fully to understand.

2. We affirm that the Bible is centrally authoritative in defining the Christian faith and thus, among other things, provides instruction in what it means to live morally.

3. There are only a few biblical texts that speak directly to the issue of homoerotic relations. Those few which do address the subject, taken at face value, speak negatively.[18]

4. Any discussion of homoerotic relations within the Bible must include a more comprehensive biblical framework that would include not only other texts related to sexuality, but also a broader understanding of Christian theology and ethics. Furthermore, this discussion should be placed within an overall framework of what it means to be Christian.

5. We have something to learn from the various ways the church throughout its history has dealt both with sexuality in general and homoerotic relations in particular, as we seek today to wrestle with these matters.

6. We believe Christians are commanded to love their neighbors as themselves. This would include repudiating any cruel behavior toward people (certainly including friends, family members, and co-workers) who are engaged in homoerotic relationships. Moreover, it would also include being loving toward gays, lesbians, and people who believe homoerotic behaviors to be wrong.

7. We believe it is important to support and nurture heterosexual married couples (and their children). Moreover, if the church were to shift positions on homosexual relationships, what is being suggested for adoption is a parallel monogamous arrangement for gays and lesbians. [*Author's note:* For some congregations, this last sentence would not sit well for a place to begin discussion, and thus is, perhaps, best deleted.]

8. Homoerotic behavior is really the issue we are wrestling with. Of course this issue can neither be separated from the lives of the people who are in homoerotic relationships nor disconnected from broader issues related to sexuality.

By affirming together as much of this as possible, the group begins to see that what is held in common is most significant. This will build trust to consider areas of difference.

In addition to discernment on the relative role of Scripture, church/tradition, Holy Spirit, and experience, contemporary techniques used in conflict resolution can be helpful to the discernment process.[19] One reason why the application of these techniques to this issue and process has been so difficult and ineffectual is that the issue is so deeply emotional and theological.[20] Also, the complexity of the issue and the community's theological commitment further complicates the conflict resolution process.[21]

It may be helpful to the discernment process to discuss the *good* we can affirm about Christian gays and lesbians who covenant together. The following statement by Kathryn Greene-McCreight could stimulate such a discussion, and prepare us to relate to such coupled people in our families and wider church. In addition to repenting of sins of hate and failures to be empathetic for their suffering resulting from exclusion and discrimination,

> [T]he church could indeed go so far as to acknowledge the "goods" which can come from homosexual relationships. The self-giving of two individuals in a committed relation-

ship can, after all, reflect the sacrificial love of Christ. The contribution to the wider community which may come of homosexual relationships can also be acknowledged as a "good," such as the time and talents given in service to the church and the love and care rendered to the adopted children of gay and lesbian couples. The church can recognize as a "good" the pastoral, preaching, and teaching ministries of gays and lesbians which further the church's witness to Christ. To recognize these goods, however, is not to sanction the sexual activity which may (or may not) accompany such relationships. It does not follow from the church's freedom to recognize these goods which may issue from homosexual relationships that the church therefore has the freedom to bless such relationships. The church has neither such freedom nor such authority. To insist on this would be to insist on consequentialist ethics, that the "ends justify the means," so to speak.[22]

When all is said and done, what matters most in our living and dying is whether we are "in Christ" and led by God's Spirit. This is *the* important issue about our identity, not sexual identity. Sexual identity should not be a core identifying feature of those born again by the grace and power of God. Whether we live or die, *who we are in Jesus Christ* is what really counts.

For Christians, prayer together is essential.[23] If we seek to discern the will of God on this matter, we need to bathe ourselves personally and corporately in prayer. When we pray, "without a trace of hypocrisy" as James 3:15 commends, we have a chance of hearing God's word and receiving direction as to just what the gospel mission for the church is for its own life and for our culture, as word of witness.

Prayer

For this reason . . . we have not ceased praying for you and asking that you may be filled with the knowledge of God's will in all spiritual wisdom and understanding, so that you may lead lives worthy of the Lord, fully pleasing to him, as you bear fruit in every good work and as you grow in the knowledge of God. May you be made strong with all the strength that comes from his glorious power, and may you be prepared to endure everything with patience, while joyfully giving thanks to the Father, who has enabled you to share in the inheritance of the saints in the light. He has rescued us from the power of darkness and transferred us into the kingdom of his beloved Son, in whom we have redemption, the forgiveness of sins. (emphasis mine)

—Colossians 1:9-14

Now may the God of peace, who brought back from the dead our Lord Jesus, the great shepherd of the sheep, by the blood of the eternal covenant, **make you complete in everything good so that you may do his will, working among us that which is pleasing in his sight, through Jesus Christ,** to whom be the glory forever and ever. Amen. (emphasis mine)

—Hebrews 13:20-21

CHAPTER NINE

CONCLUDING REMARKS: THE PATH FORWARD

Recently the scholarly journal *Religious Studies Review* carried an extensive review article by Deirdre Good in which Good looked at five recent books on homosexuality, with the question: "Are We Getting Anywhere?"[1] Reflecting the contemporary university ethos, the review lamented that we are not, in fact, getting anywhere—meaning, it appears, to achieve the normalization of homosexuality into society and church as an acceptable way of life. In her conclusion, Good pointed to the 1999 decision of the General Synod of the Reformed Church in America. While noting that in 1994 the Synod reaffirmed its position that "the practicing homosexual lifestyle is contrary to Scripture," the 1999 statement urged attention to how homosexual persons have suffered in our churches and called its members into "a process of repentance, prayer, learning, and growth in ministry."[2] Good ends the review by calling for *time* to work on the issue, knowing that such a momentous issue will continue to be with the church and society in the years to come.

Three factors must be central for the church in the journey ahead. First, we need to be more explicit on the authority of

Scripture, without recycling old fundamentalist-liberal debates (see chapter 1).

Second, we need to listen to voices from the worldwide church, from brothers and sisters outside western culture. Our life in this world includes the body of Christ worldwide. We know these days how much the lives of people around the globe are intertwined with the economic and political interests of the west, especially the U.S. We must take these worldwide voices seriously, and become more self-critical of our own culture, especially its assumptions about individual sexual freedom.

Third, we will need to be proactive in providing pastoral care of all in our congregation, for whatever sexual issues they deal with. This includes those struggling with sexual identity, and parents of those who have painful experiences dealing with the issue. In many cases this includes persons within the extended family as well. With this effort, we will need to appreciate anew the paradoxical relation between sin and grace, affirm the transforming power of salvation and identity in Jesus Christ for human character and moral choices, and live toward a "third way"[3] in which love and discipling of one another embrace each other.

In this effort we need to be sustained by the vision of the gospel, God's grace in Jesus Christ, and our central mission that grows out of that mission, as put so well by Paul. The wonderful text of Paul in 2 Corinthians 5:16-21 offers an important focus for our way forward. I include here a sermon meditation on the text:

Be Reconciled to God
2 Corinthians 5:16-21
From now on, therefore, we regard no one from a human point of view; even though we once knew Christ from a human point of view, we know him no longer in that way. So if anyone is in Christ: **new creation!!** Everything old has passed away; see, everything has become **new!**

All this is from God, who **reconciled** us to himself through Christ, and has given us the **ministry of reconciliation**; that is, **in Christ God was reconciling** the world to himself, not counting their trespasses against them, and entrusting the **message of reconciliation** to us. So we are **ambassadors for Christ**, since God is making his appeal through us; we entreat you on behalf of Christ, be **reconciled to God**. For our sake he made him to be sin who knew no sin, so that in him we might become the **righteousness of God**.

I put in bold the key words and give a literal translation of *new creation* in verse 17. I highlight the recurring emphasis on reconciliation, a wonderful gift of God. This important text declares that God's own initiative in Christ reconciles us to God's own self. This is the basis for our ministry of reconciliation.

The text begins in verse 16 with two ways of viewing Jesus Christ: the human way and a new way that no longer regards Jesus simply as a person according to the flesh. When Paul regarded Jesus as only human, he was a persecutor of Christians. He murdered them, for they were undermining Judaism. Paul had to have a strike-down, knockout encounter and be resuscitated before he came to know Jesus as the Christ, the Messiah. He had to make a 180-degree turn. Then, all things became new for him.

It happens also for us. We may not need a Damascus Road knock-down encounter, but we do need to confess our sinfulness, our participation in Adam's and Eve's turning away from God. We need to open ourselves to the light of Christ that God shines into our lives. Repenting of our sinful ways, we then look to Christ for God's forgiving, reconciling power.

In my translation of verse 17, I take it as an exclamation: New Creation—Wow! This radical new reality means we know Christ no longer from a human point of view. It's like driving through a bad snowstorm, as it once happened to

Mary and me on the northeast Pennsylvania Turnpike, then coming to a long tunnel cut through the mountain, and on the other side being greeted with dazzling sunshine and dry road. In Christ, and only in Christ, is the church God's new creation. Old things pass away; behold, all becomes new. We receive God's righteousness, enabling us to live the new life. We cannot do this on our own efforts. God in Christ empowers us. Only God can make us really new people.

Reconciliation is at the heart of the text.[4] I use here a concentric diagram of the main thought of the text to show this:

1. Through Christ, a new creation
2. All this is from God, who **reconciled** us to himself through Christ,
3. and has given us the ministry of **reconciliation;**
4. that is, in Christ God was **reconciling** the world to himself, not counting their trespasses against them and
3a. entrusting the message of **reconciliation** to us. So we are ambassadors for Christ, since God is making his appeal through us;
2a. we entreat you on behalf of Christ, be **reconciled** to God
1a. Christ became sin for us; that we might become the righteousness of God

Each unit from line 2 through 2a includes some form of the word "reconcile." Reconciliation is through God's initiative. From beginning to end it is *God's* act in Christ that reconciles humans to God. God is not pacifying divine wrath, as is sometimes emphasized, but acting to reconcile us wayward humans to God's self. God then entrusts to us reconciled humans the ministry of reconciliation.

Lines 2 and 2a reinforce this point. God is the subject; Christ is the agent through whom God does his reconciling work. We are the ambassadors who herald the good news, "Be reconciled to God." Alleluia, thank God!

In lines 3 and 3a we are enlisted into God's work of reconciliation. Here we receive our work orders: be agents of reconciliation—first reconciling people to God and then people to one another. This is the call to shalom-making, peacemaking in our world. God entrusts that word and power of reconciliation to us.

We then become ambassadors *for* or *in behalf of (hyper)* Christ. God makes his appeal through us. The appeal, "be reconciled to God," is a command. God is addressing us, "Be reconciled to me," "on behalf of (*hyper*) Christ." We honor the work of Christ when we heed this command, and give our lives to Christ and God. Only then can we as Christian believers join God and Christ in the work to *reconcile* people to God.

The last line (1a) points to Christ, who knew no sin, but came into our sinful humanity and died by the violence of humans putting him to death on the cross. Thus he became sin for us, dying on the cross as a criminal for us. All this "so that we might become the righteousness of God." God's initiative in Christ's life and work on Calvary is the means for us to be reconciled to God. Then we are called to take up the task. Christian peacemaking efforts must never lose sight of this. For here is our identity as peacemakers and our long-term empowerment for the task.

So the text as visualized shows the movement of the gospel's grand declaration: "God was in Christ, reconciling the world unto himself." God was in Christ—mystery of mysteries and miracle of miracles. When Jesus died on Calvary and was then resurrected, he bore our sins, broke the curse upon us, and set us free from shame and guilt. This is the glorious gospel news. This is the news every Christian church has for its community, in this country, and in all countries of the world. This power transcends race, culture, and politics.

Dietrich Bonhoeffer, in a sermon on loving our enemies, speaks clearly about God's prior action that makes such possible:

Even though I acted as an enemy against God's commands, God has acted as a friend toward me. Even though I did evil to him, God did good to me. [God] did not prosecute me for my sin, but instead sought me tirelessly and without exasperation. God suffered and died for me, and even that was not an action too extreme for him to take for me. By this, God has won me over. God's enemy has become God's friend. The Father has found his child again.[5]

When in the depth of our being, we feel great gratitude for God reconciling us to God's self even while we were *weak, sinners, even enemies*, then we risk seeking reconciling relationships with those who differ, even strongly, from us. Several years ago, *Christianity Today* carried an article under the title, "Waging Peace," that described how a reconciled relationship developed between a liberal and conservative Episcopalian on this issue of homosexuality. The article, written by Douglas LeBlanc, describes how the relationship of trust grew between LeBlanc, the conservative, and Louie Crew, a then-sixty-five-year-old man whose partnership with a man named Ernest began in 1974. LeBlanc writes about the movement from distrust to trust, and under the article's lead text of 2 Corinthians 5:18-19 recounts how after working together with this fellow Episcopalian he came to see his role as a reconciler among other conservatives in their attitudes toward gays. He writes, "I feel I have taken enough steps to apply the apostle Paul's words at 2 Corinthians to my particular sense of calling." He concludes the article:

I want them [liberals] to remember the discussion when they helped me better understand what it's like to fear for your safety because some thug on a bus has a finely tuned "gay radar." I want to remember that discussion when I'm with my conservative friends and talking about liberals. I want them to remember how deeply it wounds conservatives to have our motives second-guessed. I want to remember how deeply it wounds liberals to receive our written or verbal anathemas. I want them to remember and to feel in their bones that conservatives do what we do because we love the Lord Jesus, and we want to obey him. I want to keep my eyes and my heart open to recognize when my liberal friends express the same motives. . . . I'm no more in favor of blessing gay couples than I was in 1992, but I hope that by God's grace I am a humbler representative of my convictions. I know that the street clothes of a peacemaker fit me better than the armor of a political activist.[6]

May the Lord lead us on our journeys of faith to experience a more fully reconciled relationship to God and to one another.[7]

Prayer

Beloved, let us love one another, because love is from God; everyone who loves is born of God and knows God. Whoever does not love does not know God, for God is love. God's love was revealed among us in this way: God sent his only Son into the world so that we might live through him. In this is love, not that we loved God but that he loved us and sent his Son to be the atoning sacrifice for our sins. Beloved, since God loved us so much, we also ought to love one another. No one has ever seen God; if we love one another, God lives in us, and his love is perfected in us.

By this we know that we abide in him and he in us, because he has given us of his Spirit. And we have seen and do testify that the Father has sent his Son as the Savior of the world. God abides in those who confess that Jesus is the Son of God, and they abide in God. So we have known and believe the love that God has for us.

God is love, and those who abide in love abide in God, and God abides in them. Love has been perfected among us in this: that we may have boldness on the day of judgment, because as he is, so are we in this world. There is no fear in love, but perfect love casts out fear; for fear has to do with punishment, and whoever fears has not reached perfection in love. We love because he first loved us. Those who say, "I love God," and hate their brothers or sisters, are liars; for those who do not love a brother or sister whom they have seen, cannot love God whom they have not seen. The commandment we have from him is this: those who love God must love their brothers and sisters also.

—1 John 4:7-21

Interpretations of Genesis 19

Non-Sexual Interpretations	Sexual Interpretations
Jeremiah 23:14	2 Peter 2:6-10
Ezekiel 16:49-50	Jude 7
Wisdom Solomon 10:8	Jubilees (7:20-21); 16:5-6;
	20:5-6
Ecclus. 16:82	Enoch 10:4; 34:1-2
Jubilees 13:17	
Babylonian Talmud	T. B. Sanh. l09a
Sanhedrin 109a	Test. Twelve Patriarchs
Ketuboth 103a	Napth. 3:4-5; 4:1
Baba Batra 12b,	Asher 7:1
Abot 5.10	Benjamin 9:1
Erubin 49c	Levi 14:6
	3 Maccabees 2:3
	Philo, *De Abr.* 26:134-36
	Josephus *Ant.* 1.200;
	cf. *Against Apion* 2.199
	Gen. Rabbah 50:7 (Midrash)

All the entries in the last left block are from the Babylonian Talmud. Sanhedrin 109a mentions both defiling their bodies by immoral deeds and economic transgressions. Three of the Talmudic texts contain the expression "compelling (not to act) in the manner of Sodom." This phrase is exposited in the notes as meaning the refusing of favors, helping someone, even when it cost nothing, a "dog-in-the-manger" attitude. The exposition in Abot refers to four types of characters; the Sodom type is "Mine is mine; thine is thine." It is an immoral self-contained, smug, self-oriented life-style. *The Letter of Aristeas*, written between 130-70 B.C. but with some first-century A.D. additions likely (though purported to be written a century earlier) narrates a Jewish view of Gentile vices that is instructive in assessing biblical texts like Romans 1:18-32:

> The majority of other men defile themselves in their relationships, thereby committing a serious offense, and lands and whole cities take pride in it: they not only procure the males, they also defile mothers and daughters. We are quite separated from these practices.[1]

Sibylline Oracles 3:764-66 links male-to-male intercourse with adultery and doing away with infants as sins of the Gentile world. In 2:73 is a direct prohibition: "Do not practice homosexuality, do not betray information, do not murder."[2]

(Prepared for Mennonite Church Assembly Seminar, St. Louis, July 26, 1999, by Willard Swartley)

Clarity Regarding the Use of the Word "Homosexual"

Preferably, the word "homosexual" should be understood as an adjective, and not as a noun. But common usage has turned it into a noun, *homosexual(s)*, thus denoting *essence*, and reducing sexuality to static categories. More liberal secular writers advocating for gay and lesbians rights resist the static view, as chapter 5 indicates. This is to be understood in the context of a postmodern view of reality, that nothing is objectively determined, but that anything becomes what it is in accord with how humans choose to construct reality. All meaning is constructed, and all values are conferred—and some would say always with political import.

The ideological map regarding "homosexuality/homosexuals" spreads over five categories of connotation:

1. Homosexuality refers to behavior, what one *does* sexually (this is likely the biblical view, but the Bible does not use the term).

2. Homosexuality refers first and foremost to a sexual orientation that is likely not chosen, but a given; behavior is a separate matter that is chosen (this seems to be the dominant use in Mennonite church discourse).

3. Homosexuality refers to a phenomenon in which *is*

and *does* are one. The distinction between orientation and behavior is plastic, undesirable, and ontologically impossible. This has several schools of advocates:

a. conservative: *orientation* is not a given, but a "cover" for freedom to manipulate ethically (one's *desire* can and should change as one converts, undergoes therapy, or grows in Christ).

b. liberal postmodern: *orientation* connotes a static view of reality. As the gay and lesbian patron "Saint" Foucault says, "we must become what we wish to be sexually, including gay, lesbian, bisexual, transgender, etc."

c. feminist contributions: sexuality must be understood in the larger context of gender-identity. Nature and nurture are unified in gender formation and expression.

4. Homosexual(ity) refers to people who have same-sex erotic desire and choose to remain celibate or enter into monogamous covenant unions.

5. Homosexual(ity) may refer to any or all of the above, without distinction.

Because our speech these days does not normally make these distinctions, there is great possibility for misunderstanding whenever one speaks on this topic. To illustrate, in a presentation on the subject, I described 3b above, and it was later reported by a hearer that I denied the concept of *orientation* on conservative, fundamentalist, and biblical grounds. Quite the opposite is what I intended to say, to point out that the liberal university discussion of this subject no longer honors the distinction between orientation and behavior. What one *becomes* sexually arises from freedom to construct who one is. It is ironic that this view has affinity with a conservative view, in resisting the notion of orientation. But those who know the history of western thought know that these have been bedfellows before (for example, the rationalist strand in both fundamentalist and liberal theology, especially in the 1920-1950 era).

My own hesitation to own the "orientation" concept

already in the early eighties arose neither from conservative nor liberal thought, but the simple practical matter that it is extremely difficult to laud someone's homosexual nature, on the one hand, but forbid its expression, on the other. But this is what we expect of heterosexual singles also, which by far outnumber homosexual people in population. We need to launch a massive campaign of social support, encouragement, and both homosexual and heterosexual modeling of celibate lifestyles, and we must be articulate, intentional, and public about it.

While endorsing "same-sex covenant unions" seems to be a more common-sense "solution" to this conundrum, this development flies in the face of Scripture and 2,000 years of church tradition. Here I concur with John D. Roth of Goshen College that the church should not make a hasty decision on this matter, but should respect the church's centuries-long tradition of its understandings of marriage.[1] I think also we need first to examine our contemporary western culture that landed us into this situation. Few writers have undertaken to show how and why we came to be where we are culturally on this topic. David Greenberg and David A. Shank are exceptions.[2] Most writers rather debate "causes" of homosexuality in terms of given persons, which in my judgment are simply diverse and many. While there are many theories, speculations, and prejudices, I am inclined only to say: *many*.

Also, it would be quite wrong to interpret my "Cultural Analysis" (see chapter 5) as saying that the cause of any one person's homosexuality originated because of one or several factors enumerate in the western cultural legacy. That's not the point of cultural analysis. No, the purpose of seeing clearly the cultural legacy is to help us understand why we frame the topic in current discussion in peculiar and particular "western" ways. Aside from western cultural influence imported into other world cultures, I do not know of any culture besides (northern) western that thinks about this issue in categories akin to those that we think in today. I venture to say that in most cultures worldwide the issue is regarded akin to incest, as it appears in Leviticus 18 and 1 Corinthians 5-6. We may call this the primitive view, but we should not thereby depreciate it.

My resistance to climbing onto the modern bandwagon of being either "for or against," or to devise ways to settle the matter, is fundamentally a fear of being culturally blinded. I fear falling prey to the very cultural forces that we as Mennonites on various other counts have been stubborn in resisting. In some respects, I see it as analogous to the collapse of liberal pacifism in the 1930s and 40s. When the cultural pressure became so strong, many pacifists shifted sides and made defense of "the free world" a virtue, in the name of social justice and democracy. The current pressure is for justice and inclusion. And these are enormously important values. But when applied to this issue, they mute in advance a careful assessment of biblical interpretation, the church's historic position, and assessment of cultural analysis. Then, too, a distinction must be made between biblical and modern understandings of justice, as Millard Lind's several writings on this issue make evident.[3]

On the other side, the pressure to join the forces of obstinate resistance to consider and discuss the matter, since Scripture is said to be so clear is equally strong and distressing. When and if this is linked up with a spirit that breeds discrimination and hatred, or demeaning attitudes toward homosexual people, this is a worse sin. This is a travesty of Christian courtesy and grace, and also contradicts the best in the believers church tradition.

For those who struggle with homosexual attraction, I wish for them every level of love, affirmation, and acceptance as persons by all of us. I want them as friends and trusted fellow believers. I am against name-calling from both sides. To me this is a basic attitudinal issue for which we need another responsibility. Individual people who are "victims" of these cultural forces should not be blamed for the cultural "baby" that in my judgment the west and post-Christendom have conceived.

A Day of Gloom: Dying from Love[1]

What have Amos and AIDS in common? As the title suggests, a day of gloom (Amos 5:20)! Doom marks both the prophecies of Amos and the ominous threat of AIDS in our world today. In 1989 I wrote an article on AIDS for the *Gospel Herald* in the aftermath of the first International Conference on AIDS held in Toronto in early June of that year.[2] At that time, on sabbatical from Associated Mennonite Biblical Seminary at Yale Divinity School, I was following the news releases from the First International AIDS conference through articles in the *New Haven Register*. Medical and cultural analysts predicted a ninefold rise in deaths from AIDS during the nineties (but the ninefold increase occurred already by 1995, with deaths rising from one-half million to 4.5 million!). Then the August 3, 1992, issue of *Time* reported that 110 million people were predicted to die from AIDS by the year 2000. The U.S. deaths would account for 16 percent, of which 58 percent would be from male homosexual intercourse—a bit over ten million.

I was moved to see this as a warning sign, and wondered, do we not need a clear word, as the Old Testament prophets gave to Israel? Since at that time the spread of the HIV/AIDS virus was linked mostly to male homosexual intercourse and drug use, the matter was also sensitive in relation to the church's dialogue with proponents of gay and lesbian concerns.

Is the worst outcome for humans inevitable? It was for

Israel, the northern kingdom, which would soon go into exile and never return as Amos prophesied. What is the AIDS scenario for the next fifteen years? A recent article in *Christianity Today* is quite sobering, indeed depressing.[3] By 2010 over half the world's deaths will be from AIDS. And the number of deaths by 2015, *if the current exponential progression continues* will be. . . .? We do not want to know! It cannot be spoken.

What is the nature of Old Testament prophecy? The great Jewish scholar Abraham Heschel described the role of the prophets in Israel as declaring God's action of judgment amid the events of nature and history, a point diametrically opposed to modern secular conventional wisdom. The last thing compassionate Christians are inclined to do is to say that some personal or corporate calamity happened as an act of divine judgment.

In this Old Testament prophetic vein I ask: Do such events in history and nature just happen? Is there some meaning in the course of world history? If so, how do we discern it? Should not the church, in its prophetic role, see in this God's judgment? In asking this, I do not take the lonely Jeremiah or Isaiah stance, but as one among believers, I tender this perspective for discernment.

Within present Mennonite prophetic consciousness it is easier and safer to speak against economic and political "freedoms" of some that lead to oppression and death of others, than it is to speak against sexual "freedoms" or "rights" that are causative of AIDS. But can the church, if it is faithful and prophetic, keep its mouth closed when the lives of millions have ended, and will end, not by the blast of the bomb, but by a whimper from what we call sexual love?

The irony of "love" leading to so much pain and calamity forces us to rethink what love really is. Augustine appealed to Jesus' love commands as the basis for the "just war," a view that developed and dominated Christian thinking, and is still widely held today.[4] Those of us in the pacifist church

tradition believe that this use of Scripture and way of thinking is flawed. But can we see an analogy in the argument that
love justifies sexual behavior that has deadly consequences,
when we know such to be the case? In the *Christianity Today*
article, a couple working in southern Africa for thirty years
noted that in the sexual morality ethos of the 1920s-1930s
AIDS could have been contained, but not in the current ethos
of sexual freedom. Even avoidance of sexual promiscuity
does not fully protect against devastating consequences, personally and corporately.

The church is called indeed to ministries of compassion, to
be a healing, loving, and caring community for AIDS victims.
But will it also have what is most necessary? Will it have
"tough love" and say clearly to its members: Stop thinking
that sex outside of marital covenant and use of illicit drugs are
okay. They are not. To think otherwise is moral deception.

At the present time our society in its promiscuous (and
especially homosexual) sex and illicit drug use is filled with
corporate life-threatening actions as subversive and subtle in
threat to human welfare as is the nuclear arms threat (only
the nuclear threat is more public). But the AIDS plague
advances insidiously, with its scope of victimization invisible,
and only retrospectively discernible. Its horror we feel most
in our grief for loved ones and threatening medical costs. But
such concern over *how many* will die and *how high* the hos-
pital costs will be is teleological analysis, much too banal a
consideration for the biblical prophetic tradition that simply
says: God is punishing us for our hardness of heart.

The homosexual debate rages around issues of nature,
nurture, and human choice. But none of these stances
bypasses the culpability of prophetic criticism. For the
prophets would pick events that we would say are naturally
caused and declare God's judgment in that catastrophe. The
prophets believed that nature and history were in the hands
of God. Granted, biblical thought is characterized by appeal
to ultimate causes, whereas our scientific thought is oriented

to direct, immediate causes. As moderns, we would argue that AIDS is caused by a virus and contracted through unsafe sex and sharing of needles in drug use.[5] But this limiting of our analysis to empirical direct causes needs rethinking and reevaluation. What are the ultimate causes behind the immediate causes? How are the spiritual and physical interconnected?

The AIDS crisis has arisen not only from the moral deformity of our present thinking but more ultimately from the philosophical legacy of western individualism. Like a mushroom cloud over the future of human life, the modern assumption that moral value is a matter of personal decision—that individual rights transcend corporate human welfare, that what I do with my body is only my business—are the cold fusion sources of the ongoing AIDS explosion. The AIDS crisis will diminish the world population drastically if the call to conversion is not heard and our thinking does not change. More than ever before, the issues of sexual freedoms and rights will become matters of community, corporate, and global welfare.

Let us know again that God's purpose in giving the Ten Commandments is to guarantee the social health of the community. What threatened *shalom*-health was forbidden in the name of God. Hence, in the name of God and Jesus Christ who came to save life and give abundant life, personal moral actions that threaten the life of the community are sin, wrong, and must be stopped. Otherwise, we will witness the unspeakable.

Hear what the statistics now forecast. The ninefold rise in deaths from HIV/AIDS occurred already by 1995 (4.5 million). By 2000 another ninefold increase in the HIV/AIDS death or infection number advanced to somewhere around 38 million,[6] with highest percentages of population infected with HIV in sub-Sahara Africa (in Botswana the rate is currently 36 percent of the population).[7] Using 40 million as a base for the year 2000, if a ninefold increase continues every five years as it has since 1990 (and it may if it hits hard in Asia's high populations),[8] Amos' prophecy of a day of gloom will bring utter devastation over the face of the earth: 360 million by 2005; 3.24 billion by 2010, and by 2015—well, there are not that many people living on the face of the earth.[9] This is hardly what Jesus meant by his love command. It should put to rest the silly notion, "Love and do whatever you please," as an adequate moral guide.

Thank God for new medical breakthroughs that will hopefully lessen the scope of this projected tragedy. But it continues in unimaginable proportions, with staggering numbers in southern Africa, where most cases result from heterosexual intercourse. I believe the Old Testament prophets would say this is an act of God's judgment, and that God suffers with the victims (Hosea's *pathos)*. Ironically, while secular society today correlates illness with choices to smoke or drink, and fatal disease with unsafe sex, we in the church remain tongue-tied on these issues. Why is this? Are we so concerned about individual rights, personal freedom, and fear of legalism, that we withhold true compassion by failing to warn of death and teach the ways that lead to true life? Has Satan blinded our eyes; has God hardened our hearts?

AIDS Prayer
(from Mennonite Central Committee, *A Common Place*, Nov. 2002)

> *God of mercy,*
> > *grant healing and peace to your children suffering from AIDS.*
> *God of understanding,*
> > *open the minds and hearts of those of us who have not experienced the pain and devastation of AIDS.*
> *God of knowledge,*
> > *help us talk openly about the tragedy of AIDS. Help us learn and teach others about it so that ignorance and death shall not prevail.*

God of grace,
> *be with those caregivers who walk bravely and humbly with the sick.*

God of healing,
> *guide the work of doctors and researchers who search daily for a cure to AIDS.*

God of compassion,
> *teach us to walk in Jesus' path, caring for the sick, the poor and the forgotten.*

God of forgiveness,
> *forgive us the judgments we have made, as a result of our own misunderstanding, against our brothers and sisters suffering from AIDS.*

God of life,
> *be with those not yet infected with HIV and keep them in the safety of your care.*

God of wisdom,
> *make known to us our role in the struggle against AIDS, and equip us with strength and courage to follow your calling. **Amen.***

Sexuality, Marriage and Singleness, Family and Community

Chapters 2, 3, and 4 each speak about sexuality and marriage, occasioned by biblical texts addressing homosexuality. Attention, therefore, to this wider context is necessary.[1] It is also a cluster of topics that need more attention in the life of our church today.

Marriage is indeed holy, as Jesus declares when answering the Pharisee's question on divorce. Jesus quotes Genesis 2:24, "Wherefore a man shall leave his father and mother, and be joined to his wife, and they shall become one flesh." Here is a micro-realization of the divine community (three in one): here two become one. What does this mean? Scripture regards this as a mystery, which cannot be fully understood, just as the oneness of the church and Christ is a mystery (Eph. 5:21-33). Certainly, the underlying understanding is that sexual union is sacred, a gift of God. Also, that male and female in coming together in sexual union form a bond that cannot be broken. Here is a knowing, a discovering, a uniting that has no physical or conceptual parallel.

Unlike our culture's emphasis on romantic love or reducing sexual intercourse to merely an experience of pleasure, the biblical view is that a holy covenant bond and mysterious oneness are formed. A great mystery potentially awaits the united couple, that of birthing children, becoming family, and having descendants. In this aura of mystery and awe, humans may realize one aspect of God's design in sexual stewardship. The modern lingo "it's awesome" is not adequate but evokes the right notion.

On marriage, Stanley Hauerwas contributes an insightful essay, "The Public Character of Sex: Marriage as a Heroic Institution."

> [Marriage] stands as one of the central institutions of the political reality of the church, for it is a sign of our faithfulness to God's Kingdom come through the providential ordering of history. . . . Our commitment to exclusive relations witnesses to God's pledge to his people, Israel and the church, that through his exclusive commitment to them, all people will be brought into his Kingdom.
>
> Marriage so understood is a heroic task that can be accomplished only by people who have developed the virtues and character necessary for such a task. The development of such virtues and character is a correlative of a narrative that helps us understand that struggle in which we are involved. But it is exactly such a narrative that we have been lacking, or perhaps more accurately, our primary problem is that our experience of marriage has been captured by narratives that have done little for, and have perhaps even perverted, the role of marriage in the Christian community.[2]

In *Sexual Character*, Marva Dawn lists four goals for a Christian marriage. First, marriage is to serve God's larger salvation purposes, rather than be focused only on itself. Such a marriage is mostly "turned inward" and cannot satisfy a larger fulfilling life purpose. To be sustainable, marriages need an infinite goal, ever to be achieved, to fulfill God's purposes for their lives in relationship. Second, when children are part of a marriage's blessing—and that is not always possible, as Marva Dawn indicates for her own marriage—an important goal is to raise the children in the faith and pass the faith to the next generation. Third, a couple should seek to reach out beyond themselves, to others, both singles and married, to extend the strength of their union to be a blessing to others. Fourth, in marriage they can celebrate their own union as a sign of God's fidelity to us.[3]

I would add a fifth goal, to experience God's grace and forgiveness of one another in shortcomings and failures. In some cases, through harsh experiences of divorce, this may need to be extended to and through marriage failure.

In 1 Corinthians 7:6 Paul speaks of both singleness and marriage as charismas, or gifts of God. Singleness too is a sacred option, according to Paul. Here the sacred encompasses devotion to the kingdom of God, a freedom to be open to Christ in such a way that the distracting responsibilities of care for spouse, and possibly children, do not encumber time, money, and service. As far as we know, both Jesus and Paul were unmarried. Together, they set a precedent that Christians today take too casually. We are indebted to the Roman Catholic Church, for it exemplifies a model that preserves this truth. The institutions of monastery and convent arose to make this model work in a culture dominated by the marriage model.

Herein lies a great challenge for churches today. If we do well, singles in the congregation are fully incorporated into our fellowship and social life as are married folk. Both states of being, marriage or singleness, are ways of living our maleness and femaleness for the glory of God.[4] Another important dimension of the creation design is that through heterosexual marriage children are born and parenting becomes a primary task. In parenting, sexuality finds a particular form of fulfillment, to which some married couples are called, but not all. Some couples may forgo children for the same reasons some singles remain single. In such situations freedom to pursue the work of the kingdom may become a higher priority. For those married with children the gift and responsibility of bearing and rearing children is a holy calling, to the glory of God. We have much modern guidance on parenting, with changing opinion on various theories. But let us not neglect the biblical point, "to bring them up in the fear of the Lord." Here I present a counter-cultural challenge: it is the task of the whole congregation, including singles, to rear the children. The responsibility of parenting embraces both family and church community. I am sure this was understood in early church communities; we must do what we can to do this in our church life today.[5]

The vision of the biological and spiritual family must strive for a common horizon of responsibility in this time. As Dawn puts it, "All of us in the [church] community are responsible for helping [children] and youth to see that the values we hold as God's people provide for much better choices for how we live . . . the sex education of our children begins when they are tiny, and we want them from the very start to recognize the goodness of God's design."[6] The role of mentors is very important.

This task of working together to raise children in and for the faith is necessary to counter the world's agenda pushed upon us through TV, advertising, and the Internet. Our sexuality, femaleness and maleness, contribute to the parenting and formational task of home and church.

This vision for sexuality, shared by family and church, is idealistic. I don't apologize. I believe the world, with its destructive agenda for children, home, and the sanctity of singles, should apologize. The world with its cheapening of sexuality has too often raped Christians of the sanctity of sexuality.

This is a call to be counter-cultural, for the sake of our soul. We have lived through an era where the family has come under attack from many angles.[7]

We dare never be boastful, because temptation, lust, and deception are very strong all around us, and also within us. We must stand against the sins of the flesh, against Satan and his hosts, and do so in great humility, for it is only by God's grace that we resist the evil one, triumphing over temptation and sin.

It is certain that we all slip and maybe fall at some point. For this we open ourselves to the forgiving, healing power of Jesus Christ and the Christian community. Many of us represent this vision of God's design for sexuality as wounded healers.

We have learned through painful experiences, from which we desire to save others. Jesus Christ will be glorified, as we are stewards of our sexuality as God's sacred gift.

Recently a book by Stephen Barton, professor of New Testament at Durham University, England, has brought together a series of his previously published essays relating to family, sexuality, and community. I include my review of that book in Mennonite Quarterly Review *86 (April 2002): 215-17, used with permission.*

Review of Stephen C. Barton's
Life Together

Stephen C. Barton. *Life Together: Family, Sexuality, and Community in the New Testament and Today.* Edinburgh and New York: T. & T. Clark, 2001.

Barton's *Life Together* consists of essays he wrote over the last ten years and presented on various occasions. Some were previously published. Part I contains three fine essays on the family and two good essays on sexuality. Part II contains six essays on community in biblical studies, broadly conceived. Part III, with one essay on biblical interpretation, calls for current hermeneutical models to give way to a new metaphor and model, namely, the *performance* of texts in the community(ies) of those who seek to live by them. Barton is Professor of New Testament at Durham University and has published widely, including the fine book *The Spirituality of the Gospels* (Peabody, Mass.: Hendrickson, 1992).

The strength of Barton's work is its perceptive analysis of writings on these topics, e.g., Adrian Thatcher's *Liberating Sex* (1993) and Rodney Clapp's *Families at the Crossroads*

(1993), books that take different stances on family and sex. Barton summarizes the contributions of each and notes what they fail to consider. Though Thatcher utilizes the historical-critical method to discount subordinationist biblical texts as culturally bound, he is not critical enough, says Barton, in that he fails to value what those texts contribute within, despite and against their cultural setting. Thatcher's cavalier judgment against those texts ends up cutting "Christian theology off from its scriptural roots altogether" (23). Thatcher fails to see how these texts begin a process of deconstruction of the hierarchical and patriarchal cultural norms in which they were written. Clapp's otherwise good contribution, influenced by Hauerwas's emphasis on narrative, ends up with a very *general* description of how Scripture informs family values, hanging too much on the strength of the biblical "story" to sustain the family and not addressing specific issues that threaten family life in the world today. Chapter 3 presents Barton's own perceptive understanding of the New Testament on the family, and argues well for a dialectic relationship between biological and ecclesial families. Each is important to and strengthens the other.

On both family and sexuality Barton urges believers to be guided not only by the study of specific texts, since on family issues and sexual conduct one text is often claimed by one side of the debate and another text by the other side. Barton calls for considering larger, more fundamental theological questions: What kind of people do we want to be? And, what can we learn from the doctrines of Creation, Incarnation, and the Trinity to shape our understandings of relational qualities that make sexual relations and familial relations strong and genuinely Christian? Further, the doctrines of Creation and Incarnation are essential to grounding our understandings of the goodness of the body and body-relatedness. After noting dangers and inadequacies in much current talk about sexuality, he points to Paul's counsel in Corinthians: strive to build each other up in the community by the choices we make and "glorify God in your body"—both our created bodies and the church body.

Part II is less cohesive thematically. [I've omitted my review of chs. 6-8]. The section ends with a provocative essay, "Paul and the Limits of Tolerance." Here Barton cautions against "harnessing Jesus or Paul or early Christianity to the bandwagon of post-Enlightenment secular individualism and pluralism" (219). Not only do we thus cut ourselves off from the spiritual and ecclesial roots in the Scripture that nourished the Christian ethic of neighborly love, but we also undermine the particularity and distinctiveness of the truth claims inherent to the Christian faith.

Barton's final excellent essay on "New Testament Interpretation as Performance" develops a recent emphasis, indebted to Nicholas Lash, in biblical interpretation. Essentially, performance is a new metaphor or paradigm for interpretation in which *performance* of the text in the life of the church becomes authentic biblical interpretation. The concept is drawn from Alasdair MacIntyre and has been utilized by several writers (including Lash, Rowan Williams, and Frances Young), whose contributions Barton summarizes. The metaphor is drawn from the worlds of music and theater, in which performance is essentially different from analysis of the musical score or expertise in music history. So also performance of scripture is diachronic in nature—expression through time—rather than synchronic, as are most analytic methods of biblical interpretation used by the New Testament guild. Further, performance is communally expressed, in worship, Eucharist, and daily life. While this emphasis is akin to what Wayne Meeks called "the hermeneutic of social embodiment" and Richard Hays has called "Scripture-shaped community," it adds another rich dimension in that authentic interpretation expresses itself in the doing of textual meaning.

The book as a whole is a gem, rich with insight, providing an up-to-date overview of New Testament scholarship on the three themes of the subtitle. At times Barton's emphasis on the core doctrines of Christian theology appear to substitute for the specific moral guidance expressed in Scripture, e.g., in suggesting that the parable of the Good Samaritan might offer more guidance on homosexuality than explicit texts that speak of same-sex relations in scripture. This seems to be akin to what Barton critiqued in Thatcher and Clapp—substituting general moral principles or the general notion of "story" for careful examination of what these texts, given their cultural settings, contribute to present-day moral guidance. Granted, the central Christian doctrines of Creation, Incarnation, and Trinity have much to teach us for life in family, sexuality, and community, but there is no reason that these should be unhooked from or put in opposition to the more specific rules or principles. "Love of neighbor" is commanded originally amid specific rules for life in community (Lev. 19:18—in the Holiness Code, of all places!).

In this section I sketch out the main lines of thought that guided the statements on this issue by the Mennonite Church (Purdue) and General Conference (Saskatoon), as well as the Confession of Faith in a Mennonite Perspective.

Biblical Theological Framework for Mennonite Church Belief

1. Biblical teaching on sexuality is foundational for the church's moral beliefs and practice, and Scripture contains ethics for human sexuality. This may seem to be obvious but should not be taken for granted. Writing in *Christian Century* some years ago, the widely read Walter Wink said: *"There is no biblical sex ethic.* The Bible knows only a love ethic, which is constantly being brought to bear on whatever sexual mores are dominant in a given country, culture or period"[1] (*emphasis mine*). Wink cites such Old Testament cultural practices as polygamy, levirate marriage, and abhorrence of celibacy to make his point. But most Christians, certainly those in the Anabaptist-Mennonite tradition, have regarded the direction of biblical revelation as making monogamy normative and have taken biblical teaching overall to regard all genital intercourse outside the heterosexual marriage bond to be sinful.

2. Biblical ethics on sexuality are rooted in the following interrelated teachings:

a. Humans are created "in God's image," male and female (Gen. 1:26-27). Since these two declarations are parallel poetic lines in v. 27, some aspect of this maleness and femaleness appears to be very sacred. Some theologians (including Barth) have held that relationality, together with the complementarity of the sexes, is the imago dei aspect. Others have put the focus of the imago dei with the capacity to exercise dominion (v. 27ff.). I have suggested that both capacities, communion and dominion, are God-image factors. When either of these dominates and suppresses the other, we distort our God-human relationship. I take image of God (imago dei) to be more functional in meaning (like image/*tselem* in ancient Near Eastern use, where a statue represents the ruler). Thus we are called to live out the task of being and reflecting God's image in this world.

Further, in creation the body and sexuality are regarded as good, indeed, "very good." The natural body anatomy of male and female augurs for heterosexual relationship in sexual union. For this reason the prevailing view that heterosexual union is intended by creation is banal. Cultures worldwide, apart from biblical teaching, generally confirm the point (though occasional exception in practice may be cited).

b. Marriage between man and woman is God's intention for sexual union and fulfillment. Through procreation, humans too fulfill the narrative refrain, "each according to its kind." Procreation is viewed here as a privilege, responsibility, and blessing. So much so that in Old Testament life barrenness was viewed as the lack of blessing.

c. In the New Testament, however, singleness too is viewed as God's gift. In fact, Paul calls it a *charisma* (1 Cor. 7:6-7). This is true because the kingdom calling takes priority over marriage and family.

d. All sexual union outside marriage covenant is sinful, whether as fornication, adultery, homosexuality, incest, or bestiality. I cite from the *Confession of Faith in a Mennonite Perspective*: "We believe that God intends marriage to be a covenant between one man and one woman for life. Christian marriage is a mutual relationship in Christ, a covenant made in the context of the church. According to Scripture, right sexual union takes place only within the marriage relationship."[2]

e. Sexual ethics serve the health of the community. Clear boundaries in the community provide freedom within agreed upon expectations.

3. Sin for us humans is not simply a freely chosen act, but is intertwined with our fallen humanity, both a condition and an act on the part of each of us. We sin because we are sinners, and we are sinners because we sin (Rom. 5:12-17). All people are sinners, not because we choose to be, but because we are so predisposed. Yes, we are born that way.[3]

4. Sexual sins are no worse morally than other sins, even though the psychological and social consequences may be more severe. All sins, except ascribing the work of God to Satan, as I understand it, may be forgiven. Here we might be reminded of what Martin Luther said: "It is a rare and hard thing for a man (sic) to become a sinner, but so we must." The point is: we deny and hide from this reality about ourselves and our condition, and then we fail also to experience God's grace and forgiveness. Luke's Gospel majors on this point.

5. Human choice against sin is possible because of God's prior grace and initiative to bring us salvation. God offers us divine righteousness in Jesus Christ, the true human and faithful divine Son. This is our only hope in getting liberated from sin's bondage over our will and practice.

6. The predisposition to homosexual desire or other addictive desire is not sin, but the acting upon that desire is. Sexual union outside the male/female marriage relational bond is sin. This includes premarital and extramarital heterosexual and homosexual intercourse.

7. Fidelity to marital vows is the norm expected of Christians.[4] The long-held views of the Christian church that marriage is union between male and female, with potentiality for childbirth, cannot be equated or even approximated by the notion of a covenant union between two people of the same sex.

8. The church is to be a discerning community to ascertain what is to be bound and loosed. Sexual morality is not an individual matter.[5]

Statements from a variety of groups and church bodies represent perspectives similar to those above. I mention three:

"The Homosexual Movement: A Response by the Ramsey Colloquium," in *First Things* 41 (March 1994): 15-20. Named after Paul Ramsey (Princeton ethicist), the colloquium meets periodically to consider questions of morality, religion, and public life. The Statement, signed by twenty-one distinguished Jewish and Christian American scholars, addresses the impact on public morality and questions basic assumptions of the homosexual movement.

"The St. Andrew's Day Statement," printed in *The Way Forward?*, edited by Timothy Bradshaw (London: Hodder & Stoughton, 1997), 5-11. The statement focuses on biblical and theological considerations, with names of seven professors and/or church leaders from various British locations. The book consists of thirteen essays in response to this statement. They represent a wide variety of stances on the issue.

Linda L. Belleville, *A Biblical Perspective on Sexuality*. Chicago: ECC 1997. The Evangelical Covenant Church commissioned Linda Belleville to write this fine 30-page statement for the Church to answer the question: "What does the Scripture say?" It concludes with the ECC's 1996 adopted statement, "Commission on Christian Action Resolution on Human Sexuality," available from: Covenant Bookstore, 3200 West Foster Ave., Chicago, IL 60625.

Reprinted with permission from my book, Slavery, Sabbath, War, and Women: Case Issues in Biblical Interpretation. *Scottdale, Pa.: Herald Press, 1983.*

The Wider Use of the Bible: Ephesians as a Model

One of the limitations of this study has been a narrow focus on the use of the Bible. The study has illustrated the use of the Bible to address social issues that affect the structural order of a total society as well as the church's faith and practice within that order. It will be helpful, therefore, to sketch, even if in briefest form, a wider dimension of the church's use of the Bible. Such a sketch can be made by looking directly at Scripture, especially the book of Ephesians, since it was written for the purpose of addressing holistically the concerns of several churches in Asia Minor.

By following the thought structure of the Ephesians text, I identify twelve different uses of Scripture. This analysis assumes that the functions Scripture performed at the time of its writing are those it should perform today. Ephesians thus presents us with a model for the uses of Scripture.

1. Scripture describes and celebrates God's redemptive work in Christ (chapter 1). This of course has been and should be one of the church's primary uses of Scripture. The church reads the Scripture to learn what God has done and what salvation means. Ephesians 1 may well function as one of the best models in the New Testament for review of God's

salvific work (cf. Deut. 26:5-9; Josh. 24; Ps. 105, 135, 136; and Neh. 9 in the Old Testament as well as Acts 7 and 13:13ff. in the New). Scripture assists and even forms the memory of God's people.

Such a recital of God's saving acts frequently occurs in the form of praise and blessing, as is the case in Ephesians 1 (compare the Pss. and Neh. 9 mentioned above). Congregations of faith are called by Scripture to celebrate God's marvelous blessings of salvation. Read Ephesians 1:3-14 and list each blessing the text mentions, noting also the sphere or person through whom it comes and the ultimate purpose of these mighty deeds of God.

2. Scripture leads us in prayer, placing the individual needs of believers within the context of God's sovereign purposes (1:15-23; 3:14-21; 6:18-20). This too is one of the church's most essential uses of Scripture. Many prayers appear in Scripture (e.g., the Psalms and doxologies at the ends of Paul's letters). These prayers, addressing both individual and corporate needs, regularly include petition and praise. Petitions often focus on our need as believers to grow in faith, to be filled with love, and to know the hope to which we have been called. Prayer, informed by Scripture, functions for the edification of each believer and for the building up of the whole body.

Prayer may also be seen as a response of praise for what God has done. Even some of the complaints of the psalmist move finally toward a heart cry of praise and thanks (e.g., Ps. 42-43). From the writer's perspective these prayers in Ephesians are cries to God for the believers; from our perspective as believers the prayers intercede on our behalf. This double edge of prayer is instructive for us: we cry our concerns to God, and we are held up to God by the cries of our brothers and sisters. With its variety of prayers—confession, petition, and praise—Scripture is indeed an important resource for the church in its prayer. One of Scripture's functions therefore is to provide prayers for the church, leading and shaping the church's expression of prayer.

3. A third function of Scripture is to help us as believers to "tell our story." It is indeed a corporate story, as Ephesians 2 and 1:11-14 indicate. The outline of the story as presented in 2:1-10 and 2:11-22 moves from who we were, to what God did, to who we are now in Christ Jesus. The story in its broadest strokes reflects upon the time when we had no identity as a people and no salvation before God. It then moves to the pivotal event in which God took initiative to change the situation, granting us salvation, hope, and identity. Its third and final phase focuses upon and celebrates this new identity which God's people come to experience within the community of salvation. The images are rich indeed: God's handiwork, one new humanity, fellow citizens with God's people, members of God's household, a holy temple in which God dwells through the Spirit. This particular recital of the corporate story stresses the riches of God's grace (2:5-7) and the new reality of peace between former enemies (2:14-17).

Using Scripture to help us "tell our stories" is important for the continuing life of the Christian community. Especially in a pluralistic world, where many social forces compete for influencing our identity, the telling of the common Christian story plays a very significant role in the formation and development of the Christian congregation, the conference, the denominational group, and the Christian body as a whole. Without the experience of the story relived again and again in the act of telling and claiming it as our own, the survival of the congregation as a genuinely Christian congregation is in jeopardy amid the competing forces of the modern world. The resources of Scripture help us recover and maintain our Christian identity. They are not only important but absolutely essential for the life of the Christian community.

4. Scripture provides us with models for comprehending and telling our own personal role in God's salvation purpose (3:2-13). In this text Paul reminds his readers of the special role given to him through his call to be an apostle to the

Gentiles. On the one hand, his call is set firmly within the initiative of God; on the other hand, his mission contributes directly to God's kingdom purposes—uniting Jew and Gentile—which in turn serves as a testimony of God's manifold wisdom to the principalities and powers.

While none of us in today's church can recite personal vocational callings as distinctive and marvelous as Paul's, with the resources of Scripture we can understand the contribution of our lives as rooted in God's initiative and reflecting God's purpose. We should remember that the apostle Paul spent three years discerning his vocational mission; no doubt much of that time was spent reflecting upon the Scriptures and God's purposes revealed through the prophets. By spending more time in serious study of the Bible and thus seeking to understand God's salvific purposes, we can gain clearer insights into the meaning of our own commitment and call to service.

5. Scripture helps us to correlate our moral life with our Christian identity. A major part of the second half of Ephesians focuses upon the Christian walk: walk worthy of your calling (4:1-16); walk as new people, not as the pagans (4:17-32); walk in love (5:1-2); walk in light (5:3-14); and walk wisely or circumspectly (5:15-20). This major section merits detailed analysis which, however, lies beyond the scope of this brief sketch. But the main point here is the way in which specific attention is given by Scripture to the moral life of the Christian community. The "therefore" of 4:1 indicates that the realities of God's salvific work and the creation of corporate Christian identity function as the foundation of "responsibility" for the Christian moral life.

The Scriptures frequently connect the ethical imperative directly to the experiential indicative, as in 4:24. The call to put on new conduct is rooted in the experience of having been recreated in God's image. Often the Scriptures first describe and celebrate who God's people are; then they call the people to live accordingly, or as Ephesians 5:4 puts it, "as is fitting for God's people." In this way the Scriptures speak crucially to the important issue of motivation for the ethical and moral life.

6. The Scriptures help believers identify the gifts that equip various members for ministry leading to the growth and maturity of all the members (4:7-16). In its various lists of gifts (cf. Rom. 12:3-8; 1 Cor. 12:17ff.) the Scriptures provide us with patterns for identifying gifts within the Christian congregation. These lists need not be viewed as exhaustive; rather they illustrate of the way in which every person's contribution plays a significant role in the life of the body. The Scriptures teach us that these gifts are not self-serving but are given for use in ministry. The purpose of this ministry is to complete and perfect the body of Christ.

Few tasks are more urgent in the church's life today than the prayerful and deliberate discernment of the gifts of its members. Too often, however, within the current psychological trend of self-fulfillment, the quest to discern gifts is oriented too one-sidedly toward individualistic questions such as "What can I do well?" or "What will give me the greatest sense of self-fulfillment?" Conversely, the needs of the church body should not stifle the development of personal gifts nor thwart human growth. Rather, the discernment and use of each person's gifts should stand in the service of the body's corporate fulfillment.

7. Scripture is an important resource for the formation of our values and patterns of conduct (4:17-5:18). Scripture teaches us that this process of spiritual formation, as it is often called today, is rooted in the resource of God's power. It is connected directly to the decision of the human will (note the call to put off and to put on), and it manifests itself in specific traits of Christian character (4:31-32). Even within this one biblical text the agenda for spiritual formation is extensive enough to occupy any one person for most of a lifetime. Reflection upon a text then becomes a powerful resource for developing the character of the new life first within our

own spirits and then in behavioral patterns that mirror the presence of the holy.

While all of the biblical resources for use in the life of the church mentioned so far require time and commitment, this one in particular demands the dedication of one's entire being. The disciplines of prayer, meditation, self-examination, and "binding and loosing" (Matt. 18:15-18) are some of the necessary ingredients for the lifelong task of conforming ourselves more and more to the image of God.

8. The Bible contains a variety of images providing us with both vision and motivation for the formation of our Christian identity and our Christian behavioral patterns (4:4-6; 5:1-2). Examples of such images found in these Ephesians texts are "one body and one Spirit . . . one hope . . . one Lord, one faith, one baptism, one God and Father of us all . . . be imitators of God . . . Christ gave himself up for us, a fragrant offering and sacrifice to God." Such images, and the Bible is full of them, can provide us with the identity and motivational structure that assist us in the life of faith and enable us to contribute more fully and meaningfully to congregational life and kingdom work.

The importance of such images influencing specific ethical behavior cannot be easily overestimated. As various writers have pointed out, ethical decisions are not made simply within the context of given situations. Rather, patterns of character formation, intentions of the will, and self-identity resources greatly affect the way a person makes specific decisions in given situations. The biblical model is not that of situation ethics: it is rather the formation of character and conviction, inspired by biblical images and motifs, which enables one to make decisions with Christian values.

9. Scripture guides us in worship by instructing us to be filled with the Spirit, to speak to one another with psalms, hymns, and spiritual songs, and to give thanks for everything (5:18b-20). While these verses mention the basic ingredients of the worship experience, other Scriptures give us extensive

texts for singing and giving thanks (especially the Psalms and the book of Revelation).

Certainly the church has recognized this use of Scripture quite clearly throughout the ages. But the worship of the church is broader than the activity that takes place on a Sunday morning. While the Scriptures are indeed useful for corporate worship, the elements of worship as described in this text should characterize the believer's spontaneous expression of worship to God on the job, in the home, and on vacation.

10. Scripture teaches us how to correlate the gospel perspectives of new life in Christ with the prevailing social structures and patterns existing within the world (5:21-6:9). In this text Paul addresses the relationship between wives and husbands, children and parents, and slaves and masters. A most distinctive feature of the way the gospel encounters these cultural patterns is the priority and worth it places upon the person in the subordinate position in the social structure. Wives, children, and slaves are addressed directly, indicating that the gospel recognizes them as real persons and is concerned specifically about their plight. The dominant partner in the social structure is addressed on the issue of power. The specific counsel given to that partner turns the power position onto its head. Mutuality frames the instruction to wives and husbands, since the Greek text does not even contain a verb in 5:22, but has 5:22 dependent upon 5:21. Thus the perspective of the gospel moves clearly toward mutuality.

Further, both partners in the social structural pair are called to direct accountability to Christ, clearly making Christ the source of authority for the believer's conduct in social structures. Not the structures, but the Spirit of Christ himself informs the moral life.

This text is most significant for assisting the church in its use of Scripture regarding social issues. While many pages of this study have been given to the church's endeavors *in* this area, the church's fidelity to the will of God on social issues could be greatly enhanced and strengthened by careful and sustained reflection upon this one text. Other texts, to be sure, will offer the same kind of insight; what is important is the commitment to listen carefully and humbly to the accent of the text and the direction in which it calls the people of God.

11. Scripture helps us prepare for warfare against evil. (6:10-17). This Scripture, along with many others from the beginning to the end of the canon, reminds us that the Christian life is a battle. The Bible takes evil seriously and calls Christians to be vigilant in resisting temptation and refusing to do evil. Scripture also sounds an optimistic note for this task. The resources of the Christian, illustrated here by the many parts of effective and powerful armor, are adequate not only to resist the evil one, but also to conquer evil and advance the gospel of peace.

Even though the warfare reality of the Old Testament has proved difficult for the church, the structural perception it gives for the Christian line is not at all at odds with the spirit of Jesus. The Gospels clearly present Jesus in battle against evil; the epistles call believers to fight against evil; and the book of Revelation promises believers victory in the battle as they follow the faithful martyr and slain lamb, Jesus Christ. Pacifist believers especially can learn much from Scripture's warfare imagery. Not only will it save them from passivism, but it will anchor pacifist belief and action firmly within the biblical witness.

12. Scripture gives us new content for our greetings and our good-byes (1:2; 6:23-24). Paul's greeting of grace and peace (*charista* and *shalom*) not only expresses the warmth and resource of his own person but links this resource to the grace and peace from God the Father and the Lord Jesus Christ. In his good-bye, shalom is linked to love and faith, which come from God and Jesus Christ. God's grace is extended specifically to those linked to the Lord Jesus Christ

with an undying love. These ordinary greetings, filled with the reality of divine resource, testify powerfully to the way in which personal self-consciousness has been shaped by Christian identity, values, and commitments. Even the injunction to "greet one another with a holy kiss," occurring in some of Paul's other letters, should not be brushed aside too lightly. The instruction is a tender sign that old things have passed away: a whole new creation has as begun.

NOTES

Preface

1. Miroslav Volf, *Exclusion and Embrace: A Theological Explanation of Identity, Otherness, and Reconciliation* (Nashville: Abingdon, 1996), 213.

Chapter 1

1. A monthly magazine published by Mennonite Publishing House until recently.
2. This position was expressed by the Mennonite Task Force working on the issue, as well as the statements accepted by two Mennonite denominations: General Conference Mennonite Church (Saskatoon, 1986) and Mennonite Church (Purdue, 1987). See the document *Human Sexuality in the Christian Life: A Working Document for Study and Dialogue* (Newton, Kan., and Scottdale, Pa.: General Conference Mennonite Church and Mennonite Church, 1985).
3. See Christopher Seitz, "Sexuality and Scripture's Plain Sense: The Christian Community and the Law of God," in *Homosexuality, Science, and the "Plain Sense" of Scripture*, ed. David L. Balch (Grand Rapids: Eerdmans, 2000), 177-96. Seitz' article is most illuminating. It shows that the exegetical efforts of the last several decades that depart from this traditional plain sense do so by isolating texts from their interconnected Old and New Testament theological unity, and seeking then through historical-critical investigation to provide contextual meanings of the texts that refute the plain meaning and mitigate the united witness. But the historical-critical method has been around long enough for many scholars to have become skeptical of its assumptions. Postmodern deconstructionists thus argue that texts have no objective meaning, only those that interpreters give to them (p. 180). That position obfuscates endeavors from both sides of the debate. Further, those seeking Scriptural support for endorsing same-sex unions have "run into a fire wall even historical-critical endeavor could not remove. This was one of those places where the plain sense of the text did not appear to be materially affected by efforts to recover

original authorial intention or clearer sociohistorical circumstances. At a minimum, there is no positive statement backing same-sex unions in Scripture, occasional or lifelong and committed" (p. 179). Hence advocates for same-sex unions in the church are now of divided mind: either "(1) recognizing the Bible's plain sense on this issue and saying that it does not matter, over against (2) arguing that no such thing [i.e. proscription against it] is said in Scripture that plainly and directly" (p. 182). With such diverse stances on Scripture, efforts toward fruitful dialogue are jammed, and perhaps the issue must be given over to resolution by God's final judgment (p. 181). Kathryn Greene-McCreight also addresses the issue of the plain sense of Scripture and explicates how and why this reading of Scripture is more congruent with the "rule of faith" and the "rule of love" than historical-critical interpretations that seek to dislodge the traditional reading on what the Bible says about same-sex genital relations. She also includes a brief bibliographical list of key essays on "plain sense" reading of Scripture. See "The Logic of the Interpretation of Scripture and the Church's Debate over Sexual Ethics," in *Homosexuality, Science,* ed. Balch, 248-52, note 11, for bibliography.

4. The other two issues that I take up in my book—Sabbath versus Lord's day observance and Christian participation or non-participation in war—do not make the same types of appeal. But the arguments illustrate exegetical and hermeneutical matters. The overall purpose of the book was to present these issues in biblical interpretation for discussion and discernment, rather than to seek to resolve each issue. Certain hypotheses regarding stance in interpretation and outcome on the issues were put forward in the Introduction. Each chapter, devoted to slavery, Sabbath, war, and women respectively, concludes with hermeneutical learning from the arguments put forth in opposing sides of the debates. Learning from this study will show up here and there in this book as well.

5. This is not to say that discrimination in the two cases is equally wrong in a moral sense. The institution's religious beliefs and moral standards as they are reflected in its policies affect the moral judgment as well.

6. See Willard M. Swartley, *Slavery, Sabbath, War, and Women* (Scottdale, Pa.: Herald Press, 1983), 201-02, 258-69.

7. See Donald J. Wold, *Out of Order: Homosexuality in the Bible and the Ancient Near East* (Grand Rapids: Baker Books, 1998); Martti Nissinen, *Homoeroticism in the Biblical World: A Historical Perspective,* trans. Kirsi Stjerna (Minneapolis: Fortress,

1998); Robert A. Gagnon, *The Bible and Homosexual Practice* (Nashville: Abingdon Press, 2001).

8. Swartley, *Slavery, Sabbath*, 201.

9. The *Gospel Herald* editor thought I should seek more substantiation of the statistical forecast. I also read his response as thinking the article too alarmist. But as we now know, the forecast was on the underside of reality.

10. Marion Soards, *Scripture and Homosexuality: Biblical Authority and the Church Today* (Louisville: Westminster/John Knox Press, 1994), 26.

11. Walter Moberly, "The Use of Scripture in Contemporary Debate about Homosexuality," *Theology* 103 (July-Aug. 2000): 253.

12. Swartley, *Slavery, Sabbath*, 215-24.

13. *Confession of Faith in a Mennonite Perspective* (Scottdale, Pa.: Herald Press, 1995), 23-24. Other resources are Appendix 1 in Swartley, *Slavery, Sabbath*, 235-49; Paul Achtemeier, *Inspiration and Authority: Nature and Function of Christian Scripture* (Peabody, Mass.: Hendrickson, 1999); and for a description of various models, Robert Gnuse, *The Authority of the Bible: Theories of Inspiration, Revelation and the Canon of Scripture* (Mahwah, N.J.: Paulist Press, 1985).

14. Jer. 30:2; Jer. 36; 2 Tim. 3:16.

15. 2 Pet. 1:21.

16. Exod. 20:1; Jer. 1:9-10; Gal. 1:11-12; Heb. 1:1-4.

17. John 1:14, 18; Rev. 19:13.

18. Prov. 30:5; John 10:35.

19. Isa. 55:10-11; John 20:31.

20. Matt. 5:17; Luke 24:27; Acts 4:11.

21. Mark 7:13; Acts 5:29-32; Col. 2:6-23.

22. Ps. 1:2; 1 Tim. 4:13; 2 Tim. 3:15-17.

23. Acts 15:13-20; Heb. 4:2-8, 12.

24. Good resources for use of Scripture for moral formation now abound. I recommend Kenneth Boa, *Conformed to His Image: Biblical and Practical Approaches to Spiritual Formation* (Grand Rapids: Zondervan, 2001); Stephen E. Fowl and L. Gregory Jones, *Reading in Communion: Scripture & Ethics in Christian Life* (Grand Rapids: Eerdmans, 1991); M. Robert Mulholland Jr., *Shaped by the Word: The Power of Scripture in Spiritual Formation* (Nashville, Tenn.: The Upper Room, 1985). The widely read books by Richard Foster and Dallas Willard, *The Divine Conspiracy: Rediscovering Our Hidden Life in God* (San Francisco: HarperSanFrancisco, 1998), are most important for spiritual

nurture. For an overview of the biblical drama from a moral perspective see Alan Kreider, *Journey Toward Holiness* (Scottdale, Pa.: Herald Press, 1987). For a pilgrimage genre of reflection on key biblical teachings see J. Nelson Kraybill, *On the Pilgrim's Way* (Scottdale, Pa.: Herald Press, 1999). For a recent scholarly collection of essays on the topic see William P. Brown, ed., *Character and Scripture: Moral Formation, Community, and Biblical Interpretation* (Grand Rapids: Eerdmans, 2002). For sustained study of Scripture directly, I recommend the Believers Church Bible Commentary series (Scottdale, Pa.: Herald Press) and The NIV Application Commentary series (Grand Rapids: Zondervan). Both have similar formats, explaining a text, locating it within larger canonical dialogue, noting how the text has been understood historically, and appropriating it for church ministries.

25. On the latter, David Augsburger, in an interview article by Associated Press with Fuller Theological Seminary faculty on the reasons why divorce rates are just as high in the evangelical churches as they are in American society generally, says that three factors are responsible: individualism, narcissism, and consumerism (*The Elkhart Truth*, 8 December 2002, AA8). To these three, evangelicals have succumbed as well as other denominations.

Chapter 2

1. Ulrich W. Mauser, "Creation, Sexuality, and Homosexuality in the New Testament," in *Homosexuality and Christian Community*, ed. Choon-Leong Seow (Louisville: Westminster/John Knox Press, 1996), 48.

2. Ibid., 47.

3. Both Gen. 1:1 and 1:26 strikingly contain a plural noun for God (*Elohim*) and a singular verb (*bara*).

4. I am aware that in rare cases babies are born without clearly defined sexual gender or may evidence both forms (in which case doctors decide which, according to the more prominent). But this highlights the rule.

5. Karl Barth, *Church Dogmatics: A Selection*, selected by Helmut Gollwitzer and trans. by G. W. Bromiley (New York: Harper and Bro., 1961), 194.

6. Anne Hershberger and Willard Kraybill, eds., *Sexuality: God's Gift* (Scottdale, Pa.: Herald Press, 2000), 26. See the good treatment of five "foundation stones" for a positive view of sexuality (pp. 17-31).

7. *Human Sexuality in the Christian Life: A Working Document for Study and Dialogue* (Newton, Kan., and Scottdale, Pa.: General Conference Mennonite Church and Mennonite Church, 1985), 37.

8. Ted Grimsrud helpfully presents six scholars' interpretations of Scripture in his essay "Six Perspectives on the Homosexuality Controversy," in *To Continue the Dialogue: Biblical Interpretation and Homosexuality*, ed. C. Norman Kraus (Telford, Pa.: Pandora Press U.S., 2001), 187-208. Three of these Grimsrud identifies as "restrictive" positions (Grenz, Schmidt, Hays) and three as "inclusive" (Helminiak, Nissinen, and Scanzoni and Mollenkot). Some restrictive churches, however, have also become inclusive, such as one in Grand Rapids, Mich., which ministers to gays and lesbians. Don Blosser's article "Why Does the Scripture Divide Us? A Conversation on Same-sex Attraction," in the same volume (121-47), is also pertinent here. Both articles are helpful, though some overlap occurs between them. Blosser cites Schmidt at length as a foil to delve deeper into what these texts really say and mean. Nissinen is then cited to provide a cultural interpretation of *why* same-sex relations were opposed by biblical writers, i.e., gender transgression in a patriarchal context where femaleness was considered inferior to maleness. Hence the question: Does the Bible condemn same-sex relations for reasons that are not part of our world today, thereby suggesting that the texts do not speak to our situation?

9. Thomas E. Schmidt, *Straight and Narrow: Compassion and Clarity in the Homosexuality Debate* (Downers Grove, Ill.: InterVarsity, 1995), 29ff.

10. I present these new interpretations, as well as counter views, throughout chapters 2-4.

11. These are: John McNeill, *The Church and the Homosexual* (Kansas City, Mo.: Sheed, Andrews, & McMeel, 1976); John Boswell, *Christianity, Social Tolerance, and Homosexuality* (Chicago: University of Chicago Press, 1980); Robin Scroggs, *The New Testament and Homosexuality* (Philadelphia: Fortress, 1983). A fourth source, James B. Nelson' chapter, "Gayness and Homosexuality: Issues for the Church," in his book, *Embodiment: An Approach to Sexuality and Christian Theology* (Minneapolis: Augsburg, 1978), has also been influential especially in seminary circles.

12. The foremost contributions here, in order of publication are: J. Robert Wright, "A Case Undemonstrated," *Anglican*

Theological Review 66 (1984): 79-94; David F. Wright, "Homosexuals or Prostitutes? The Meaning of ARSENOKOITAI (1 Cor. 6:9, 1 Tim. 1:10)," *Vigiliae Christianae* 38 (1984): 125-53; Richard B. Hays, "Relations Natural and Unnatural: A Response to John Boswell's Exegesis of Romans 1," *Journal of Religious Ethics* 14 (1986): 184-215; David F. Wright, "Early Christian Attitudes to Homosexuality," *Studia Patristica* 18:2 (1989): 329-34 [see here Bernadette Brooten's related article in *Studia Patristica* 18:1 (1985): 287-91]; Lynne C. Boughton, "Biblical Texts and Homosexuality: A Response to John Boswell," *Irish Theological Quarterly* 58:2 (1992): 141-53; David F. Malick, "The Condemnation of Homosexuality in Romans 1:26-27" and "The Condemnation of Homosexuality in 1 Cor. 6:9," *Bibliotheca Sacra* 151 (1993): 327-40, 479-92; Marion Soards, *Scripture and Homosexuality: Biblical Authority and the Church Today* (Louisville: Westminster/John Knox Press, 1994); J. Glen Taylor, "The Bible and Homosexuality," *Themelios* 21 (Oct. 1995): 4-9; Gerald D. Coleman, *Homosexuality: Catholic Teaching and Pastoral Practice* (Mahwah, N.J.: Paulist Press, 1995), 56-72; Thomas E. Schmidt, *Straight and Narrow*; Stanley Grenz, *Welcoming But Not Affirming* (Louisville: Westminster/John Knox, 1998). Robert Gagnon, *The Bible and Homosexual Practice: Texts and Hermeneutics* (Nashville: Abingdon Press, 2001). This latter work is by far the most extensive (520 pages) and incisively critical of scholarly works that mute the texts to preclude authoritative relevance for the contemporary situation. This list is not complete, for numerous articles in edited collections (see Bibliography) could also be included.

13. Richard B. Hays, "Awaiting the Redemption of Our Bodies: The Witness of Scripture Concerning Homosexuality," *Sojourners* 20 (July 1991), 17-21.

14. Richard B. Hays, *The Moral Vision of the New Testament: Cross, Community, New Creation* (San Francisco: HarperCollins, 1996), 379-406.

15. Cited by C. Burr drawing from David Halpern's *One Hundred Years of Homosexuality,* in *Homosexuality in the Church: Both Sides of the Debate,* ed. Jeffrey S. Siker (Louisville, Westminster/John Knox Press, 1994), 117. Herman C. Waetjen informs us in "Same-Sex Sexual Relations in Antiquity and Sexuality and Sexual Identity in Contemporary American Society," in *Biblical Ethics and Homosexuality: Listening to Scripture,* ed. Robert L. Brawley (Louisville: Westminster/John Knox Press, 1996), 113, that the

first English use of the term was in the 1892 *Oxford English Dictionary*.

16. While this point is held generally, both Bernadette J. Brooten and Robert A Gagnon, on opposite sides of the issue, provide evidence from Greek writings that similar conceptions did exist in antiquity (see chapter 6, "But Is Our Situation Different?").

17. Peter Coleman, after carefully assessing the hospitality explanation by Bailey for Genesis 19, concludes that the traditional understanding remains viable: homosexual lust was a prompting factor: *Christian Attitudes to Homosexuality* (London: SPCK, 1980), 34.

18. Lynne C. Boughton, "Biblical Texts and Homosexuality," 142; Grenz, *Welcoming But Not Affirming*, 36. The first questioning of this common understanding came in 1955 with Derrick Sherwin Bailey's *Homosexuality and the Western Tradition* (London: Longmans, Green & Co., 1955), 5. John Boswell, in *Christianity, Social Tolerance*, made the suggestion a veritable fact: "There is no sexual interest of any sort in this incident" (p. 95).

19. Coleman, *Homosexuality: Catholic Teaching*, 61.

20. Seow, *Homosexuality and Christian Community*, 15-16, takes this to mean not homosexuality but intercourse with divine beings, as in Jude 6 (also in *Biblical Ethics*, ed. Brawley, 22). But this cannot be maintained. Verse 6, in speaking of the fall of the angels, makes no mention of Gen. 6:1-4, or the "Watchers Myth." The parallel between verses 6 and 7 consists of similar types of rebellion against God's order. On this, see J. Daryl Charles, *1-2 Peter, Jude*, Believers Church Bible Commentary (Scottdale, Pa.: Herald Press, 1999), 296-97. All three examples in verses 5-7 consist of unnatural or out of order rebellion.

21. Boughton, "Biblical Texts," 144-45. A Korean environmentalist "evangelist" once visited me in my office to challenge me (and the Associated Mennonite Biblical Seminary where I teach) that it is crucial to teach the laws of Leviticus 11. If we don't, he claimed, we will reap ecological disaster. To eat the wrong kind of seafood will rape the sea of its "cleansing system" and thus the waters will become poisoned. Rather, eat only those fish that belong to the food system, the clean ones that have both fins and scales.

22. Seow, Choon-Leong, "A Heterotextual Perspective," in *Homosexuality and Christian Community*, ed. Seow, 14.

23. Moskala, Jirí, "Categorization and Evaluation of Different Kinds of Interpretation of the Laws of Clean and Unclean Animals in Leviticus 11," *Biblical Research* 46 (2001): 5-41.

24. Mary Douglas, *Purity and Danger: An Analysis of the Concepts*

of *Pollution and Taboo*, rev. ed. (London: Routledge & Kegan Paul, 1966), 55. A variation of this view, "a social symbolic system that identified certain natural boundaries in order to protect the society from destructive or dangerous powers," is expressed in the note on Leviticus 11 in *The Access Bible: New Revised Standard Version* (New York: Oxford University Press, 1999), 136.

25. Moskala, "Categorization," 40-41.

26. This point cannot apply to OT portions outside this section. *Toevah* is used frequently in Proverbs, e.g., and does not carry such a specific connotation.

27. William J. Webb, *Slaves, Women, and Homosexuals: Exploring the Hermeneutics of Cultural Analysis* (Downers Grove, Ill.: InterVarsity Press, 2001), 197-99.

28. Webb addresses rather briefly the relation between the cultural and transcultural (ibid., 24-25) but seems to assume that elements of transcultural value can be deduced as principles of universal significance and thus applied to all cultures. More needs to be said about the relation between a particular cultural practice or historical event and its universal relevance. On this point I stress that all divine revelation is intertwined with historical and cultural particularity, and that in itself does not put its authority on discount: Willard M. Swartley, *Slavery, Sabbath, War, and Women* (Scottdale, Pa.: Herald Press, 1983), 233. The particularity of Jesus and biblical claims as a whole permeates both John H. Yoder's and Stanley Hauerwas' ethical-theological contributions. This is a point of gospel offense. That moral norms must be "universalized" in order to be authoritative is not the assumption of biblical realism that has power to change the world: John H. Yoder, *Body Politics: Five Practices of the Church before the Waiting World* (Scottdale, Pa.: Herald Press, 2001). See also Stanley Hauerwas, *The Peaceable Kingdom: A Primer in Christian Ethics* (Notre Dame: Univ. Press, 1983), xxiv, 28, and *passim*. I think Webb would agree; clarity is needed in *how* the particular and the universal are related, specifically in biblical moral teachings.

29. Gagnon, *The Bible and Homosexual Practice*, 128-41.

30. *De Abrahamo* 136-37.

31. *On the Special Laws* 3.39; cf. *On the Contemplative Life* 62.

32. *Against Apion* 2.199.

33. Ibid., 2.273-75.

34. Gagnon, *The Bible and Homosexual Practice*, 163. As I point out in my review of Gagnon in *The Mennonite Quarterly Review* 76:2

(April 2002): 221-22, the accuracy of this latter point may be contested. Carl S. Keener's and Douglas E. Swartzendruber's essay "The Biological Basis of Homosexuality" in *To Continue the Dialogue*, ed. Kraus, 166-73, provides extensive citation of sources, with more than several related to this issue, and suggests that Gagnon's fourth point is questionable, perhaps untenable. Whether animal practices can be used for grounds to argue for human moral practice is still another issue. My comments on Genesis 1-2 above would indicate caution in this regard, since animals do not have the moral capacity to distinguish right from wrong or the potential for covenant relationship, both of which make humans unique. This too means that in the final analysis it is not nature but revelation and moral discernment that determine whether same-sex relations are right, wrong, or something else. See Elizabeth Moberly, *Homosexuality: A New Christian Ethic?* (Cambridge: James Clark & Co. Ltd., 1983) for the latter option.

35. This chapter does not take up the longer agenda of examining both honorable and destructive sexual practices throughout the Old Testament. Keith Graber Miller does this in a helpful way in "Guidelines from the Gift-Giver: Sexuality and Scripture," in *Sexuality: God's Gift*, ed. Hershberger, 35-38.

Chapter 3

1. Lorraine Ali and Julie Scelfo, "Choosing Virginity," *Newsweek* (9 December 2002): 61.

2. Robert A. Gagnon, *The Bible and Homosexual Practice* (Nashville: Abingdon Press, 2001), ch. 3. In my review of his book in *The Mennonite Quarterly Review* 76:2 (April 2002): 221-22, I say this in sum of this chapter:

Compared to others, Gagnon's treatment of Jesus on the topic is most distinctive. He shows convincingly that the myth of a sexually tolerant Jesus does not stand up to careful textual examination. Jesus is strict against adultery and divorce, on the latter more than Paul, who makes some exceptions (1 Cor. 7). Jesus' acceptance of sinners includes the call to repentance and to transformation, and his treatment of sexual sinners is no different from his treatment of other sinners. Generalizing from the parable of the Good Samaritan to seeing the homosexual as the "new Samaritan" in our midst may be appealing, but the parable in its Lukan context gives no warrant for such a notion. It calls rather to reconceptualize the "enemy" as a "neighbor" (226). Jesus' zeal to save the "lost" and "sick" for us "includes those engaged in homosexual practice." Gagnon's concluding sentence reflects the hope-bestowing spirit of his work as a whole: "Concretely, this means visiting their homes, eating with them, speaking and acting out of love rather than hate, communicating the good news about God's rule, throwing a party when they repent and return home, and then reintegrating them fully into communities of faith" (228).

3. On this matter, the fine, provocative article by Michael J. McClymond should be pondered seriously: "The Last Sexual Perversion: An Argument in Defense of Celibacy," *Theology Today* 57:2 (July 2000): 217-31.

4. Paula Fredriksen, a Jewish New Testament scholar, rightly points out a fundamental difference in Torah teaching and Judaism between what is "unclean" (purity law) and moral sin. Being unclean (in the eyes of Levitical law) is not regarded as sin. It requires purification. Moral sin (sometimes called religious or spiritual impurity), some of which is called "an abomination" to the Lord (Lev. 18:25, 28-30; cf. 20:3), requires repentance and atonement through sacrifice. See her excellent discussion in *Jesus of Nazareth, King of the Jews* (New York: Alfred Knopf, 1999), 62-69.

5. See my treatment of this in my chapter, "Luke's Transforming of Tradition: Eirēnē and Love of Enemy" in *The Love of Enemy and Nonretaliation in the New Testament*, Studies in Peace and Scripture (Louisville: Westminster/John Knox Press, 1992), 163-65). Further, the translation *innocent* is wrong in Luke 23:47. The KJV *righteous* is correct here (see *ibid.*, 164). For fuller comment, see Willard M. Swartley, *Israel's Scripture Traditions and the Synoptic Gospels: Story Shaping Story* (Peabody, Mass.: Hendrickson, 1994), 137-38, 234 and note 95.

6. See Millard Lind's chapter, "Transformation of Justice: From Moses to Jesus," in *Monotheism, Power, and Justice: Collected Old Testament Essays*. Text-Reader Series, no. 3 (Elkhart, Ind.: Institute of Mennonite Studies, 1990), 82-103.

7. For an excellent treatment of justice in Jesus and Paul, see Christopher D. Marshall's contribution emphasizing restorative justice, *Beyond Retribution: A New Testament Vision for Justice, Crime, and Punishment* (Grand Rapids: Eerdmans, 2001), especially 35-95. For an understanding of how justice has meant different things to major thinkers through time, and how the concept can be used to serve various ideological agendas, see Alasdair

MacIntyre, *Whose Justice? Which Rationality?* (Notre Dame, Ind.: University of Notre Dame Press, 1988).

8. Three key studies on church discipline are: John Howard Yoder's essay, "Binding and Loosing," originally published in *Concern* 14 (1967), and now printed as an appendix in a second important study by John White and Ken Blue, *Healing the Wounded: The Costly Love of Church Discipline* (Downers Grove, Ill.: InterVarsity Press, 1985)—a book I highly recommend. Yoder's work is also now available in shortened form in *Body Politics: Five Practices of the Church before the Waiting World* (Scottdale, Pa.: Herald Press, 2001), 1-13. The third important resource is Marlin Jeschke, *Discipling in the Church: Recovering a Ministry of the Gospel*, 3d ed. (Scottdale, Pa.: Herald Press, 1988).

9. Richard B. Hays, *The Moral Vision of the New Testament: Cross, Community, New Creation* (San Francisco: HarperCollins, 1996), 97-104.

10. Another possibly pertinent text is Jesus' genealogy in Matthew 1, where all the women mentioned are known by a sexual shadow. This indicates that God in his purposes uses those who bear a social stigma, even in the procreation line that leads to the Messiah. While this point may be relevant, it also has a sharp edge against homosexuality, since such cannot lead to procreation, a point of no small significance from an Old Testament/Jewish prioritizing of values. I do not think proscription against homosexuality is essentially related to the need to bear children/men to keep Israel's army strong, as one paper on homosexuality suggests. This flies in the face of the Old Testament theology of warfare, where God is the Warrior, and numbers can be drastically reduced, as with Gideon, to prove who wins the battles. The New Testament tempers this priority of bearing children, especially in the value placed on celibacy for the kingdom. This signals a crucial difference between Judaism and New Testament Christianity.

11. This latter case is especially fraught since 1 Tim. 6:1-6 and other New Testament texts presume the continuing institution of slavery even among church members. Granted, it is put on a new footing within the fellowship, but not directly protested or condemned as an institution. Walter Wink, in his article, "Homosexuality and the Bible," in *Homosexuality and Christian Faith: Questions for Conscience for the Churches*, ed. Wink (Minneapolis: Fortress Press, 1999), puts the issue of homosexuality in parallel to the slavery issue several times. What he fails to notice is that slavery, while *accepted* in the culture of and in Scripture, is *now* in our time considered

morally *wrong* in principle. A homosexual sexual relationship, however, was considered *wrong* in and by Scripture, and some *now* in our time are thinking it may be *right* in some situations. It is one thing to move from a "right" or "okay" practice in ancient times to a morally "wrong" now, but quite another to move from a clear "wrong" then to an affirming "right" now.

12. This is a considered use of the term, in that Guy F. Hershberger used it to resolve the issue of war in the Old Testament in his book, *War, Peace, and Nonresistance*, rev. ed. (Scottdale, Pa.: Herald Press, 1953), 25. Perhaps here is a striking analogy for seeking to understand how God regards same-sex relations. In conversation with me about the homosexuality issue several years ago, my nephew compared same-sex union to Israel's desire for kingship. While such does not represent God's declared will in Genesis or in Jesus, yet God can and does work through the people. Indeed, God birthed the messianic hope from within the institution of kingship, though not without a running critique of it in the Old Testament (Hos. 8:4; 13:11) and from Jesus himself (see Mark 8:27-33). For more see Millard Lind, *Yahweh Is A Warrior* (Scottdale, Pa.: Herald Press, 1980), especially chapters 7-8.

13. Specifically, in the new Mennonite Church denominations, Canada and the U.S.

14. In our culture I believe that most homosexuals have not chosen so to be (though some have) and that not all can be changed in orientation and desire (though some can and have been). Testimonies to both realities are numerous. That some choose same-sex relationships is evident from Bernadette Brooten's statement that for numerous lesbians, it is "a choice and a public act within the current condition of patriarchy": *Love Between Women: Early Christian Responses to Female Homoeroticism* (Chicago: University of Chicago Press, 1996), 243. I believe it is possible for many to change behavior, but such people need support of a prayer group, confession of known sin and renunciation of evil, and possibly reparative therapy. See further comments in chapter 5.

15. In reading Jewish psychiatrist Jeffrey Satinover's account of the politicization forces at work in leading psychiatric, psychological, and social work professional associations, I realize that this force cannot be resisted in mainline American society. See Satinover, *Homosexuality and the Politics of Truth* (Grand Rapids: Baker Books, 1996), 31-48.

16. Kathryn Greene-McCreight "The Logic of the Interpretation of Scripture and the Church's Debate over Sexual Ethics," in

Homosexuality, Science, and the "Plain Sense" of Scripture, ed.
David L. Balch (Grand Rapids: Eerdmans, 2000), 260.

Chapter 4

1. Richard B. Hays, "Relations Natural and Unnatural: A Response
   to John Boswell's Exegesis of Romans 1," *Journal of Religious
   Ethics* 14 (1986): 200.

2. Karl Barth interprets this to mean that the Gentiles also do not
   know that they do not know. Because their sinful behavior blinds
   them to see what could be seen in God's self-manifestation in
   nature, they end up worshiping visible nature rather than the
   invisible Creator. However, both Romans 1:21 and 1:32 do speak
   of knowledge of God. The difference turns on the issue of "willful
   refusal" or simply not knowing what they might have been able
   to know if their deeds were not suppressing the truth.

3. John Toews, in his forthcoming commentary on *Romans*,
   Believers Church Bible Commentary Series (Scottdale, Pa.: Herald
   Press), recognizes this point also. How could Paul describe
   Gentiles so categorically, when, having grown up in Tarsus in
   Cilicia, he would have known many devout Gentiles (and indeed
   Jews as well), as the Gospel narrative shows (Matt. 8:5-12; Acts
   10-11)? Further, Paul devoted his life in mission to the Gentiles,
   and was their advocate to be included in principle into God's salvation history, upon repentance of sins and belief in the name of
   the Lord Jesus Christ. I suggest then that the normal commentary
   reading of this section is wrong in this regard.

4. Ibid. Toews' view is similar to Jouette M. Bassler's in "Divine
   Impartiality in Paul's Letter to Romans," *Novum Testamentum*
   26 (1984): 47ff. Grieb in *The Story of Romans*, 25-28, proposes
   that this text is descriptive of all Jews and Gentiles, "with special
   emphasis, however, on Gentiles." Grieb holds that Paul plays on
   the stereotypical portrayals ("misunderstandings," Grieb says, "to
   challenge the tendencies of each group to judge and despise the
   other,") of both Gentiles and Jews to prepare for his conclusion
   that no one is justified by works and *all* have sinned and fallen
   short of God's glory (Rom. 3:20, 23). Grieb sees numerous echoes
   or allusions to the Genesis 1-3 narrative in Romans 1:18ff. First,
   the expression "images in the likeness of" (1:23) echoes Genesis
   1:26. Second, "serving the creature rather than the One who created it" (Rom. 1:25) alludes to the serpent's role as "creature" in
   Genesis 3. Further, the "lie" occurs in both texts (Rom. 1:25 and

what the serpent says). Even Paul's order in Romans 1:26-27, mentioning females before males, may reflect Genesis 3: Eve's seduction, then Adam's. These echoes and allusions could be regarded as further substantiating John Toews' view that the stereotypical list of Gentile sins is shockingly (subversively?) directed to Jews. My own tentative resolution of this conundrum (the text does not mention Gentiles in Rom. 1:18-32) is to emphasize *all*, both Jew and Gentile, in this order, as it occurs in Romans 1:16. This interpretation is strengthened if one extends the unit to 2:3, as Toews does. The "whoever you are" in 2:1 makes good sense then.

5. It seems to me that this is true even if we affirm Nolland's view, that 2:15 is a "pincer movement" to catch all people here that were not caught in 1:18-32: John Nolland, "Romans 1:26-27 and the Homosexuality Debate," *Horizons in Biblical Theology* 22:1 (June 2000): 42, 46.

6. John Boswell, *Christianity, Social Tolerance, and Homosexuality* (University of Chicago Press, 1980), 112-3.

7. Hays, "Relations Natural and Unnatural," 188-89, 200. See also Richard B. Hays, *The Moral Vision of the New Testament: Cross, Community, New Creation* (San Francisco: HarperCollins, 1996), 383-89.

8. Compare with Hays' use of Chrysostom in "Relations Natural and Unnatural," 202.

9. Christopher Seitz, "Sexuality and Scripture's Plain Sense: The Christian Community and the Law of God," in *Homosexuality, Science, and the "Plain Sense" of Scripture*, ed. David L. Balch (Grand Rapids: Eerdmans, 2000), 177-96. See note 3 in chapter 1 for explication of "plain sense."

10. A. Katherine Grieb, *The Story of Romans: A Narrative Defense of God's Righteousness* (Louisville: Westminster/John Knox Press, 2002), 30; William R. Schoedel, "Same-Sex Eros: Paul and the Greco-Roman Tradition," in *Homosexuality, Science*, ed. Balch, 45-46, 48, 51, 67-68; David E. Fredrickson, "Natural and Unnatural Use in Romans 1:24-27: Paul and the Philosophic Critique of Eros," in *Homosexuality, Science*, ed. Balch, *passim*. Numerous texts from the world contemporary to the New Testament utilize the distinction between 'natural' (*kata physin*) and 'unnatural' (*para physin*). See Victor P. Furnish, *The Moral Teaching of Paul: Selected Issues*, rev. ed. (Nashville: Abingdon, 1985), 58-67.

11. Jeffrey Satinover, *Homosexuality and the Politics of Truth* (Grand Rapids: Baker Books, 1996), 150-54.

12. Robert A. Gagnon, *The Bible and Homosexual Practice*, (Nashville: Abingdon Press, 2001), 256-57.

13. David E. Fredrickson, "Natural and Unnatural Use in Romans 1:24-27: Paul and the Philosophic Critique of Eros," in *Homosexuality, Science,* ed. Balch, 207-18, 222.

14. Robin Scroggs, *The New Testament and Homosexuality* (Philadelphia: Fortress, 1983), 44-62. Scroggs cites Greek authors who regard pederasty as according to nature (*kata physin*, 46-49) and others who regard it against nature (*para physin*, 59-62). For critique of pederasty as the referent in Rom. 1:26-27, see Gagnon, *The Bible and Homosexual Practice*, 359-60, last part of note 16.

15. See note 38 of this chapter for Scroggs' conclusion regarding appropriation to the current relevance for the church.

16. Two levels apply: whether the exegesis is correct (Boswell and others do not concur), and whether our present situation is free from pederasty. The sad pedophilia crisis facing the Roman Catholic Church (in Boston and with Cardinal Bernard Law) may suggest otherwise. John Richard Neuhaus, editor of *First Things* magazine, contends that the current scandal in the Catholic Church is really about homosexuality. This problem is among a minority of priests; most are faithful to their chastity vows. See Neuhaus, "The Public Square: Scandal time," *First Things* 122 (April 2002): 61-64, and no. 124 (June/July 2002): 75-85. This view that pedophilia and homosexuality are linked, generally repudiated, gains credence when one examines pedophilia advocacy literature as well as the two-stage revision in the APA removal of first "ego-syntonic" disorders and then later "ego-dystonic" disorders, which includes unwanted homosexual acts. See Jeffrey Satinover for discussion of both these points: *Homosexuality and the Politics of Truth*, 62-65.

17. J. Glen Taylor, "The Bible and Homosexuality," *Themelios* 21 (Oct. 1995), 6.

18. William Countryman, *Dirt, Greed, and Sex: Sexual Ethics in the New Testament and Their Implications for Today* (Philadephia: Fortress Press, 1988), 30.

19. Ibid., 113-14.

20. Ibid., 117.

21. Countryman considers 1 Corinthians 6:9, reviewing Boswell's and Scroggs' differing proposals, but concludes that since *malakos* simply means 'soft' and *arsenokoites* occurs only here without clear meaning it is best to understand it in the same way as he suggested for Rom. 1:24, a purity issue. Ibid., 117-23.

22. Ibid., 240-43. These principles are: "1. Membership in the Christian community is in no way limited by purity codes. . . . 2. Christians must respect the sexual property of others and practice detachment from their own. . . . 3. Where, in late antiquity, sexual property belonged to the family through the agency of the male householder, in our own era it belongs to the individual. . . . 4. The gospel can discern no inequality between men and women as they stand before God's grace. . . . 5. Marriage creates a union of flesh, normally indissoluble except by death. . . . 6. The Christian's sexual life and property are always subordinate to the reign of God."

23. For an excellent discussion of this passage, with up-to-date treatment of scholarly and churchly perspectives, see Thomas Yoder Neufeld, *Ephesians*, Believers Church Bible Commentary (Scottdale, Pa.: Herald Press, 2002), 253-67; 275-89.

24. While I believe a basic distinction between purity laws and moral codes needs to be maintained, I do notice a sliding between them by Paul in Romans 6:16-20. For more on this, see Gagnon, *The Bible and Homosexual Practice*, 276.

25. Schoedel, "Same-Sex Eros," in *Homosexuality, Science*, ed. Balch, 43-72.

26. Brian Blount, "Reading and Understanding the New Testament on Homosexuality," in *Homosexuality and Christian Community*, ed. Choon-Leong Seow (Louisville: Westminster/John Knox Press, 1996), 34, takes a similar approach, citing a longer list of writings of Paul's contemporaries. He concludes, "they all have similar condemnation of homosexual behavior, and they all associate homosexual activity with idolatry, lust, and a disregard for the natural order. Paul's attitude on homosexuality was no different than that of his contemporaries."

27. The argument runs throughout Schoedel, "Same-sex Eros," in *Homosexuality, Science*, ed. Balch. He also notes damages to the aggressor adult male in Philo's writings (p. 50).

28. Ibid., 72.

29. Ibid.

30. Many writers contrast this emphasis to Jesus, who taught and lived an egalitarian view of men and women. See Elisabeth Schüssler Fiorenza, *In Memory of Her* (New York: Crossroad, 1983), 97-242. The assumed dichotomy between Jesus and Paul in this argument is highly questionable on three counts: (1) Jesus is presented through the theological and ethical lenses of Matthew, Mark, Luke, and John, which in time are later than

Paul; (2) on the issue of divorce, an analogous issue, Paul is more flexible than Jesus (cf. Mark 10 and 1 Cor. 7); and (3) the alleged silence of the Gospels on homosexuality cannot be adduced to prove anything, as shown in chapter 3.

31. Bernadette J. Brooten, *Love Between Women: Early Christian Responses to Female Homoeroticism* (Chicago: University of Chicago Press, 1996), 302. Brooten critically analyzes the plethora of explanations of Romans 1 and shows that virtually all are not persuasive exegetically (that this comes from one committed to lesbianism is telling). For noting other scholars who hold virtually the same interpretation as Brooten, see Gagnon, *The Bible and Homosexual Practice*, 361, note 19, and 362-64, note 25. This is the dominant interpretation of scholars these days.

32. John Nolland, "Romans 1:26-27 and the Homosexuality Debate," *Horizons in Biblical Theology* 22:1 (June 2000): 32-57.

33. Ibid., 52. Nolland finds only one other text that sets male and female homosexuality in close parallel relationship: Plato, *Laws* 1.2 (636B-C). Here also, Nolland writes, the "unnatural has nothing to do with usurping men's roles."

34. Walter Wink, ed., *Homosexuality and Christian Faith: Questions for Conscience for the Churches* (Minneapolis: Fortress Press, 1999), 48.

35. In contrast to Wink, Christopher Seitz, "Sexuality and Scripture's Plain Sense," in *Homosexuality, Science*, ed. Balch, 177-78, 195-96, seeks to understand the scriptural texts on same-sex relations within a larger framework of "a *connected* Old and New Testament witness to God in Christ" for discussing specific texts related to homosexuality. Rather than atomize these texts one by one, as is often done by "explaining" them against a proposed historical and cultural context, Seitz calls for a theologically interconnected canonical witness that adheres to the "rule of faith" and the "rule of love." This is a sound hermeneutic for all topics, not only moral issues. For more on Seitz, see note 3, chapter 1.

36. Brooten, *Love Between Women*, 242, speaks to this point, saying that Greco-Roman writings show notions of orientation also, i.e., preferences for same-sex relations along class, status, and rank cultural categories; orientation-notions included pedophilia. Gagnon, *The Bible and Homosexual Practice*, and Schoedel, "Same-Sex Eros," concur.

37. Scroggs suggests that what is condemned in 1 Corinthians 6:9 is a specific form of pederasty, especially regarded as debased, "the effeminate call-boy" (*malakos*). The active partner who hires him

is designated by the term *arsenokoites*. This, he says, is a far cry from loving same-sex relations (although one could imagine certain same-partner friendships developing in this practice). Scroggs, *The New Testament and Homosexuality*, 106-8.

The proposal that 1 Corinthians 6:9 denotes only one specific form of homosexual relations is difficult to maintain, since the literary context in 1 Corinthians 5 is incest in the extended family setting (the admonition not to take cases to the secular court [6:1-6] was likely occasioned by this incest case, since incest was proscribed by local law). The later portion of 1 Corinthians 6 deals with sexual admonitions more broadly.

38. Brian Rosner points out that the occurrence of *arsenokoites* in Sibylline Oracles 2:73, a Jewish writing contemporary to Paul, may be a later Christian addition. *Paul, Scripture & Ethics: A Study of 1 Corinthians 5-7* (Grand Rapids: Baker Books, 1999), 120, and end of appendix 1.

39. David F. Wright, "Homosexuals or Prostitutes? The Meaning of ARSENOKOITAI (1 Cor. 6:9, 1 Tim 1:10)," *Vigiliae Christianae* 38 (1984): 128ff.

40. Jacob Elias, "Homosexuality and Scripture: Outline for Class Presentation."

41. Gagnon, *The Bible and Homosexual Practice*, 327.

42. Anthony C. Thiselton, *The First Epistle to Corinthians*, The New International Greek Testament Commentary (Grand Rapids: Eerdmans, 2000), 452.

43. Ibid., 449. Thiselton acknowledges that Vasey (in *Strangers and Friends*) is likely right, at least in part, that much of the homosexuality Christians saw was connected to idolatry, slavery, and social domination (451). But he demurs on Dale Martin's view, in *The Corinthian Body* (p. 33), that Paul's teaching is only against a lifestyle not suitable to one's gender, whose sexual attractions vary since people stand at different positions on the male-female spectrum (449).

44. Ibid., 451.

45. Jacob Elias, *1 & 2 Thessalonians*, Believers Church Bible Commentary (Scottdale, Pa.: Herald Press, 1995), 137-42.

46. Larry O. Yarbrough, *Not Like the Gentiles: Marriage Rules in the Letters of Paul* (Atlanta: Scholars Press, 1985), 75-76.

47. Jeffrey S. Siker, "Homosexual Christians, the Bible, and Gentile Inclusion: Confessions of a Repenting Heterosexist," in *Homosexuality in the Church: Both Sides of the Debate*, ed. Jeffrey S. Siker (Louisville: Westminster/John Knox Press, 1994), 178-94.

48. Kathryn Greene-McCreight makes an excellent, sustained critique of Siker's article in "The Logic of the Interpretation of Scripture and the Church's Debate," in *Homosexuality, Science*, ed. Balch, 253-59.

Chapter 5

1. See here the articles by George R. Brunk, III, Marlin E. Miller, and Willard M. Swartley in *Essays on Biblical Interpretation: Anabaptist-Mennonite Perspective*, ed. Willard M. Swartley (Elkhart, Ind.: Institute of Mennonite Studies, 1984), 203-64. Brunk demonstrates the historical-critical method at work in a study of the Emmaus road narrative in Luke 24. Miller critically analyses the philosophical rationalist presuppositions of the historical-critical method. Swartley describes current trends in biblical studies that go beyond the historical method. In the intervening years since 1984 these trends have proliferated. But most retain a "critical" component, marking them also as children of the Enlightenment. For more on evaluation of the historical-critical method see Peter Stuhlmacher, *Historical Criticism and the Theological Interpretation of Scripture: Toward a Hermeneutics of Consent* (Philadelphia: Fortress Press, 1977). For an up-to-date description of the recent rapprochement of narrative criticism with the historical, see Mark Allen Powell, *Chasing the Eastern Star* (Louisville, Ky.: Westminster/John Knox Press, 2001).

2. In some literature the theories are regarded as either an "essentialist" type (genetics/biology) or a "constructionist" type. Later in this chapter this topic emerges in relation to postmodern thinking, which seems to opt for the latter approach. It would seem to me that "developmental" theories fit somewhere in between, since they figure into the nature/nurture modes of description.

3. Barbara G. Wheeler, "Living Together in the Light of Christ," in *Theology, News, and Notes* (Fuller Theological Seminary) 50:2 (Winter 2003): 7-11.

4. In *Christian Century* (Issues 12 and 17, 2002). See also Gagnon's lengthy reply to Wink, "Are There Universally Valid Sex Precepts? A Critique of Walter Wink's Views on the Bible and Homosexuality," *Horizons in Biblical Theology* 24:1 (June 2002): 72-125.

5. J. Richard Middleton and Brian J. Walsh, *Truth Is Stranger Than It Used to Be: Biblical Faith in a Postmodern Age* (Downers Grove, Ill.: InterVarsity Press, 1995), 20-21.

6. Ibid., 32.
7. Robert N. Bellah, *Habits of the Heart* (New York: Harper & Row, 1985), 50. Cf. Middleton and Walsh, *Truth Is Stranger,* 22. See also Ronald Sider and Jacques Ellul on this topic.
8. This observation has been used to argue that greed itself is the real sin here, and that same-sex relations in that context meant economically exploitative uses of sex. But I doubt that interpretation. As the vice lists in Paul indicate, greed is often listed together with fornication or other sexual sins (Eph. 5:3: "But fornication or impurity of any kind, or greed, must not even be mentioned among you"). William Countryman does extensive study of greed in writings contemporary with the New Testament (several centuries before and after) that show the relation of greed to sexual practice, reinforcing the exploitative aspect as the sin to be avoided. But it does not mean that sexual transgression can be reduced to greed.
9. Approximately one million women, aged 15-19 are unmarried and pregnant each year in the U.S. Approximately 19 percent of black women, 13 percent of Hispanic women, and 8 percent of white women, aged 15-19, become pregnant. The U.S. has the highest rate of teenage pregnancy and childbirth in the developed world—twice as many pregnancies as Canada or England. Alan Guttmacher Institute, *Sex and America's Teenagers* (New York: Alan Guttmacher Institute, 1994).
10. See Margot Adler, *Drawing Down the Moon,* rev. and expanded ed. (New York: Penguin, 1997).
11. Jeffrey Satinover, *Homosexuality and the Politics of Truth* (Grand Rapids: Baker Books, 1996), 229-43.
12. David Greenberg, *The Construction of Homosexuality* (Chicago: University of Chicago Press, 1988). Don Browning's insightful review reflects on implications, "Rethinking Homosexuality," *Christian Century* (11 October 1989): 911-13.
13. Abraham Smith, "The New Testament and Homosexuality," *Quarterly Review* 11:4 (1991): 19. Also, Martti Nissinen, *Homoeroticism in the Biblical World* (Minneapolis: Fortress Press, 1998), 70.
14. Michael J. McClymond, "The Last Sexual Perversion: An Argument in Defense of Celibacy," *Theology Today* 57:2 (July 2000): 219.
15. Several important readings on this topic are: Ibid., 217-31; Gerald Biesecker-Mast, "Living as Though We Were Not Married," *Christian Living* 47:6 (September 2000): 21-24; Sarah Hinlicky, "Subversive Virginity," *First Things* 88 (October 1998): 14-16;

Kathleen Norris, "Celibate Passion," *Christian Century* (March 1996): 331-33.

16. In a conversation with my father-in-law, Bishop John E. Lapp before his death in 1988, he said he thought that homosexuality is a pastoral care issue, and should be handled in that context. David Schroeder seems to suggest the same in his essay, together with congregational discernment: "Homosexuality: Biblical, Theological, and Polity Issues," in *To Continue the Dialogue: Biblical Interpretation and Homosexuality*, ed. C. Norman Kraus (Telford, Pa.: Pandora Press U.S., 2001), 71-72.

17. Wheeler, "Living Together in the Light of Christ," 8.

18. For a review of professional views and literature on causation theory, see Daniel L. Buccino, "Homosexuality and Psychosis in the Clinic: Symptom or Structure," in *Homosexuality and Psychoanalysis*, eds. Tim Dean and Christopher Lane (Chicago: University of Chicago Press, 2001), 265-87.

19. This is the view, for example, of Mary Stewart van Leeuwen, *Gender & Grace* (Downers Grove, Ill.: InterVarsity, 1990), 225.

20. This view, made popular by Freud, dominated psychological and psychiatric theory for years, but is no longer widely respected in this regard. However, the work of psychologist Elizabeth Moberly (British) holds that relationships between same-sex parent and child are crucially causative. Her treatment approach works with such issues and has had significant results. See *Homosexuality: A New Christian Ethic?* (Cambridge: James Clark & Co. Ltd., 1983).

21. See here Satinover's helpful discussion, *Homosexuality and the Politics of Truth*, 147-51.

22. See Carl S. Keener and Douglas E. Swartzendruber, "The Biological Basis of Homosexuality," in *To Continue the Dialogue*, ed. Kraus, 148-73; and Willard Kraybill, "The Gift and Same-Sex Orientation," in *Sexuality: God's Gift*, eds. Anne Hershberger and Willard Kraybill (Scottdale, Pa.: Herald Press, 2000), 99-117.

23. MIT, Harvard, and Yale educated Jewish psychiatrist Jeffrey Satinover identifies and describes numerous organizations, with some evaluative comment. See *Homosexuality and the Politics of Truth*, 196-209. He values Leanne Payne's Pastoral Care Ministries highly.

24. Lee Birk, "The Myth of Classical Homosexuality," in *Homosexual Behavior: A Modern Appraisal*, ed. Judd Marmor (New York: Basic Books, 1980), 386-87. Birk begins his essay saying, "there is no such unitary thing as 'homosexuality'" (376).

25. Satinover, *Homosexuality and the Politics of Truth*, 185-87.

26. Robert L. Spitzer, "Commentary: Psychiatry and Homosexuality," *Wall Street Journal* (23 May 2001).

27. Joseph Nicolosi, "What Does Science Teach Us About Human Sexuality?, in *Caught in the Crossfire: Helping Christians Debate Homosexuality*, eds. Sally B. Geiss and Donald E. Messer (Nashville: Abingdon Press, 1994), 67-77. David A. Shank, *Mennonite Weekly Review* (29 February 1996), reports that the 1994 *Journal of American Psychoanalytic Association* speaks of a one-third successful change rate of those who came for help. But the Fall 2001 issue of JAPA indicates some rethinking of the "changes goals" in its members' counseling practices. The "change" issue is most controversial, as reflected in the *Newsweek* articles on the topic (17 August 1998): 46-53. The Human Rights Campaign Foundation has published a booklet of fourteen testimonies from those who have been "saved" from "Ex-Gay" ministries under the title, *Finally Free: Personal Stories: How Love and Self-Acceptance Saved Us from "Ex-Gay" Ministries* (Washington, D.C.: The Human Rights Campaign Foundation, 2000). The strong effort to promote the gay and lesbian agenda, culturally and politically, and to discount "change-potential" within American society, even in the Roman Catholic context, is described well by John C. Cort, "The Unwelcome Ex-'Gay' Phenomenon," *New Oxford Review* (October 2001): 33-36.

28. Robert A. Gagnon, *The Bible and Homosexual Practice* (Nashville: Abingdon Press, 2001), 420-29.

29. Within the Mennonite context, see groups mentioned in note 10, chapter 7. Greg and Joy Wallace, who spoke on homosexuality at Clinton Frame Mennonite Church in northern Indiana on September 30, 2000, witness to this fact, having lived heterosexually now for thirteen years after each had lived as gay and lesbian even longer before marriage to each other. See report in *Mennonite Weekly Review* (5 October 2000): 1, 10.

30. Satinover, *Homosexuality and the Politics of Truth*, 169.

31. Warren Throckmorton, "Attempts to Modify Sexual Orientation: A Review of Outcome Literature and Ethical Issues," *Journal of Mental Health Counseling* 20 (October 1998): 286.

32. Leanne Payne, *The Broken Image: Restoring Personal Wholeness Through Healing Prayer* (Grand Rapids: Baker Books, 1996), 59-121. Payne describes twenty related types of developmental hurt or trauma, one beginning even in the womb, which in one way or another distorts sexual identity. Through "healing of memories" prayer, these wounds can be healed, and heterosexual identity

restored. This view is similar to that of British psychologist Elizabeth Moberly (*Homosexuality: A New Christian Ethic?*), who regards homosexuality not as sin, but a wound needing to be healed.

33. Richard B. Hays, "Awaiting the Redemption of the Body," *Sojourners* 20 (July 1991): 17-21.

34. Mary Stewart van Leeuwen, "To Ask a Better Question: The Heterosexuality-Homosexuality Debate Revisited," *Interpretation* 51 (April 1997): 144, 155.

35. Some gays and lesbians reacted negatively to Simon LeVay's announcement that brain-size may determine sexual preferences. See *Newsweek* (9 September 1991): 52.

36. See the *Newsweek* article by John Leland, "Bisexuality," (17 July 1995): 44-50. Leland refers to bisexuality as "the wild card of our erotic life." Beth Firestein and essayists in *Bisexuality: The Psychology and Politics of an Invisible Minority* (Thousand Oaks, Calif.: Sage Publishing, 1996), propose that "sexual identity is not immutable for all individuals" (24), that we need to think of at least five different types of preference (31), and that some persons long for at least two "types of relationship concurrently" (191).

37. Marva Dawn, *Sexual Character: Beyond Technique to Intimacy* (Grand Rapids: Eerdmans, 1993), 105-9.

38. See David A. Shank, "On the Exegesis of an Ethos," unpublished paper, 1993, 1-27. Mark Thiessen Nation's quote from Camille Paglia, an ex-Catholic describing the sordid side of the gay world, illustrates one aspect of the sexual entropy Williams explicates (see note 40 below). See Nation, "Fruit of the Spirit or Works of the Flesh? Come Let Us Reason Together," in *To Continue the Dialogue*, ed. Kraus, 234. Cf. Thomas E. Schmidt, *Straight and Narrow: Compassion and Clarity in the Homosexuality Debate* (Downers Grove, Ill.: InterVarsity, 1995), 100-30.

39. Greenberg, *The Construction of Homosexuality*, and Martti Nissinen, *Homoeroticism in the Biblical World: A Historical Perspective*, trans. Kirsi Stjerna (Minneapolis: Fortress, 1998). Several of the excellent essays in *The Way Forward?: Christian Voices on Homosexuality and the Church*, edited by Timothy Bradshaw (London: Hodder & Stoughton, 1997), reflect the same direction of thought. Herman C. Waetjen, "Same-Sex Sexual Relations in Antiquity and Sexuality and Sexual Identity in Contemporary American Society," in *Biblical Ethics and Homosexuality: Listening to Scripture*, ed. Robert L. Brawley (Louisville: Westminster/John Knox Press, 1996), 103-16, has

advanced similar views, showing how modern western people conceive of sexuality: "Originating as a culture production from the sciences of physiology, anatomy, and psychology, sexuality individuates human beings according to their sexual predilection and thereby establishes sexual identity apart from the taxonomy of male and female and its conventionally designed roles" (112).

40. Michael Williams, "Romans 1: Entropy, Sexuality and Politics," *Anvil* 10:2 (1993): 105-10.

41. Robert Goss, *Jesus Acted Up: A Gay and Lesbian Manifesto* (San Francisco: HarperCollins, 1994).

42. Ron Fogleman, review of Goss's book, *Jesus Acted Up*, *Critical Review* 7 (1994), 508-11.

43. Ibid.

44. Robert Goss, *Queering Christ: Beyond "Jesus Acted Up"* (Pilgrim Press, 2002), 228-38. Leland, "Bisexuality," also makes this same point.

Chapter 6

1. Willard M. Swartley, *Slavery, Sabbath, War and Women: Case Issues in Biblical Interpretation* (Scottdale, Pa.: Herald Press, 1983), 54, 146-47, 213, 221, 231 speak to this. See also chapter 5 for its treatment of western culture.

2. Ronald Sider, "Loving people the way Jesus loved people," *Gospel Herald* (21 November 1995): 2.

3. John D. Roth, "Binding and Loosing: Why the Mennonite Church does not regard same-sex marriages as a Christian option," parts 1 and 2, *The Mennonite* 2 (19 January 1999): 4-6; (26 January 1999): 5-8.

4. Robert A. Gagnon, *The Bible and Homosexual Practice* (Nashville: Abingdon Press, 2001), 341-486. I include a slightly revised section here from my review of Gagnon's book in *The Mennonite Quarterly Review* 76 (April 2002): 220-21.

5. Gagnon, *The Bible and Homosexual Practice*, 350, note 8, and similar views from different writers (351-60). Robin Scroggs, *The New Testament and Homosexuality* (Philadelphia: Fortress Press, 1983), 45-46, cites Aeschines.

6. Bernadette J. Brooten, *Love Between Women: Early Christian Responses to Female Homoeroticism* (Chicago: University of Chicago Press, 1996), 242, and William R. Schoedel, "Same-Sex Eros: Paul and the Greco-Roman Tradition," in *Homosexuality, Science, and the "Plain Sense" of Scripture*, ed. David L. Balch (Grand Rapids: Eerdmans, 2000), 43-72.

7. Anthony Thiselton, "Can Hermeneutics Ease the Deadlock?" in *The Way Forward?: Christian Voices on Homosexuality and the Church*, edited by Timothy Bradshaw (London: Hodder & Stoughton, 1997), 184. Thiselton locates his interpretation of the relevant texts within an analysis of leading contemporary hermeneutical theories. The commendations for Gagnon's book, whether from those who agree or disagree with his non-acceptance of homosexual practice, concur that this study represents thorough and important analysis of biblical interpretation and hermeneutical debates. Marion Soards describes it as a "tour de force that cannot be easily set aside." Jürgen Becker says it "contains the most sophisticated and convincing examination of the biblical data to date." Similarly, Martti Nissinen rightly comments that it "cannot be ignored in future debate even by those who hold discordant views." John Nolland notes that it "is delightfully free of tired traditional arguments." James Barr regards it as "a brilliant, original, and highly important work, displaying meticulous scholarship, and indispensable even for those who disagree with the author." John Barton notes that it "shows the weakness of many modern discussions." Jerome Murphy-O'Connor commends it for its "incisive logic, prudent judgment, and exhaustive research." In his recent article, J. I. Packer, "Why I Walked," *Christianity Today* 47 (January 2003): 48-49, calls it essential reading and that to disregard it disqualifies one from serious discussion of the issue.

8. Walter Wink, *Engaging the Powers* (Minneapolis: Fortress Press, 1996).

9. Here remarriage is considered part of the transaction, in accord with Jewish divorce custom. That divorce and remarriage were linked is expressed in the Jewish Mishnah Gittim 9.3, which describes the bill of divorce used at that time. In the bill of divorce the husband announces that he is divorcing his wife and she is free to marry another man. One of the reasons for which divorce was permitted was not bearing children. After ten years, either husband or wife was permitted to divorce and marry another in order to fulfill the command to be fruitful and multiply. For full treatment of divorce and remarriage see George Ewald, *Jesus and Divorce* (Scottdale, Pa.: Herald Press, 1991).

10. Robert A. Gagnon, "The Bible and Homosexual Practice: Theology, Analogies, and Genes," *Theology Matters* 7 (November/December 2001): 4-7.

11. Walter Moberly, "The Use of Scripture in Contemporary Debate about Homosexuality," *Theology* 103 (July-August 2000): 254.

12. Ibid., 253.
13. Richard B. Hays, *The Moral Vision of the New Testament: Cross, Community, New Creation* (San Francisco: HarperSanFrancisco, 1996), 3-10, but then demonstrated throughout the entire book.
14. Ibid., 390.
15. Ibid., 392.
16. Ibid., 392-93.
17. Ibid., 394.
18. Ibid., 395.
19. Ibid., 396.
20. Ibid., 397-98.
21. Charles H. Cosgrove, *Appealing to Scripture in Moral Debate: Five Hermeneutical Rules* (Grand Rapids: Eerdmans, 2002). Cosgrove outlines the scope of his work in his "Introduction." The five types of assumptions that function in the uses of hermeneutical rules are: The Rule of Purpose. The purpose (or justification) behind a biblical moral rule carries greater weight than the rule itself. The Rule of Analogy. Analogical reasoning is an appropriate and necessary method for applying Scripture to contemporary moral issues. The Rule of Countercultural Witness. There is a presumption in favor of according greater weight to countercultural tendencies in Scripture that express the voice of the powerless and marginalized than to those tendencies that echo the dominant culture of their time. The Rule of the Nonscientific Scope of Scripture. Scientific (or "empirical") knowledge stands outside the scope of Scripture. The Rule of Moral-Theological Adjudication. Moral-theological considerations should guide hermeneutical choices between conflicting plausible interpretations. Cosgrove clarifies that these are not his concocted rules, except for this formulation of them, but "rules" that operate in hermeneutical debate. His book undertakes a close analysis of how these rules function, and with what legitimacy or illegitimacy. His notes also introduce the reader to key sources of the last several decades on the connection of Scripture to contemporary moral issues. For a summary of six alternative views and differing models, including my own proposal, see Swartley, *Slavery, Sabbath, War, and Women*, 204-24. For more extensive analysis see Hays, "Five Representative Hermeneutical Strategies," in *Moral Vision*, 215-90, and his formulation of "*Normative Proposals*," 291-310.
22. William J. Webb, *Slaves, Women, and Homosexuals: Exploring*

the Hermeneutics of Cultural Analysis (Downers Grove, Ill.: InterVarsity Press, 2001), 30-31.

23. Ibid., 95-105.
24. Ibid., 106-10.
25. Ibid., 250.
26. See Webb's chart in ibid., 69.
27. See his summary in ibid., 250-53.
28. John Boswell, *Same-Sex Unions in Premodern Europe* (New York: Villard Books, 1994), 178-93, 298-99, 333-41, 350-51. One of the prayers translated and cited by Boswell is as follows, with two alternate versions in his footnotes, one anachronistically literal and with the title "Prayer for Making Brothers," and another tendentiously slanted, entitled "Prayer for Homosexual Marriage." This is the version he uses in the text:

Prayer for Same-Sex Union
O Lord our God, who hast granted unto us all things necessary for salvation and didst command us to love one another and to forgive one another our failings, protect in thy holiness, Lord and lover of good, these thy servants who love each other with a love of the spirit and have come into thy holy church to be blessed and consecrated by Thee. Grant them unashamed faithfulness, true love, and as Thou didst vouchsafe unto thy holy disciples thy peace, bestow also on these servants all those things needed for salvation and eternal life.
(*Antiphon*) For thou are merciful and loving, God, and thine is unending glory, Father and Son and Holy Spirit.

The prayer continues with a priest citing quite a generic prayer for blessing. Also in note 85 on page 299, Boswell says, "This prayer is one of the most common components of same-sex union ceremonies, and this is one of the earliest versions of it." It is from A.D. 1027/29 in Greek, with manuscript in the National Library in Paris (#213).

29. See Robin Darling Young's revealing review in *First Things* 47 (November 1994), 43-48. Young, a theology professor teaching church history at the Catholic University of America, points out that she and her traveling scholar partner, Susan Ashbrook Harvey of Brown University, were offered one such prayer by an archbishop in St. Mark's Church in Jerusalem as a gift after their arduous travel and study together in eastern Turkey and Syria. It was blessing upon them as sisters in their labors. It, of course, had no sexual connotations, for them or for the priest. As a historian

Young shows how Boswell distorts the historical record, making texts serve the gay union cause, which in their original context (as at one place Boswell briefly acknowledges), had quite another meaning. The issue hinges to a great extent upon the translation and meaning of *adelphopoiēsis*, literally, the "making of brothers" or "sisters." Indeed, liturgies were used to dedicate "brothers" (or "sisters") to spiritual friendship, to avoid quarrel and conflict, as they undertook together special missions in the work of the church. No priest or patriarch using such blessings in the medieval period would recognize or even dream of the meanings Boswell reads into these texts, says Young. Enough said, especially for Mennonites who either still customarily address or can remember when we addressed fellow church members as brothers and sisters, and in some settings with a holy kiss, as Paul mentions in several of his letters.

30. Stanley J. Grenz, *Welcoming, But Not Affirming: An Evangelical Response to Homosexuality* (Louisville: Westminster/John Knox Press, 1998), 64-80. Grenz draws on the historical work of both Derrick Sherwin Bailey and David Greenberg.

31. Ibid., 65.

32. Ibid., 66.

33. Councils at Paris (1212) and Rouen (1214), though, forbade nuns from sleeping together: Ibid., 69.

34. Ibid., 73-75.

35. Ibid., 71-72.

Chapter 7

1. Here note Peter L. Berger and Thomas Luckmann, *The Social Construction of Reality* (Garden City, N.Y.: Doubleday, 1966), 36-37, and philosopher Martha Nussbaum, *Love's Knowledge* (Oxford University Press, 1990), 286-313, arguing that, congruent with social learning, we learn our emotions in the same way we learn our beliefs.

2. I am also keenly aware that another alternative is church splits. Often when discipline is undertaken it may result in splitting as well. But if undertaken in a spirit of love and care, it can also be restorative and healing in effect.

3. Richard B. Hays, "Homosexuality," in Richard B. Hays, *The Moral Vision of the New Testament: Cross, Community, New Creation* (San Francisco: HarperSanFrancisco, 1996), 400.

4. Ibid.

5. Ibid., 401.

6. James B. Nelson, *Embodiment: An Approach to Sexuality and to Christian Theology* (Minneapolis: Augsburg Press, 1979), 189-96.

7. Nelson's extended critique (ibid.) of Barth is surely in error on one point: that Barth appeals to "natural law and idolatry" (Nelson, 190). With Barth's famous "*Nein*" to Emil Brunner in 1938, the first of the two appeals cannot be correct. Karl Barth's discussion of the matter is found in most extensive form in *The Doctrine of Creation*, vol. 3, pt. 4 of *Church Dogmatics*, trans. by G. W. Bromiley (Edinburgh: T. & T. Clark, 1961), within his 124-page treatment of "Man and Woman" (116-240) as part of his larger section on "Freedom in Fellowship." Within this lengthy discussion of humans created as man and woman, Barth takes up tendencies to rebel against the divine creation. Not natural law but "command of God" or "obedience to the divine command" dominates this entire section. He mentions Simone de Beauvoir as illustrating "flight from one's own sex," a conception and emphasis derived from Sartre's existentialism (ibid., 161-62). Later Barth comments on "male or female seclusion" that may arise for various reasons, some enforced and some in response to an emergency. But the desire to pursue this in situations of freedom marks a turn away from God's creation intention. These first steps, he says, may be indicative of a "malady called homosexuality. This is the physical, psychological, and social sickness, the phenomenon or perversion, decadence and decay, which can emerge when man refuses to admit the validity of the divine command in the sense in which we are now considering it," (ibid., 166). I include this citation for historical perspective. Few theologians today would put it this way, but it is important to reflect on how earlier theologians understood homosexuality, and to remind ourselves of the journey we have come.

8. Barth's position is also described by A. James Reimer, "Homosexuality: A Call for Compassion and Moral Rigor," in *To Continue the Dialogue: Biblical Interpretation and Homosexuality*, ed. C. Norman Kraus (Telford, Pa.: Pandora Press U.S., 2001), 183. Utilizing Edward Batchelor's collections of articles to describe various theological positions, *Homosexuality and Ethics* (New York: The Pilgrim Press, 1980), Reimer describes also Helmut Thielicke's position, "which considers homosexual acts as intrinsically imperfect, as a departure from the biblical view, but is willing to consider making exceptions under certain extreme conditions." Thielicke also urges that if change is possible it be

actively sought (Reimer, 183-84). Reimer then examines a third view that considers homosexual practice to be morally neutral in itself, but as requiring moral assessment as to its openness to mutuality, repudiating power, and domination in the relationship (he cites Gregory Baum for this view). While Reimer is drawn to this latter view because of "the weight it places on the sin of domination and the importance of mutuality," he objects to this position's "disregard . . . of the biblical view of the 'normativity' of heterosexual relationships." He thus leans toward Thielicke's position but is uncomfortable with his use of the word *perversion* to characterize homosexual acts as deviation from the created order (Reimer, 184-85).

9. Gerald D. Coleman, *Homosexuality: Catholic Teaching and Pastoral Practice* (Mahwah, N.J.: Paulist Press, 1995), 8-9.

10. The learning of such groups as Day Seven (Enos Martin in Harrisburg, Pa.) and Transformed by Grace (Reba Place, Evanston, Ill.) can inform pastors of how to function in the counseling process. In certain cases deliverance ministry has been effective—as I have once witnessed it—in breaking the power of compulsion toward homosexual thoughts and acts.

11. Walter Moberly, "The Use of Scripture in Contemporary Debate about Homosexuality," *Theology* 103 (July-August 2000): 256, points out the hermeneutical analogy between incest and homosexuality. He notes that an increasing number of voices are saying that if incest is conducted in a harmless way, but in consensual agreement between adults, the difference between this claim and the case that has been made for similar homosexual relations is nil. What we must come to terms with is the ancient notion of taboo and ask if we no longer have need for it.

12. We might also identify "accepting" congregations as *congregations of risk*. For those who feel certain that they are about the kingdom's business in accepting sexually active homosexuals and affirming homosexual relations, it means risk in the positive sense—giving up one's own and the congregation's security for the sake of the kingdom. For those of us who consider this to be the impact of our neo-pagan world-culture intertwined into the bondage of the will in fallen humanity, it is a risk to salvation and standing before God for both the person and the congregation. Some have suggested identifying such congregations as *congregations of refuge*, suggesting that these congregations be havens of mercy for gays and lesbians. This has merit but does not say all that needs to be said. I suggest combining the two suggestions:

congregations of risk and refuge. Both sides of the reality must be acknowledged.

13. I say this despite John Boswell's claims in *Same-Sex Unions in Premodern Europe* (New York: Villard Books, 1994). See Robin Darling Young's revealing review in *First Things* 47 (November 1994): 43-48. See notes 28-29 for chapter 6.

14. The congregation might teach that homosexual covenants are defective in relation to marriage. Marlin Miller had used this word for second marriages in that they continue to be encumbered with experiences and obligations from the first marriage. But, in reality, a homosexual covenant union is no marriage at all, since it does not participate in two basic criteria of a marriage: heterosexual genital intercourse and potentiality for procreation, unless celibacy vows are taken within marriage for kingdom service purposes.

15. For a penetrating short essay on this text, see William H. Willimon, "Matthew 5:43-48," *Interpretation* 57 (2003): 60-63.

Chapter 8

1. Jeffrey S. Siker, "Gentile Wheat and Homosexual Christians: New Testament Directions for the Heterosexual Church," in *Biblical Ethics and Homosexuality: Listening to Scripture*, ed. Robert L. Brawley (Louisville: Westminster/John Knox Press, 1996), 135-51.

2. Harold S. Bender presented this some years ago. For similar content, see his article, "Seminary and Congregation: Communities of Discernment," in *Education for Peoplehood: Essays on the Teaching Ministry of the Church*, Text Reader Series, no. 8 (Elkhart, Ind.: Institute of Mennonite Studies, 1997): 179-97. See also Luke Timothy Johnson's analysis of Acts 15 for decision-making by the church in *Scripture and Discernment* (Nashville: Abingdon Press, 1996), 87-108.

3. Paul S. Minear, *The Obedience of the Faith: The Purposes of Paul in the Epistle to the Romans*, Studies in Biblical Theology, Second Series 19 (Naperville, Ill.: Alec R. Allensen Inc., 1971).

4. Ibid., 8-20.

5. For an illustration of this on the issue of homosexuality, see Mark Thiessen Nation, "Fruit of the Spirit or Works of the Flesh? Come Let Us Reason Together," in *To Continue the Dialogue: Biblical Interpretation and Homosexuality*, ed. C. Norman Kraus (Telford, Pa.: Pandora Press U.S., 2001), 223-44. In his essay, Nation cites the views of both Wolfhart Pannenberg and Eugene R. Rogers Jr.

For Pannenberg the church's acceptance of homosexual practice means it will cease to be "the one, holy, catholic, and apostolic Church." Rogers, upping the ante at the other end, says, "if straight Christians do not move to affirm monogamous gay and lesbian marriages, then they are in danger of losing their salvation!" Clearly, we need voices from groups four and five (of Minear's list) if the church is to deal lovingly and fruitfully with this issue.

6. Minear, *The Obedience of the Faith*, 17-20, lists a total of twelve principles or axioms from Romans 14.

7. See A. James Reimer, "Homosexuality: A Call for Compassion and Moral Rigor," in *To Continue the Dialogue*, ed. Kraus, 175-77. For a good accessible survey of church tradition, see Stanley J. Grenz, *Welcoming But Not Affirming: An Evangelical Response to Homosexuality* (Louisville: Westminster/John Knox Press, 1998), 64-80. See my summary on pages 112-13.

8. See Don Blosser, "Why Does the Scripture Divide Us? A Conversation on Same-Sex Attraction," and Ted Grimsrud, "Six Perspectives on the Homosexuality Controversy," both in *To Continue the Dialogue*, ed. Kraus, 121-47; 187-208. These interpretations are problematic, as shown in chapters 2-4.

9. In this regard, this issue differs from the slavery, war, and women issues I wrote about in 1983.

10. For Anabaptist-Mennonites, the faith community appealing to Scripture is also a source of authority. But the faith community is not of one mind. The irony is that those who take a position differing from the church's stance appeal to the authority of the discerning community (often defined as congregation). But then this group is offended when the larger community with a differing view disciplines the congregation.

11. Marion Soards, *Scripture and Homosexuality: Biblical Authority and the Church Today* (Louisville: Westminster/John Knox Press, 1994), 46. See Alasdair MacIntyre, *Whose Justice? Which Rationality?* (Notre Dame, Ind.: University of Notre Dame Press, 1988), for application of this question to the point of justice and rationality. Whose understanding counts?

12. Richard B. Hays, *The Moral Vision of the New Testament: Cross, Community, New Creation* (San Francisco: HarperCollins, 1996), 210-11; also 398-400.

13. Marcus Smucker, "Psychological Dynamics: Being Gay or Lesbian," in *To Continue the Dialogue*, ed. Kraus, 45-61.

14. See Carl S. Keener and Douglas E. Swartzendruber, "The Biological Basis of Homosexuality," in *To Continue the Dialogue*,

ed. Kraus, 148-73. See also Charles H. Cosgrove's treatment of "The Rule of Nonscientific Scope," in *Appealing to Scripture in Moral Debate: Five Hermeneutical Rules* (Grand Rapids: Eerdmans, 2002), 116-53.

15. As I put it in my review of the Keener and Swartzentruber article in *To Continue the Dialogue*, ed. Kraus, the article covers the field well, and raises also the delicate issue of how complicated causation is—the mix of biological-genetic and environmental influence: "The Church and Homosexuality: Review Essay," *The Mennonite Quarterly Review* 76 (April 2002): 215-30. In my "Response" in the Kraus volume, I also said that *is* does not determine *ought* (pp. 287-88). Evil or war does not provide the moral authority to tell us whether we should or should not fight, for example. What one experiences does not in itself serve as the basis of moral obligation. In fact, most moral proscriptions and prescriptions originated to protect the morality of behavior from being based on desires. This point has a philosophical history. Ayn Rand, in *The Virtue of Selfishness*, saw the point clearly when she advocated fulfillment of our innate selfishness as a basic virtue—a point at odds with Christian morality. For more on science and homosexuality, see Stanton L. Jones and Mark A. Yarhouse, "The Use, Misuse, and Abuse of Science in the Ecclesiastical Homosexuality Debates," in *Homosexuality, Science, and the "Plain Sense" of Scripture*, ed. David L. Balch (Grand Rapids: Eerdmans, 2000), 73-120. See also their book, *Homosexuality: The Use of Scientific Research in the Church's Moral Debate* (Downers Grove, Ill.: InterVarsity, 2000). Also, for more sources, see Robert A. Gagnon, *The Bible and Homosexual Practice* (Nashville: Abingdon Press, 2001), 396, note 83. See the general study by Alice Ogden Bellis and Terry Hufford, *Science, Scripture, and Homosexuality* (Cleveland: Pilgrim Press, 2002). In the final analysis it is difficult to sort out the influences of nurture and nature. See Willard Kraybill, "The Gift and Same-Sex Orientation," in *Sexuality: God's Gift*, eds. Anne Hershberger and Willard Kraybill (Scottdale, Pa.: Herald Press, 2000). If it were determined that same-sex preference is genetically caused, would that make it morally right to practice same-sex relations? Hardly, since biological evidence for violent crime already exists. See "Gray Matters," *Newsweek* (27 March 1995): 53.

16. Mark Thiessen Nation, "Fruit of the Spirit or Works of the Flesh?" in *To Continue the Dialogue*, ed. Kraus, 223-44. While all the articles in *To Continue the Dialogue* contribute to the discernment

process, the ones by Schroeder, Reimer, and Nation are crucial. Schroeder's guidelines for decision-making are helpful (pp. 62-75).

17. Ibid., 225-26.

18. On this point I would want to know why seven or eight is few. If I count the texts in the Bible where *reconciliation/reconcile* occurs in the sense of humans becoming reconciled to God, I find only five, all Pauline (Rom. 5:10-11; 11:15; 2 Cor. 5:18-20; Col. 1:20-22; Eph. 2:16). The word itself is repeated and occurs three times each in Romans 5 and 2 Corinthians 5, similar to recurring emphasis on same-sex practices in Romans 1. Does this lessen the significance of reconciliation as a moral mandate? I do not mean to compare the theological significance of these two topics, but only register discomfort with regarding seven or eight texts spread over the canon as inconsequential.

19. Helpful resources on this are John Paul Lederach, *The Journey Toward Reconciliation* (Scottdale, Pa.: Herald Press, 1999); and Carolyn Schrock-Shenk and Lawrence Ressler, eds., *Making Peace with Conflict: Practical Skills for Conflict Resolution* (Scottdale, Pa.: Herald Press, 1999).

20. Carolyn Schrock-Shenk, "Commanded to Keep Wrestling and Wrestling and Wrestling," in *To Continue the Dialogue*, ed. Kraus, 245-55.

21. A major study of discernment in relation to Scripture can be found in the two books by Luke Timothy Johnson, *Decision Making in the Church: A Biblical Model* (Philadelphia: Fortress Press, 1983) and *Scripture and Discernment: Decision Making in the Church* (Nashville: Abingdon Press, 1996). Both are helpful.

22. Kathryn Greene-McCreight, "The Logic of the Interpretation of Scripture and the Church's Debate," in *Homosexuality, Science*, ed. Balch, 259. On this point see John Stott, *Same-Sex Partnership?: A Christian Perspective* (Grand Rapids: F. H. Revell, 1998).

23. For two excellent books on prayer, see Arthur Paul Boers, *Lord, Teach Us to Pray* (Scottdale, Pa.: Herald Press, 1992); and John Koenig, *Rediscovering New Testament Prayer* (San Francisco: HarperSanFrancisco, 1992).

Chapter 9

1. Deirdre Good, "The New Testament and Homosexuality: Are We Getting Anywhere?" *Religious Studies Review* 26 (2000): 307-12.

2. Ibid., 311.

3. For use of this term on this topic, see Richard A. Kauffman, "A Third Way between Fight and Flight," *The Mennonite* (2 May 2000): 6-8.
4. For exposition of text in full, see V. George Shillington, *2 Corinthians*, Believers Church Bible Commentary (Scottdale, Pa.: Herald Press, 1998), 126-41.
5. Dietrich Bonhoeffer, "Loving Our Enemies: Dietrich Bonhoeffer's Sermon on Romans 12:16-21," trans. by Evan Drake Howard, *The Reformed Journal* (April 1985): 18.
6. Douglas LeBlanc, "Waging Peace," *Christianity Today* (9 July 2001): 42-47.
7. As James Alison puts it in his insightful and provocative book (though I do not agree with his exegesis at crucial points), may the path ahead be *Faith Beyond Resentment*, the title of his book, written in the Catholic context. He imaginatively leads us to "fraternal relations" that make all people children of the one Father, rather than tribally following earthly fathers. He also calls for empathy for those marginalized through accusations of pedophilia. His is a bold endeavor, highly theological and artful in its Scripture exposition, spiced with Girardian themes.

Appendix 1

1. J. H. Charlesworth, ed., *The Old Testament Pseudepigrapha*, vol. 2 (New York: Doubleday, 1985), 23.
2. *Idem*, vol. 1 (New York: Doubleday, 1983), 347.

Appendix 2

1. John D. Roth, "Binding and Loosing: Why the Mennonite Church does not regard same-sex marriages as a Christian option," parts 1 and 2, *The Mennonite* 2 (19 January 1999): 4-6; (26 January 1999): 5-8.
2. David Greenberg, *The Construction of Homosexuality* (Chicago: University of Chicago Press, 1988); David A. Shank, "On the Exegesis of an Ethos." Unpub. paper, 1993.
3. Millard Lind, *Monotheism, Power, and Justice: Collected Old Testament Essays*, Text Reader Series, no. 3 (Elkhart, Ind.: Institute of Mennonite Studies, 1990), especially chapter 7.

Appendix 3

1. This essay is included here not to blame homosexual people for the AIDS tragedy. My work above suggests that the issue is part and

parcel of our larger culture. Within this context it is fair to say, and needs to be said, that AIDS is not unrelated to homosexuality. The fact continues that about fifty percent of HIV cases in the U.S. are caused by homosexual intercourse of some type, especially among males ages 13-19. See Committee on Adolescence, *Pediatrics* 92 (October 1993): 632. For those of us who value human life, this is a cause for alarm.

2. The article was not printed because the editor felt I needed more data to support the numbers, even though it was in the news those days that around a half million people had already died from AIDS. The article sat in my files. Thus now I sense a need to confess: I stuffed it.

3. Timothy C. Morgan, "Have We Become Too Busy with Death?" *Christianity Today* (7 February 2000): 34-39. See also the articles by Eugene F. Rivers III and Jacqueline C. Rivers "The Fight for the Living: Aids, Orphans, and the Future of Africa," *Sojourners* (July-August 2000): 18-23 and the article in *Newsweek* (11 June 2001): 36-51.

4. See the persuasive brief article by Darrell Cole, "Good Wars," *First Things* (October 2001): 27-31. For an excellent review and analysis of the "just war" theory, see John D. Roth, *Choosing Against War: A Christian View: "A Love Stronger Than Our Fears"* (Intercourse, Pa.: Good Books, 2002), 32-61. See the entire book for the strength of the pacifist view and how to work toward transformation of conflict and violence. On this see also John Paul Lederach, *The Journey Toward Reconciliation* (Scottdale, Pa.: Herald Press, 1999).

5. Even medical and health considerations challenge the truth of this. See Jeffrey Satinover, *Homosexuality and the Politics of Truth* (Grand Rapids: Baker Books, 1996), 49-70, and Thomas Schmidt, *Straight and Narrow* (Downers Grove, Ill.: Intervarsity, 1995), 112-30.

6. Morgan, "Have We Become Too Busy," based on 1999 figures, used the number of 36 million. The 2001 *Newsweek* article used the 2000 data report and claimed 42 million. Rivers and Rivers, "The Fight for the Living" (see note 3) report 34 million in Africa, two-thirds of the total world number, which would be 51 million, of HIV incidence to date. The same article reports that 11.5 million have already died in Africa. The December 1, 2001, AIDS Day news report cited 22 million having died from AIDS and 36 million currently infected with HIV.

7. At the time of writing, October 18, 2001, the International Jubilee 2000 organization e-mailed its listserv to request calls to U.S.

Senators and members of Congress to support the Global Health
Fund, since $7-10 billion is needed to curb AIDS in sub-Sahara.
Over 5,000 people are dying each day.
8. An Associated Press article (30 November 2002) by Christopher
Bodeen projected ten million to be infected in China by 2010: *The
(Elkhart) Truth* (1 December 2002): AA1.
9. I believe the situation in southern Africa is unique. In southern
Africa many men leave their homes for long periods of time, from
Botswana and other countries, and work in the mines of South
Africa. While they are living there in basic shelter dormitories, the
temptation of extramarital (some homosexual) relations is very,
very great (Morgan, "Have We Become Too Busy," 38). Upon
their return home, some to numerous wives, the HIV virus, if contracted in the dorms, spreads rampantly. I indeed hope and pray
the exponential growth will not continue, that funding for, as well
as reduced costs for, medication will become immediately available.

Appendix 4

1. Ulrich W. Mauser, "Creation, Sexuality, and Homosexuality in the
New Testament," in *Homosexuality and Christian Community*,
ed. Choon-Leong Seow (Louisville: Westminster/John Knox Press,
1996), 37-49.
2. Stanley Hauerwas, *A Community of Character: Toward a
Constructive Christian Social Ethic* (Notre Dame, Ind.: University
of Notre Dame Press, 1981), 184-93.
3. Marva Dawn, *Sexual Character: Beyond Technique to Intimacy*
(Grand Rapids: Eerdmans, 1993), 111-15.
4. Roman Catholics affirm singleness, but also highly honor marriage.
In the gorgeous St. John's Basilica in Des Moines, Iowa, the two
texts at the front of the apse next to the nave are on marriage
("Wherefore shall a man leave. . . .") and healing ("If any is sick
among you. . . ."). If the Roman Catholic Church puts the marriage
text up front, when they highly value celibacy, maybe Protestants
and Anabaptist-oriented churches should somewhere inscribe: "I
wish that all were as I am, unmarried to be free from anxieties and
the affairs of the world, and thus be more available for kingdom
work" (based on 1 Cor. 7:6, 32-33).
5. In my church at Doylestown, Pennsylvania, two single women
influenced much of my spiritual formation.
6. Dawn, *Sexual Character*, 26.
7. For a hard-hitting critique of the modern cultural demolition of

marriage and family, see Maggie Gallagher, *The Abolition of Marriage: How We Destroy Lasting Love* (Washington, D.C. : Regnery, 1996). See also Kari Jenson Gold's review article of *The Abolition of Marriage* in *First Things* 65 (1996), 45-48. For resources on earlier influences threatening the family, see Ross T. Bender, *Christians in Families* (Scottdale, Pa.: Herald Press, 1982), 48-56, 109-24. For a helpful resource to reclaim Christian response, see Rodney Clapp, *Families at the Crossroads: Beyond Traditional and Modern Options* (Downers Grove, Ill.: InterVarsity Press, 1993). See also Don S. Browning, et al, *From Culture Wars to Common Ground: Religion and the American Family Debate* (Louisville, Ky.: Westminster/ John Knox Press, 1997). Other volumes are forthcoming in this series.

Appendix 6

1. Walter Wink, *Christian Century* (7 November 1979): 1082, 1085. A version of this article appeared also in *Fellowship* (March-April 1997): 12-15. His article in Walter Wink, ed., *Homosexuality and Christian Faith: Questions for Conscience for the Churches* (Minneapolis: Fortress Press, 1999), softened his emphasis a bit.
2. *Confession of Faith in a Mennonite Perspective*, article 19 (Scottdale, Pa.: Herald Press, 1995), 72.
3. See also Richard B. Hays, *The Moral Vision of the New Testament: Cross, Community, New Creation* (San Francisco: HarperCollins, 1996), 390, 401.
4. See also ibid., 401.
5. John D. Roth, "Binding and Loosing: Why the Mennonite Church does not regard same-sex marriages as a Christian option," parts 1 and 2, *The Mennonite* 2 (19 January 1999), 4-6; (26 January 1999), 5-8.

BIBLIOGRAPHY

Denotes books consisting of essays that represent various positions on homosexuality.

Achtemeier, Paul. *Inspiration and Authority: Nature and Function of Christian Scripture.* Peabody, Mass.: Hendrickson, 1999.

Adler, Margot. *Drawing Down the Moon.* Rev. and expanded. New York: Penguin, 1977.

Ali, Lorraine and Julie Scelfo. "Choosing Virginity." *Newsweek* (9 December 2001): 60-71.

Alison, James. *Faith Beyond Resentment: Fragments Catholic and Gay.* New York: Crossroad Publishing, 2001.

Bailey, Derrick Sherwin. *Homosexuality and the Western Tradition.* London: Longmans, Green & Co., 1955.

*Balch, David L., ed. *Homosexuality, Science, and the "Plain Sense" of Scripture.* Grand Rapids: Eerdmans, 2000.

Balswick, Judith K. and Jack O. *Authentic Human Sexuality: An Integrated Approach.* Downers Grove, Ill.: InterVarsity Press, 1999.

Barnhouse, Ruth Tiffany. *Homosexuality: A Symbolic Confusion.* New York: Seabury Press, 1977.

Barth, Karl. *The Doctrine of Creation.* Vol. 3, pt. 4 of *Church Dogmatics.* Translated by G. W. Bromiley. Edinburgh: T. & T. Clark, 1961.

———. *Church Dogmatics: A Selection.* Selected by Helmut Gollwitzer and translated by G. W. Bromiley. New York: Harper and Bro., 1961.

Barton, Stephen C. *Life Together: Family, Sexuality, and Community in the New Testament and Today.* New York: T. & T. Clark, 2001.

Bassler, Jouette M. "Divine Impartiality in Paul's Letter to the Romans." *Novum Testamentum* 26 (1984): 43-58.

*Batchelor, Edward, ed. *Homosexuality and Ethics*. New York: The Pilgrim Press, 1980.

Bellah, Robert N., et al. *Habits of the Heart: Individualism and Commitment in American Life*. New York: Harper & Row, 1985.

Belleville, Linda L. *A Biblical Perspective on Sexuality*. Chicago: Evangelical Covenant Church, 1997.

Bellis, Alice Ogden and Terry L. Hufford. *Science, Scripture, and Homosexuality*. Cleveland: Pilgrim Press, 2002.

Bender, Ross T. *Christians in Families*. Scottdale, Pa.: Herald Press, 1982.

Berger, Peter L. and Thomas Luckmann. *The Social Construction of Reality*. New York: Doubleday, 1966.

Biesecker-Mast, Gerald J. "Mennonite Public Discourse and the Conflicts over Homosexuality." *Mennonite Quarterly Review* 72 (April 1998): 275-300.

Birk, Lee. "The Myth of Classical Homosexuality." In *Homosexual Behavior: A Modern Appraisal*, edited by Judd Marmor, 376-90. New York: Basic Books, 1980.

Blount, Brian K. "Reading and Understanding the New Testament on Homosexuality." In *Homosexuality and Christian Community*, edited by Choon-Leong Seow, 28-38. Louisville: Westminster/John Knox Press, 1996.

Boa, Kenneth. *Conformed to His Image: Biblical and Practical Approaches to Spiritual Formation*. Grand Rapids: Zondervan, 2001.

Boers, Arthur Paul. *Lord, Teach Us to Pray*. Scottdale, Pa.: Herald Press, 1992.

Bonhoeffer, Dietrich. "Loving Our Enemies: Dietrich Bonhoeffer's Sermon on Romans 12:16-21." Translated by Evan Drake Howard. *The Reformed Journal* (April 1985): 18-21.

Borg, Marcus. *Jesus: A New Vision*. San Francisco: HarperSanFrancisco, 1987.

Boswell, John. *Christianity, Social Tolerance, and Homosexuality*. Chicago: University of Chicago Press, 1980.

———. *Same Sex-Unions in Premodern Europe*. New York: Villard Books, 1994.

Boughton, Lynne C. "Biblical Texts and Homosexuality: A Response to John Boswell." *Irish Theological Quarterly* 58:2 (1992): 141-53.

*Bradshaw, Timothy, ed. *The Way Forward?: Christian Voices on Homosexuality and the Church*. London: Hodder & Stoughton, 1997.

*Brawley, Robert L., ed. *Biblical Ethics and Homosexuality: Listening to Scripture*. Louisville: Westminster/John Knox Press, 1996.

Brooten, Bernadette J. *Love Between Women: Early Christian Responses to Female Homoeroticism*. Chicago: University of Chicago Press, 1996.

———. "Patristic Interpretations of Romans 1:26." *Studia Patristica* 18:1 (1985): 287-91.

Brown, William P., ed. *Character and Scripture: Moral Formation, Community, and Biblical Interpretation*. Grand Rapids: Eerdmans, 2002.

Browning, Don S., et al. *From Culture Wars to Common Ground: Religion and The American Family Debate*. Louisville, Ky.: Westminster/John Knox Press, 1997.

———. "Rethinking Homosexuality." Review of David Greenberg, *The Construction of Homosexuality*. In *The Christian Century* (11 October 1989): 911-13.

Charles, J. Daryl. *1-2 Peter, Jude*. Believers Church Bible Commentary. Scottdale, Pa.: Herald Press, 1999.

Clapp, Rodney. *Families at the Crossroads*. Downers Grove, Ill.: InterVarsity Press, 1993.

Coleman, Gerald D. *Homosexuality: Catholic Teaching and Pastoral Practice*. Mahwah, N.J.: Paulist Press, 1995.

Coleman, Peter. *Christian Attitudes to Homosexuality.*
London: SPCK, 1980.

Committee on Adolescence, for the American Academy of
Pediatrics. "Homosexuality and Adolescence."
Pedatrics 92 (October 1993): 631-34.

Confession of Faith in a Mennonite Perspective. Scottdale,
Pa.: Herald Press, 1995.

Cort, John C. "The Unwelcome Ex-'Gay' Phenomenon."
New Oxford Review (October 2001): 33-36.

Cosgrove, Charles H. *Appealing to Scripture in Moral
Debate: Five Hermeneutical Rules.* Grand Rapids:
Eerdmans, 2002.

Countryman, William. *Dirt, Greed, and Sex: Sexual Ethics
in the New Testament and Their Implications for
Today.* Philadephia: Fortress Press, 1988.

Davies, Bob and Lori Rentzel. *Coming Out of Homosexuality.*
Downers Grove, Ill.: InterVarsity, 1994.

Dawn, Marva. *Sexual Character: Beyond Technique to
Intimacy.* Grand Rapids: Eerdmans, 1993.

Dean, Tim and Christopher Lane, eds. *Homosexuality and
Psychoanalysis.* Chicago: University of Chicago
Press, 2001.

Douglas, Mary. *Purity and Danger: An Analysis of the
Concepts of Pollution and Taboo.* Rev. ed. London:
Routledge & Kegan Paul, 1966.

Elias, Jacob. *1 & 2 Thessalonians.* Believers Church Bible
Commentary. Scottdale, Pa.: Herald Press, 1995.

Ellul, Jacques. *The Meaning of the City.* Translated by
Dennis Pardee. Grand Rapids: Eerdmans, 1970.

Ewald, George R. *Jesus and Divorce: A Biblical Guide for
Ministry to Divorced Persons.* Scottdale, Pa.: Herald
Press, 1991.

Firestein, Beth A., ed. *Bisexuality: The Psychology and
Politics of an Invisible Minority.* Thousand Oaks,
Calif.: Sage Publishing, 1996.

Fogleman, Ron. Review of Robert Goss, *Jesus Acted Up: A Gay and Lesbian Manifesto*. In *Critical Review* 7 (1994), 508-11.

Foucault, Michel. *The History of Sexuality*. Vol. 1, *Introduction*. Translated by Robert Hurley. New York: Pantheon Books, 1978.

Fowl, Stephen E. and L. Gregory Jones. *Reading in Communion: Scripture & Ethics in Christian Life*. Grand Rapids: Eerdmans, 1991.

Fredrickson, David E. "Natural and Unnatural Use in Romans 1:24-27: Paul and the Philosophic Critique of Eros." In *Homosexuality, Science, and the "Plain Sense" of Scripture*, edited by David L. Balch, 197-222. Grand Rapids: Eerdmans, 2000.

Fredriksen, Paula. *Jesus of Nazareth, King of the Jews*. New York: Alfred Knopf, 1999.

Friesen, Walter. "My Witness about Biblical Faith and Homosexuality." In *On Biblical Interpretation*. Booklet 4, 5-40. Goshen, Ind.: N.p, n.d.

Furnish, Victor P. *The Moral Teaching of Paul: Selected Issues*. Rev. ed. Nashville: Abingdon, 1985.

Gagnon, Robert A. *The Bible and Homosexual Practice: Texts and Hermeneutics*. Nashville: Abingdon Press, 2001.

———. "A Comprehensive and Critical Review Essay of *Homosexuality, Science, and the 'Plain Sense' of Scripture*." Part 1. *Horizons in Biblical Theology* 22 (December 2000): 174-243.

———. "Are There Universally Valid Sex Precepts? A Critique of Walter Wink's Views on the Bible and Homosexuality," *Horizons in Biblical Theology* 24:1 (June 2002): 72-125.

———. "The Bible and Homosexual Practice: Theology, Analogies, and Genes." *Theology Matters* 7 (November-December 2001):1-15.

Gallagher, Maggie. *The Abolition of Marriage: How We Destroy Lasting Love.* Washington, D.C.: Regnery, 1996.

*Geiss, Sally B. and Donald E. Messer, eds. *Caught in the Crossfire: Helping Christians Debate Homosexuality.* Nashville: Abingdon Press, 1994.

Gnuse, Robert. *The Authority of the Bible: Theories of Inspiration, Revelation and the Canon of Scripture.* Mahwah, N.J.: Paulist Press, 1985.

Good, Deirdre. "The New Testament and Homosexuality: Are We Getting Anywhere?" *Religious Studies Review* 26 (October 2000): 307-12.

Goss, Robert. *Jesus Acted Up: A Gay and Lesbian Manifesto.* San Francisco: HarperCollins, 1994.

————. *Queering Christ: Beyond "Jesus Acted Up."* Cleveland: Pilgrim Press, 2002.

Greenberg, David. *The Construction of Homosexuality.* Chicago: University of Chicago Press, 1988.

Greene-McCreight, Kathryn. "The Logic of the Interpretation of Scripture and the Church's Debate." In *Homosexuality, Science, and the "Plain Sense" of Scripture*, edited by David L. Balch, 253-59. Grand Rapids: Eerdmans, 2000.

Grenz, Stanley J. *Welcoming, But Not Affirming: An Evangelical Response to Homosexuality.* Louisville: Westminster/John Knox Press, 1998.

Grieb, A. Katherine. *The Story of Romans: A Narrative Defense of God's Righteousness.* Louisville: Westminster/John Knox Press, 2002.

Grimsrud, Ted. "Six Perspectives on the Homosexuality Controversy." In *To Continue the Dialogue: Biblical Interpretation and Homosexuality*, edited by C. Norman Kraus, 187-208. Telford, Pa.: Pandora Press U.S., 2001.

————. "What Would Jesus Do?" In *On Biblical Interpretation.* Booklet 4, 41-55. Goshen, Ind.: N.p., n.d.

Hauerwas, Stanley. *A Community of Character: Toward a Constructive Christian Social Ethic.* Notre Dame, Ind.: University of Notre Dame Press, 1981.

———. *The Peaceable Kingdom: A Primer in Christian Ethics.* Notre Dame, Ind.: Notre Dame University Press, 1983.

Hays, Richard B. "Awaiting the Redemption of Our Bodies: The Witness of Scripture Concerning Homosexuality." *Sojourners* 20 (July 1991): 17-21.

———. *The Moral Vision of the New Testament: Cross, Community, New Creation.* San Francisco: HarperSanFrancisco, 1996.

———. "Relations Natural and Unnatural: A Response to John Boswell's Exegesis of Romans 1." *Journal of Religious Ethics* 14 (1986): 184-215.

*Hershberger, Anne and Willard Kraybill, eds. *Sexuality: God's Gift.* Scottdale, Pa.: Herald Press, 2000.

Hershberger, Guy F. *War, Peace, and Nonresistance.* Rev. ed. Scottdale, Pa.: Herald Press, 1953.

Human Sexuality in the Christian Life: A Working Document for Study and Dialogue. Newton, Kan., and Scottdale, Pa.: General Conference Mennonite Church and Mennonite Church, 1985.

Jersild, Paul. *Spirit Ethics: Scripture and the Moral Life.* Minneapolis: Fortress Press, 2000.

Jeschke, Marlin. *Discipling in the Church: Recovering a Ministry of the Gospel.* 3d ed. Scottdale, Pa.: Herald Press, 1988.

Jewett, Robert. "The Social Context and Implications of Homoerotic References Romans 1:24-27." In *Homosexuality, Science, and the "Plain Sense" of Scripture,* edited by David L. Balch, 223-41. Grand Rapids: Eerdmans, 2000.

Johnson, Luke Timothy. *Decision Making in the Church: A Biblical Model.* Philadelphia: Fortress Press, 1983.

———. *Scripture and Discernment: Decision Making in the Church.* Nashville: Abingdon Press, 1996.

Jones, Stanton L. "The Loving Opposition: Speaking the Truth in a Climate of Hate." *Christianity Today* (19 July 1993): [page]

———— and Mark A. Yarhouse. *Homosexuality: The Use of Scientific Research in the Church's Moral Debate.* Downers Grove, Ill.: InterVarsity Press, 2000.

————. "The Use, Misuse, and Abuse of Science in the Ecclesiastical Homosexuality Debates." In *Homosexuality, Science, and the "Plain Sense" of Scripture*, edited by David L. Balch, 73-120. Grand Rapids: Eerdmans, 2000.

Kauffman, Richard A. "A Third Way between Fight and Flight." *The Mennonite* (2 May 2000): 6-8.

Keener, Carl S. and Douglas E. Swartzendruber. "The Biological Basis of Homosexuality." In *To Continue the Dialogue: Biblical Interpretation and Homosexuality*, edited by C. Norman Kraus, 148-73. Telford, Pa.: Pandora Press U.S., 2001.

Koenig, John. *Rediscovering New Testament Prayer.* New York: HarperSanFrancisco, 1992.

*Kraus, C. Norman, ed. *To Continue the Dialogue: Biblical Interpretation and Homosexuality.* Telford, Pa.: Pandora Press U.S., 2001.

Kraybill, J. Nelson. *On the Pilgrim's Way.* Scottdale, Pa.: Herald Press, 1999.

Kreider, Alan. *Journey Toward Holiness.* Scottdale, Pa.: Herald Press, 1987.

LeBlanc, Douglas. "Waging Peace." *Christianity Today* (9 July 2001): 42-47.

Lederach, John Paul. *The Journey Toward Reconciliation.* Scottdale, Pa.: Herald Press, 1999.

Leland, John. "Bisexuality." *Newsweek* (17 July, 1995): 44-50.

Lind, Millard. *Monotheism, Power, and Justice: Collected Old Testament Essays.* Elkhart, Ind.: Institute of Mennonite Studies, 1990.

————. *Yahweh Is a Warrior*. Scottdale, Pa.: Herald Press, 1980.

MacIntyre, Alasdair. *Whose Justice? Which Rationality?* Notre Dame, Ind.: University of Notre Dame Press, 1988.

Malick, David F. "The Condemnation of Homosexuality in Romans 1:26-27." *Bibliotheca Sacra* 151 (1993): 327-40.

————. "The Condemnation of Homosexuality in 1 Cor. 6:9." *Bibliotheca Sacra* 151 (1993): 479-92.

*Marmor, Judd, ed. *Homosexual Behavior: A Modern Appraisal.* New York: Basic Books, 1980.

Marshall, Christopher D. *Beyond Retribution: A New Testament Vision for Justice, Crime, and Punishment.* Grand Rapids: Eerdmans, 2001.

Martin, Dale B. "*Arsenokoitês* and *Malakos*: Meanings and Consequences." In *Biblical Ethics and Homosexuality: Listening to Scripture*, edited by Robert L. Brawley, 117-36. Louisville: Westminster/John Knox Press, 1996.

————. *The Corinthian Body*. New Haven, Conn.: Yale University Press, 1995.

McClymond, Michael J. "The Last Sexual Perversion: An Argument in Defense of Celibacy." *Theology Today* 57:21 (July 2000): 217-31.

McNeill, John. *The Church and the Homosexual*. Kansas City: Sheed, Andrews, & McMeel, 1976.

Middleton, J. Richard and Brian J. Walsh. *Truth Is Stranger Than It Used to Be: Biblical Faith in a Postmodern Age*. Downers Grove, Ill.: InterVarsity Press, 1995.

Miller, Keith Graber. "Guidelines from the Gift-Giver: Sexuality and Scripture." In *Sexuality: God's Gift*, edited by Anne Hershberger and Willard Kraybill, 33-48. Scottdale, Pa.: Herald Press, 2000.

Miller, Patrick D. "What the Scriptures Principally Teach." In *Homosexuality and Christian Community*, edited by Choon-Leong Seow, 53-63. Louisville: Westminster/John Knox Press, 1996.

Minear, Paul S. *The Obedience of the Faith: The Purposes of Paul in the Epistle to the Romans*. Studies in Biblical Theology, Second Series 19. Naperville, Ill.: Alec R. Allensen Inc., 1971.

Moberly, Elizabeth. *Homosexuality: A New Christian Ethic?* Cambridge: James Clark & Co. Ltd., 1983.

———. "Homosexuality and Truth." *First Things* 71 (March 1997): 30-33.

Moberly, Walter. "The Use of Scripture in Contemporary Debate about Homosexuality." *Theology* 103 (July-August 2000): 251-58.

Moskala, Jirí. "Categorization and Evaluation of Different Kinds of Interpretation of the Laws of Clean and Unclean Animals in Leviticus 11." *Biblical Research* 46 (2001): 5-41.

Mulholland, M. Robert, Jr. *Shaped by the Word: The Power of Scripture in Spiritual Formation*. Nashville: The Upper Room, 1985.

Nation, Mark Thiessen. "Fruit of the Spirit or Works of the Flesh? Come Let Us Reason Together." In *To Continue the Dialogue: Biblical Interpretation and Homosexuality*, edited by C. Norman Kraus, 223-44. Telford, Pa.: Pandora Press U.S., 2001.

Nelson, James B. *Embodiment: An Approach to Sexuality and to Christian Theology*. Minneapolis, Augsburg Press, 1978.

Neuhaus, Richard John. "The Public Square: In the Case of John Boswell." *First Things* 41 (1994): 56-58.

———. "The Public Square: Scandal time." Part 1 and 2. *First Things* 122 (April 2002): 61-64; 124 (June-July 2002): 75-85.

Nicolosi, Joseph. "What Does Science Teach Us About Human Sexuality? In *Caught in the Crossfire: Helping Christians Debate Homosexuality*, edited by Sally B. and Donald E. Messer, 67-77. Nashville: Abingdon Press, 1994.

Nissinen, Martti. *Homoeroticism in the Biblical World: A Historical Perspective.* Translated by Kirsi Stjerna. Minneapolis: Fortress Press, 1998.

Nolland, John. "Romans 1:26-27 and the Homosexuality Debate." *Horizons in Biblical Theology* 22 (June 2000): 32-57.

Packer, J. I. "Why I Walked." *Christianity Today* 47 (January 2003): 47-50.

Payne, Leanne. *The Broken Image: Restoring Personal Wholeness Through Healing Prayer.* Grand Rapids: Baker Books, 1996.

Powell, Mark Allen. *Chasing the Eastern Star.* Louisville, Ky.: Westminster/John Knox, 2001.

Pronk, Pim. *Against Nature? Types of Moral Argumentation Regarding Homosexuality.* Grand Rapids: Eerdmans, 1993.

Ramsey Colloquium. "The Homosexual Movement: A Response by the Ramsey Colloquium." *First Things* 41 (March 1994): 15-20.

Reimer, A. James. "Homosexuality: A Call for Compassion and Moral Rigor." In *To Continue the Dialogue: Biblical Interpretation and Homosexuality,* edited by C. Norman Kraus, 174-86. Telford, Pa.: Pandora Press U.S., 2001.

Rogers, Eugene F., Jr. *Sexuality and the Christian Body: Their Way Into The Triune God.* Oxford: Blackwell, 1999.

Rosner, Brian S. *Paul, Scripture & Ethics: A Study of 1 Corinthians 5-7.* Grand Rapids: Baker Books, 1999.

Roth, John D. "Binding and Loosing: Why the Mennonite Church does not regard same-sex marriages as a Christian option." Part 1 and 2. *The Mennonite* (19 January 1999): 4-6; (26 January 1999): 5-8.

———. *Choosing Against War: A Christian View: "A Love Stronger Than Our Fears."* Intercourse, Pa.: Good Books, 2002.

Satinover, Jeffrey. *Homosexuality and the Politics of Truth*. Grand Rapids: Baker Books, 1996.

Schoedel, William R. "Same-Sex Eros: Paul and the Greco-Roman Tradition." In *Homosexuality, Science, and the "Plain Sense" of Scripture*, edited by David L. Balch, 43-72. Grand Rapids: Eerdmans, 2000.

Schroeder, David. "Homosexuality: Biblical, Theological, and Polity Issues." In *To Continue the Dialogue: Biblical Interpretation and Homosexuality*, edited by C. Norman Kraus, 62-75. Telford, Pa.: Pandora Press U.S., 2001.

Schmidt, Thomas E. *Straight and Narrow: Compassion and Clarity in the Homosexuality Debate*. Downers Grove, Ill.: InterVarsity, 1995.

Schüssler Fiorenza, Elisabeth. *In Memory of Her*. New York: Crossroad, 1983.

Scroggs, Robin. *The New Testament and Homosexuality*. Philadelphia: Fortress Press, 1983.

*Seow, Choon-Leong, ed. *Homosexuality and Christian Community*. Louisville: Westminster/John Knox Press, 1996.

———. "Textual Orientation." In *Biblical Ethics and Homosexuality: Listening to Scripture*, edited by Robert L. Brawley, 17-34. Louisville: Westminster/John Knox Press, 1996.

Shank, David A. "Change Is Possible." *Mennonite Weekly Review* (29 February 1996).

———. "On the Exegesis of an Ethos." Unpublished paper. 1993.

Shillington, V. George. *2 Corinthians*. Believers Church Bible Commentary. Scottdale, Pa.: Herald Press, 1998.

Shrock-Shenk, Carolyn. "Commanded to Keep Wrestling and Wrestling and Wrestling." In *To Continue the Dialogue: Biblical Interpretation and Homosexuality*, edited by C. Norman Kraus, 245-55. Telford, Pa.: Pandora Press U.S., 2001.

———— and Lawrence Ressler, eds. *Making Peace with Conflict: Practical Skills for Conflict Resolution.* Scottdale, Pa.: Herald Press, 1999.

Sider, Ronald. "Loving people the way Jesus loved people." *Gospel Herald* (21 November 1995): 2.

*Siker, Jeffrey S., ed. *Homosexuality in the Church: Both Sides of the Debate.* Louisville: Westminster/John Knox Press, 1994.

————. "How to Decide? Homosexual Christians, the Bible, and Gentile Inclusion." *Theology Today* 51 (July 1994): 219-34.

Skinner, Douglas B. "Is Homosexuality a Sin? An Evangelical Perspective." *Lexington Theological Quarterly* 35 (Fall 2000): 157-68. See counterpoint article by Wray.

Smith, Abraham. "The New Testament and Homosexuality." *Quarterly Review* 11:4 (1991): 18-32.

Smucker, Marcus. "Psychological Dynamics: Being Gay or Lesbian." In *To Continue the Dialogue: Biblical Interpretation and Homosexuality*, edited by C. Norman Kraus, 45-61. Telford, Pa.: Pandora Press U.S., 2001.

Soards, Marion. *Scripture and Homosexuality: Biblical Authority and the Church Today.* Louisville: Westminster/John Knox Press, 1994.

Spitzer, Robert L. "Commentary: Psychiatry and Homosexuality." *Wall Street Journal* (23 May 2001).

Stott, John R. *Same-Sex Partnerships? A Christian Perspective.* Grand Rapids: F. H. Revell, 1998.

Stuhlmacher, Peter. *Historical Criticism and the Theological Interpretation of Scripture: Toward a Hermeneutics of Consent.* Translated by Roy A. Harrisville. Philadelphia: Fortress Press, 1977.

Swartley, Willard M. "The Church and Homosexuality: Review Essay." *Mennonite Quarterly Review* 76 (April 2002): 215-30.

————. *Israel's Scripture Traditions and the Synoptic Gospels: Story Shaping Story.* Peabody, Mass.: Hendrickson, 1994.

————. *Slavery, Sabbath, War, and Women: Case Issues in Biblical Interpretation.* Scottdale, Pa.: Herald Press, 1983.

————, ed. *Essays on Biblical Interpretation: Anabaptist-Mennonite Perspectives.* Elkhart, Ind.: Institute of Mennonite Studies, 1984.

————, ed. *The Love of Enemy and Nonretaliation in the New Testament.* Louisville: Westminster/John Knox Press, 1992.

Switzer, David K. *Pastoral Care of Gays, Lesbians, and their Families.* Minneapolis: Fortress Press, 1999.

Taylor, J. Glen. "The Bible and Homosexuality." *Themelios* 21 (October 1995), 4-9, 105-10.

Thielicke, Helmut. *The Ethics of Sex.* Translated by John W. Doberstein. New York: Harper & Row, 1964.

Thiselton, Anthony C. *The First Epistle to Corinthians.* The New International Greek Commentary. Grand Rapids: Eerdmans, 2000.

————. "Can Hermeneutics Ease the Deadlock? Some Biblical Exegesis and Hermeneutical Models." In *The Way Forward?: Christian Voices on Homosexuality and the Church*, edited by Timothy Bradshaw, 145-96. London: Hodder & Stoughton, 1997.

Throckmorton, Warren. "Attempts to Modify Sexual Orientation: A Review of Outcome Literature and Ethical Issues." *Journal of Mental Health Counseling* 20 (October 1998): 283-304.

Toews, John E. *Romans.* Believers Church Bible Commentary Series. Scottdale, Pa.: Herald Press, forthcoming.

Van Leeuwen, Mary Stewart. *Gender & Grace: Love, Work & Parenting in a Changing World.* Downers Grove, Ill.: InterVarsity Press, 1990.

———. "To Ask a Better Question: The Heterosexuality-Homosexuality Debate Revisited." *Interpretation* 51 (April 1997): 143-58.

Volf, Miroslav. *Exclusion and Embrace: A Theological Explanation of Identity, Otherness, and Reconciliation.* Nashville: Abingdon, 1996.

Waetjen, Herman C. "Same-Sex Sexual Relations in Antiquity and Sexuality and Sexual Identity in Contemporary American Society." In *Biblical Ethics and Homosexuality: Listening to Scripture*, edited by Robert L. Brawley, 106-16. Louisville: Westminster/John Knox Press, 1996.

Webb, William J. *Slaves, Women, and Homosexuals: Exploring the Hermeneutics of Cultural Analysis.* Downers Grove, Ill.: InterVarsity Press, 2001.

Wheeler, Barbara G. "Living Together in the Light of Christ." *Theology, News, and Notes* [Fuller Theological Seminary] 50:2 (Winter 2003): 7-11.

White, John and Ken Blue. *Healing the Wounded: The Costly Love of Church Discipline.* Downers Grove, Ill.: InterVarsity Press, 1985.

White, Mel. *Stranger at the Gate: To Be Gay and Christian in America.* New York: Penguin Books: 1995.

Willard, Dallas. *The Divine Conspiracy: Rediscovering Our Hidden Life with God.* San Francisco: HarperSanFrancisco, 1998.

Williams, Michael. "Romans 1: Entropy, Sexuality and Politics." *Anvil* 10:2 (1993): 105-10.

Willimon, William H. "Matthew 5:43-48." *Interpretation* 57 (2003): 60-63.

Wink, Walter. *Engaging the Powers.* Minneapolis, Fortress Press, 1996.

*———, ed. *Homosexuality and Christian Faith: Questions for Conscience for the Churches.* Minneapolis: Fortress Press, 1999. Earlier influential versions of this article appeared in *The Christian Century* (7 November 1979):

1082-86, and the FOR publication, *Fellowship* (April 1997): 12-15.

Wold, Donald J. *Out of Order: Homosexuality in the Bible and the Ancient Near East.* Grand Rapids: Baker Books, 1998.

Wray, Judith Hoch. "Is Homosexuality a Sin: What Do We Discern?" *Lexington Theological Quarterly* 35 (Fall 2000): 169-75.

Wright, David F. "Early Christian Attitudes to Homosexuality." *Studia Patristica* 18:2 (1989): 329-34.

———. "Homosexuals or Prostitutes? The Meaning of ARSENOKOITAI (1 Cor. 6:9, 1 Tim 1:10)." *Vigiliae Christianae* 38 (1984): 125-53.

Wright, J. Robert. "A Case Undemonstrated." *Anglican Theological Review* 66 (1984): 79-94.

Yarbrough, O. Larry. *Not Like the Gentiles: Marriage Rules in the Letters of Paul.* Atlanta: Scholars Press, 1985.

Yoder, John H. *Body Politics: Five Practices of the Church before the Waiting World.* Scottdale, Pa.: Herald Press, 2001.

———. "Binding and Loosing." *Concern.* A Pamphlet Series for Questions of Renewal. No. 14. Scottdale, Pa.: Herald Press, 1967.

Yoder Neufeld,Thomas. *Ephesians.* Believers Church Bible Commentary. Scottdale, Pa.: Herald Press, 2002.

Young, Robin Darling. "Gay Marriage: Reimagining Church History." *First Things* 47 (November 1994): 43-48.

AUTHOR AND PERSON INDEX

For noncanonical references, including sources from the Apocrypha, Pseudepigrapha, Mishnah, and Talmud, see pp. 140-41, 192 n38, and 199 n9. For Philo, Josephus, and Greek and Roman writers see the Author and Person Index.

SUBJECT INDEX

THE AUTHOR

Willard M. Swartley is professor of New Testament at Associated Mennonite Biblical Seminary and New Testament editor of the Studies in Peace and Scripture Series. He has served as dean of the seminary, director of the Institute of Mennonite Studies, and as New Testament Editor of the Believers Church Bible Commentary Series. Among other titles, he is the author of *Mark: The Way for All Nations* and *Slavery, Sabbath, War, and Women: Case Studies in Biblical Interpretation,* and editor of *The Love of Enemy and Nonretaliation in the New Testament.*